PUBLICATIONS OF THE GERMAN HISTORICAL INSTITUTE,
WASHINGTON, D.C.

Edited by Hartmut Lehmann,
with the assistance of Kenneth F. Ledford

Genoa, Rapallo, and European Reconstruction in 1922

One of the largest twentieth-century summit meetings, the Genoa Conference of 1922 was also a notable failure as a consequence of the gulf between the Allies and Germany, between the West and Soviet Russia, and among the World War I victors and their small allies. This book, a unique international collaboration, presents various perspectives on the Genoa Conference: its leadership, its goals, and its outcome. The authors present new findings on such topics as the sensational Rapallo Treaty between Germany and Russia, the strategies of the Little Entente and the small neutral powers, and the policy of the United States toward European debts. Readers will find contrasting as well as complementary views in this volume.

THE GERMAN HISTORICAL INSTITUTE, WASHINGTON, D.C.

The German Historical Institute is a center for advanced study and research whose purpose is to provide a permanent basis for scholarly cooperation between historians from the Federal Republic of Germany and the United States. The Institute conducts, promotes, and supports research into both American and German political, social, economic, and cultural history, into transatlantic migration, especially in the nineteenth and twentieth centuries, and into the history of international relations, with special emphasis on the roles played by the United States and Germany.

Genoa, Rapallo, and European Reconstruction in 1922

Edited by
CAROLE FINK
AXEL FROHN
and
JÜRGEN HEIDEKING

GERMAN HISTORICAL INSTITUTE
Washington, D.C.

CAMBRIDGE UNIVERSITY PRESS
Cambridge
New York   Port Chester   Melbourne   Sydney

Published by the Press Syndicate of the University of Cambridge
The Pitt Building, Trumpington Street, Cambridge CB2 1RP
40 West 20th Street, New York, NY 10011, USA
10 Stamford Road, Oakleigh, Melbourne 3166, Australia

First published 1991

Printed in the United States of America

Library of Congress Cataloging-in-Publication Data
Genoa, Rapallo, and European Reconstruction in 1922 / edited by Carole Fink, Axel
Frohn, and Jürgen Heideking.
p.   cm.
Includes bibliographical references.
ISBN 0-521-41167-X (hardback)
1. Genoa Conference (1922)   2. Reconstruction (1914–1939)
3. Europe – Politics and government – 1918–1945.   4. Germany – Foreign relations –
Soviet Union.   5. Soviet Union – Foreign relations – Germany.   I. Fink, Carole.
II. Frohn, Axel.   III. Heideking, Jürgen.
D655.G46   1991
940.5′1 – dc20   91-2393
                                                                       CIP

British Library Cataloguing in Publication Data
Genoa, Rapallo, and European reconstruction in 1922.
1. Genoa Conference, 1922. Europe, history, 1918–1939. World War 1
I. Fink, Carole   II. Frohn, Axel   III. Heideking, Jürgen
940.3141

ISBN 0-521-41167-X hardback

Contents

Illustrations List

Maps List

Abbreviations List

ADAP	*Akten zur Deutschen Auswärtigen Politik*
A Fin Arch.	Austria: Finanz- und Hofkammerarchiv (Austrian Finance Ministry Archives)
AHHSt	Austria: Haus-, Hof- und Staatsarchiv (Austrian Private, Court, and National Archive)
BMAE	Belgium: Ministère des Affaires Etrangères, archive (Belgian Foreign Ministry Archive)
CAMZV	Czechoslovakia: Archiv Ministerstva Zahraničních Věcí (Czechoslovak Foreign Ministry Archive)
CAUML	Czechoslovakia: Archiv Ústavu Marxismu-Leninismu (Czechoslovak Institute for Marxism-Leninism Archive)
CSUA	Czechoslovakia: Státní Ústřední Archiv (Czechoslovak State Central Archives)
DBFP	*Documents on British Foreign Policy*
DDI	*I Documenti Diplomatici Italiani*
DDS	*Documents Diplomatiques Suisses*
DVP SSSR	*Dokumenty Vneshnei Politiki SSSR*
FAN	France: Archives Nationales (French National Archives)
FMAE	France: Ministère des Affaires Etrangères, archive (French Foreign Ministry Archive)
FMF	France: Ministère de l'Economie et des Finances, archive (French Ministry of Economics and Finance Archive)
FSHV	France: Service Historique de l'Armée, Vincennes (French Army Historical Service Archive)
FRUS	*Papers Relating to the Foreign Relations of the United States*

GB CAB	Great Britain: Cabinet Papers
GB Cmd	Great Britain, Parliament, Papers by Command
GB FO	Great Britain: Foreign Office Records
Germ. AA T-120	Germany: Microfilmed Records of the German Foreign Ministry
Germ. PA AA	Germany: Politisches Archiv des Auswärtigen Amts (Political Archive of the German Foreign Ministry)
Germ. ZSAP	Germany: Zentrales Staatsarchiv, Potsdam (German Central State Archives)
H MOL Küm	Hungary: Magyar Országos Levéltár, Külügyminisztérium (Hungarian Foreign Ministry Archive)
HZ	*Historische Zeitschrift*
IACS	Italy: Archivio Centrale dello Stato (Italian Central State Archives)
IASBI	Italy: Archivio Storico della Banca d'Italia (Bank of Italy Archive)
IMAE	Italy: Ministero degli Affari Esteri, Archivio Storico (Italian Foreign Ministry Archive)
JACFR	Japan: Advisory Council on Foreign Relations
JFMA	Japan: Foreign Ministry Archive
LNA	League of Nations Archive
NEP	New Economic Policy
RSFSR	Russian Soviet Federated Socialist Republic
SAF	Switzerland: Archive Fédérale (Swiss Federal Archives)
USDS	United States: Records of the Department of State, National Archives
USFRB	United States: Federal Reserve Bank of New York Archive
USHHPL	United States: Herbert Hoover Presidential Library
USTD	United States: Records of the Treasury Department
USTD NA	United States: Records of the Treasury Department, National Archives
VfZG	*Vierteljahrshefte für Zeitgeschichte*

Introduction

CAROLE FINK, AXEL FROHN, AND JÜRGEN HEIDEKING

Over a half century ago, in January 1929, the French historians Marc
Bloch and Lucien Febvre issued a moving appeal for international col-
laborative inquiry.[1] These two World War I veterans, coeditors of a
new scholarly journal, the *Annales,* were committed to comparative
history: to a history that transcended conventional national, disciplin-
ary, and chronological barriers and treated historical subjects with as
large a view as possible. Although they did not lack esteem for the work
of the solitary scholar, Bloch and Febvre considered cooperative
inquiry to be an indispensable reinforcement to gathering documentation, testing theories, and formulating useful hypotheses.[2]

This volume of original essays by recognized scholars of the history
of international relations represents a modest effort to meet this challenge: to tap the rich but dispersed archival resources of over a dozen
states and a considerable amount of scholarly literature. Drawing on a
variety of experiences and perspectives in an effort to comprehend the
problem of European reconstruction after World War I, the contributors have demonstrated a dedicated commitment to collective, comparative research.

From April 10 to May 19, 1922, delegates from thirty-four nations
met in the north Italian city of Genoa to deliberate on the economic
reconstruction and political stabilization of Europe. This conference, a
key event of European diplomacy in the interwar period, provides an
ideal research subject for a multinational study. In the wake of the Great
War, the Russian Revolution, and the Paris Peace Treaties, the Genoa
Conference brought together ideological enemies as well as victors,
vanquished, and neutrals. Its prospect produced not only a welter of

1 "Nos enquêtes collectives," *Annales d'histoire économique et sociale* 1 (1929):58–9.
2 Carole Fink, *Marc Bloch: A Life in History* (Cambridge, 1989).

1

speeches and paper but also a conjuncture of hope and fear, vision and memory, universality and narrowness.

The scholarly undertaking that led to this book originated in Moscow in the fall of 1987 at an international conference cosponsored by the Association Internationale d'Histoire Contemporaine de l'Europe (AIHCE) and the Institute of General History of the USSR on the theme of the Great October Revolution and Europe. Spurred by *glasnost,* the Soviet and Western scholars who attended this conference were able to share fresh, critical insights concerning the initial relations between Lenin's Russia and the West. One result, initiated by the conference host, A. O. Chubarian, vice-president of AIHCE and director of the Institute of General History of the Academy of Sciences of the USSR, was the founding of a study group under the AIHCE, chaired by Carole Fink, whose mandate was to sustain and expand the Moscow spirit by conducting an international inquiry into the Genoa Conference. Invitations were issued to all interested scholars of European diplomacy of the early 1920s, and the study group held its first meeting in Geneva in June 1988. At this meeting members identified common themes and planned a conference to discuss their findings.

Hartmut Lehmann, director of the German Historical Institute in Washington, whose program emphasizes the strengthening of international scholarly cooperation and the promotion of innovative conceptual and methodological approaches to research, wholeheartedly agreed to host this gathering in 1989. From June 14 to 17, the Institute was the site of a lively research conference. In his plenary address, the president of the AIHCE, Jacques Bariéty, underscored the group's mission of working for the opening of essential archives for research. That night, at the outset of the revolutionary changes sweeping Eastern Europe, speakers from East and West voiced their hopes for increased contact and collaboration. During the conference's five working sessions, twenty-five participants heard formal papers and debated still-controversial issues of European politics and diplomacy in 1922.

Thirteen historians, representing diverse scholarly traditions and national points of view, were invited to contribute their findings to this volume. Up-to-date inventories and finding aids of all the documentary material available to scholars worldwide are essential research tools.[3] Therefore, in addition to their essays, the participants were asked to

---

3 See, e.g., Axel Frohn, *Guide to Inventories and Finding Aids of German Archives at the German Historical Institute* (Washington, D.C., 1989).

provide information on archival sources most important to their research. Along with the much-used British, French, German, and American records, the authors examined documentation in Austria, Belgium, Czechoslovakia, Hungary, Italy, Japan, the Netherlands, and Switzerland, as well as in the League of Nations archive in Geneva. They also gained access to industrial and bank archives and to the private papers of businessmen in the United States, Great Britain, Germany, and Italy as a means of supplementing official records. According to those who have used them, the state archives of Eastern Europe are now gradually opening. As to private papers, there are valuable collections pertaining to the key political actors in 1922. Some have only recently been utilized (Carl von Schubert; Andrea Torre); others have just become available (Aristide Briand) or may be used with restrictions (Edouard Beneš); and some are still missing (Francesco Giannini, E. F. Wise).

After almost forty years of near silence over the Genoa Conference,[4] in the 1960s a steady stream of literature began to appear, reflecting not only shifts in world politics but also the increased availability of archival resources. Many of the early works fell into the context of either the Cold War or (as a result of the unprecedented accessibility of captured German records) the debate over continuity in German foreign policy from Bismarck to Hitler. In the 1970s and 1980s historical literature advanced from traditional studies of national policy to more differentiated treatments of international diplomacy, including two monographs on the Genoa Conference itself.[5] A new generation of scholars has taken a broader view of post–World War I international relations; they have investigated short-term and persistent economic and financial patterns along with specific political and diplomatic developments; they have balanced the role of ideology with personal and symbolic factors in the conduct of foreign policy; and they have pictured the Europe of the 1920s as part of an increasingly interdependent world.[6]

---

4 There were three contemporary accounts: John Saxon Mills, *The Genoa Conference* (New York, 1922); Louis Fischer, *Oil Imperialism: The International Struggle for Petroleum* (New York, 1926); and Jean de Pierrefeu, *La Saison diplomatique: Gênes (avril–mai 1922)* (Paris, 1928).
5 Carole Fink, *The Genoa Conference: European Diplomacy, 1921–1922* (Chapel Hill and London, 1984); and Stephen White, *The Origins of Détente: The Genoa Conference and Soviet–Western Relations, 1921–1922* (Cambridge, 1985).
6 For the 1960s: George F. Kennan, *Russia and the West under Lenin and Stalin* (New York, 1961); and Theodor Schieder, "Die Entstehungsgeschichte des Rapallo-Vertrags," *HZ* 204 (1967):545–609. For the 1970s and 1980s: Charles S. Maier, *Recasting Bourgeois Europe: Stabilization in France, Germany, and Italy in the Decade after World War I* (Princeton, 1975, new ed. 1989); and Stephen Schuker, *American "Reparations" to Germany, 1919–1933: Implications for the Third World Debt Crisis* (Princeton, 1988).

Meanwhile, we have gained a better understanding of the various actors: Britain, the "troubled giant," wavering between the Empire and Europe; France, oscillating between legitimate security concerns and attempts to weaken and dominate its eastern neighbor; Germany, divided between "fulfillers" and "defiers," "Westerners" and "Easterners"; Soviet Russia, torn between pragmatic NEP-men and orthodox Bolsheviks; and a fragmented and contentious Eastern Europe. There have been useful investigations of the role and relative importance of the neutral countries, the political isolationism and economic expansionism of the United States, and Japan's growing interest in European and world affairs. On a broader multinational level, we now have new insights into how the United States' debt policy toward the Allies affected their handling of the reparation question in the 1920s[7] and how events in Lenin's Russia shaped Anglo–French politics and policies.[8]

The Europe that emerged after World War I was divided in many ways.[9] Borders had been dramatically redrawn. New states came into existence in Eastern Europe (Finland, Estonia, Latvia, Lithuania, and Poland); Austria, independent Hungary, and Czechoslovakia succeeded the dissolved Habsburg Monarchy; and the kingdoms of Serbia and Montenegro together with Croatia and other parts of the Dual Monarchy now formed the Kingdom of the Serbs, Croats, and Slovenes, which changed its name to Yugoslavia in 1929. In addition, former Austro–Hungarian territories had to be ceded to Poland, Romania, and Italy. Under duress, Germany returned Alsace-Lorraine to France, relinquished some frontier areas to Belgium and Denmark, and yielded the former Prussian provinces of Posen and West Prussia along with the industrial districts of Upper Silesia to Poland. Allied forces occupied the Rhineland and the Memel territory, while the Free City of Danzig and the Saarland operated under League of Nations high commissioners. Bulgaria lost West Thrace, and its access to the Aegean Sea, to Greece; the new states of Poland and Czechoslovakia soon developed their own conflict over the Teschen region; and in the early 1920s Poland seized Vilna from Lithuania and annexed vast parts of White

7 See, e.g., Denise Artaud, *La question des dettes interalliées et la reconstruction de l'Europe, 1917–1929*. 2 vols. (Lille and Paris, 1978).
8 See, e.g., Richard H. Ullman, *The Anglo-Soviet Accord* (Princeton, 1973).
9 For the 1919–23 settlements see, e.g., Sally Marks, *The Illusion of Peace: International Relations in Europe, 1918–1933* (New York, 1976), 1–25; and Karl Dietrich Bracher, *Die Krise Europas 1917–1975*, 3rd ed. (Frankfurt, Berlin, and Vienna, 1980), 23–33.

Russia and the Ukraine, thereby increasing European tensions as well as the number of disputed territories.

Russia had not been present at the Paris Peace Conference and was therefore unable to affect its proceedings. Neither could the Allies, whose military intervention in the Russian civil war failed, influence the Bolshevik ruling powers. After the October Revolution and the foundation of the Third International in Moscow in March 1919, Russia had become the center of the Communist movement and the main ideological foe of the West, and thus was no longer available to serve as France's traditional ally against Germany. France turned to the new states in Eastern Europe to establish a *cordon sanitaire* to contain Soviet Russia and to create a security system to deter Germany.[10] Czechoslovakia, Yugoslavia, and Romania formed the "Little Entente" to defend the status quo against Hungary's revisionism, and Poland concluded treaties with France and Romania as well as with Finland, Estonia, and Latvia (the "Baltic Entente") as a protection against Germany and Russia. Thus, a series of political alignments and military alliances reinforced the separation between victors, neutrals, and vanquished and created a vast chasm between Soviet Russia and the West. The League of Nations, established to reconcile narrow national interests, was unable to overcome these divisions. Originally guided by the principles of universality and equality of all nations, the League suffered from the United States' political disengagement from Europe, the absence of Soviet Russia, and the exclusion of Germany.[11]

President Woodrow Wilson's program "to make the world safe for democracy" seemed to be successful in the early postwar period when most European states established democratic parliamentary systems, but the greater part of the political leaders and elites were unable to master the challenges of founding the new states and defending their sovereignty and territorial integrity as well as their democratic institutions. From the early 1920s onward, nationalism, rather than the common basis of democratic constitutions, became the determining factor in international relations. The new nation states in Eastern Europe achieved self-determination for their ethnic majorities but did not solve

---

10 See Piotr S. Wandycz, *France and Her Eastern Allies, 1919–1925* (Minneapolis, 1962); and Raymond Poidevin and Jacques Bariéty, *Frankreich und Deutschland. Die Geschichte ihrer Beziehungen 1815–1975* (Munich, 1982), 295–340.

11 See Jürgen Heideking, "Völkerbund und Vereinte Nationen in der internationalen Politik," *Aus Politik und Zeitgeschichte: Beilage zur Wochenzeitung "Das Parlament,"* Sept. 10, 1983.

the problem of their large national minorities: the Germans in Czechoslovakia, Poland, Hungary, Romania, Yugoslavia, and the Baltic states;
the Jews in Poland and Romania; the Ukrainians and White Russians
in Poland; the Magyars in Czechoslovakia, Romania, and Yugoslavia;
and so forth.[12] The hate and enmity of the war, the losses of the defeated
nations, the unfulfilled hopes and unsettled aims of the victorious powers and the new states, the rising tide of nationalism, the most difficult
and severe structural problem of the minorities, and the rejection of the
terms of the Paris Peace Treaties, particularly in Germany and Hungary
but also in Italy, made a determined, if not forcible, revisionism one of
the basic destabilizing factors in European politics.

The Great War brought about not only the death of millions of people, devastation, famine, and disease, but also an enormous degree of
economic and financial dislocation, social disruption, and structural
change. After the Bolshevik revolution, the temporary loss of Soviet
Russia as a market for Western goods and investments and a source of
raw materials appeared to thwart European recovery and reconstruction. Furthermore, the political reorganization of Europe caused the
disintegration of large economic areas, industrial stagnation, the erec-
tion of trade barriers, and the obstruction of traffic and commerce on
the major railroad lines from central to eastern and southeastern Europe
and the Danube. On the eve of the Genoa Conference inflation was one
of the predominant economic problems, not only in the European
countries but also in the United States and Japan. In Poland, Germany,
and Austria it rendered currencies almost worthless, and in November
1923 the German inflation reached historically unknown proportions.[13] Victors, vanquished, and neutrals alike suffered high unemployment rates, which throughout the 1920s were particularly severe
in Great Britain.[14] The European Allies' internal as well as external
indebtedness far exceeded that of the defeated nations, which to some

12 For the minority problem see Carlile A. Macartney, *National States and National Minorities*
(London, 1934); Erwin Viefhaus, *Die Minderheitenfrage und die Entstehung der Minderheiten-
schutzverträge auf der Pariser Friedenskonferenz 1919. Eine Studie zur Geschichte des Nationalitäten-
problems im 19. und 20. Jahrhundert* (Würzburg, 1960); and Pablo de Azcarate, *La Société des
Nations et la protection des minorités* (Geneva, 1969).

13 See Otto Büsch and Gerald D. Feldman, eds., *Historische Prozesse der deutschen Inflation, 1914–
1923* (Berlin, 1980); Carl-Ludwig Holtfrerich, *Die deutsche Inflation, 1914–1923* (Berlin,
1980); Gerald D. Feldman et al., eds., *The Experience of Inflation: International and Comparative
Studies* (Berlin and New York, 1984), and *Konsequenzen der Inflation* (Berlin, 1989); and Table
2 in the Appendix.

14 See Sidney Pollard, *The Development of the British Economy, 1914–1967*, 2nd ed. (New York,
1969), 242–54; Anne Orde, *British Policy and European Reconstruction after the First World War*
(Cambridge, 1990); and Table 1 in the Appendix.

degree explains the bitter struggle over German reparations and the significance of the Bolsheviks' refusal to pay czarist Russia's debts.[15] In this situation the Genoa Conference of 1922 represented a unique effort to focus on the reconstruction of Europe by dramatically effacing the distinction between winners and losers through a face-to-face encounter that dealt with economic and financial realities.

This volume has several themes that need to be underscored. The first is its emphasis on the interdependence of world politics and economics, of which the statesmen of 1922 were only partially, or grudgingly, aware. The second is that the contributors, while recognizing the significance of historical and structural factors, have stressed human decision making and action as the basis of Genoa's origins, course, and failure. And the third is the acknowledgment of the crucial role of contingency and accident. The essays document several instances of grave misperceptions and misunderstandings; there are also some illuminating references to unintended consequences to third parties and outsiders. Finally, the history of the Genoa Conference is replete with examples of the exaggerated images held by one participant of another, of distortions that grew instead of diminished through personal contact, and of instances in which the cost of reconciliation was deemed more threatening than the price of continued estrangement.

The Genoa Conference failed for several reasons. Early studies, which primarily blamed the Rapallo Treaty, have given way to multicausal interpretations. Besides the German–Soviet collusion, there were the conference's faulty preparation, indecisive leadership, and poor organization, along with the mounting forces of domestic opposition and the growing weakness and weariness of the conciliators. Below the surface was the seemingly insuperable practical difficulty of accommodating national security and prosperity with international economic cooperation and peace.

In the first three chapters, Carole Fink, Andrew Williams, and Peter Krüger analyze the underlying political realities that both spurred and impeded the Genoa Conference's prospects. Fink treats the evolution of postwar revisionist sentiments and shows how unresolved problems, such as Poland's eastern borders, the economic collapse of Austria, and

15 See, e.g., Harvey E. Fisk, *The Inter-Ally Debts: An Analysis of War and Post-War Public Finance, 1914–1923* (New York and Paris, 1924); Leo Pasvolsky and Harold G. Moulton, *Russian Debts and Russian Reconstruction: A Study of the Relation of Russia's Foreign Debts to Her Economic Recovery* (New York, 1924) and *War Debts and World Prosperity* (London, 1932); Marc Trachtenberg, *Reparation in World Politics: France and European Economic Diplomacy, 1916–1923* (New York, 1980), 213–59; and Tables 3 and 4 in the Appendix.

the question of minorities, intensified the forces of change. She describes the hopes raised by the Genoa Conference, which began as a major revisionist effort but soon turned to a "fine tuning" of the status quo and ended in frustration. Williams investigates the official British policy toward Soviet Russia in the context of economic aims as well as ideological and personal rivalries within the government. In particular he notes the opposition of the conservative Foreign Office to David Lloyd George's ambitious plan for European reconstruction. Finally, Krüger presents new information from the records of the German Foreign Ministry about the negotiation of the Rapallo Treaty and Anglo–German contacts at Genoa.

Chapter 4 illuminates the intricacies of the factious reparations problem, which remains in dispute even among some of the authors represented here. Sally Marks asks penetrating questions about the conduct of German foreign policy and presents a broad European perspective on the reparations issue in 1922. In Chapter 5, Manfred Berg, whose study centers on the economic and financial ties between Germany and the United States, focuses on Weimar's two major statesmen, Walther Rathenau and Gustav Stresemann, and their revisionist concepts for Germany's reintegration into the world economy. In Chapter 6, Stephen Schuker documents America's estrangement from the Old World: choosing a "businesslike" approach to the problems of European reconstruction, the U.S. government called at the same time for disarmament, a cut in Germany's reparations payments, and the fulfillment of Allied war-debt obligations.

Specific features of Soviet–Western negotiations before and during the Genoa Conference are the topic of Chapters 7–9. Anne Hogenhuis-Seliverstoff (Chapter 7) details the elements of French financial and economic diplomacy toward Soviet Russia, largely conditioned by the desire to create a united front among Russia's prewar creditors. She also explains the shifting position of Soviet negotiators against the background of internal Russian developments. A. A. Fursenko (Chapter 8) shows that the competition for Russian oil concessions had become one of the most important issues in international economic relations, pitting the United States against the major European powers, and Giorgio Petracchi (Chapter 9) describes the Italian political and commercial strategy as well as the attitude of Italian businessmen and bankers toward Soviet Russia.

Chapters 10 and 11 are devoted to the political and economic difficulties encountered by the "successor states" after World War I. Frank

Hadler reappraises the extremely active diplomacy of Czechoslovak Foreign Minister Edouard Beneš, and Magda Ádám gives a critical evaluation of the Little Entente. In Chapter 12, Antoine Fleury sheds new light on the role of the neutral countries, and in Chapter 13, Takako Ueta documents the attentive participation of the Japanese as well as their cautious wait-and-see strategy at Genoa.

It is evident that the themes of this book have a broad resonance for the rest of the twentieth century. Some of the East European problems posed at the Genoa Conference, such as unrecognized boundaries and minority questions, remain unresolved today. Also, the impending reconstruction of Eastern Europe and the Soviet Union will once more present the challenge of reconciling seemingly incompatible social, legal, economic, and political systems. Today, as in the 1920s, national, regional, and world organizations compete for dominance over the handling of economic and financial, as well as social, questions; and now, as then, great- and small-power diplomacy is conducted through a variety of permanent and ad hoc institutions. In these days, to be sure, there is a far greater integration of Western Europe, a deeper involvement in Europe by the United States and Japan, and a mounting realization – particularly on environmental questions – of the interdependence of global decision making. Moreover, Germany's role in Europe, despite the considerable cost of unification, appears far more politically and economically stable than after World War I. The years to come will show whether today's statesmen in East and West are able to meet the challenges of a reconstruction of Europe more creatively and far-sightedly than their predecessors in 1922.

1

Beyond Revisionism: The Genoa Conference of 1922

CAROLE FINK

Revisionist sentiment against the Paris Peace Treaties erupted even before the ink was dry. The victorious wartime coalition quickly unraveled, starting with Keynes's vicious attacks and America's defection, France's insistent demands for enforcement and Britain's vacillations, Italy and Japan's dissatisfaction and dissociation, and the small East European client states' factiousness and rivalries. The defeated Reich used all means at its disposal to protest the injustice of the Treaty of Versailles; it applied diplomacy and propaganda to widen breaches among the Allies, appeal to the sympathy of the neutral nations, and, while warning of the menace of bolshevism, explore a future Berlin–Moscow entente to counterbalance the Allies' domination of Europe. Lenin's Russia and the organs of the new Communist International militated against a peace settlement that had ringed Moscow with hostile regimes. The former wartime neutrals – the Netherlands, Scandinavia, and Switzerland – blamed the postwar inflation and economic contraction on a peace settlement that had disrupted traditional commercial, manufacturing, transport, and communications systems and erected onerous barriers. The specter of huge Allied war debts and enemy reparations payments, of heavy military expenditures and mounting reconstruction costs, of high taxes and tariffs, and of growing restiveness in the colonial world, all dampened the prospects of European economic recovery.

Europe's poets and philosophers lamented the postwar "wasteland" and the West's spiritual decline, and ordinary citizens faced the repercussions of a bad end to a terrible war. Franz Kafka, for example, paid sorely for his decision to opt for Czech citizenship; prevented by visa complications from taking spa cures for his tuberculosis in either Austria or Italy, he was forced to recuperate in the unfamiliar (and unfriendly) mountains of Slovakia. In a Strasbourg newly liberated by

11

France, all the German professors of the illustrious Kaiser Wilhelms Universität were summarily dismissed and chased across the Rhine; their local students had to be retrained in French. Vast numbers of people were arbitrarily rewarded or penalized for the results of the treaties: buying a rail ticket, registering a child in school, obtaining a job, and purchasing land were everyday reminders of a new order of dominant and subordinate people. In Eastern Europe the Allies had devised Minority Treaties to guarantee the rights of racial and religious minorities that were placed under the authority of the new League of Nations. Despite the hopes kindled by these treaties, they were narrowly implemented because the Allies, their client states, and the League preferred to consolidate rather than disrupt the new peace settlement. Nevertheless, revisionist sentiment could not be permanently quelled without firm, united victors and docile, inactive losers. This would not be.

The year 1921 signaled the necessity for adjustments in the peace settlement. Things had not settled down. The Allied camp was badly split over an array of European and colonial issues. Germany grudgingly accepted a considerably scaled-down reparations figure in May but then threatened to default. Soviet Russia, exhausted by civil and foreign wars, disease, and famine, signed treaties with Poland and its Baltic neighbors and made overtures to the West, offering vague terms of debt repayment and alluring trade and investment opportunities in return for aid and recognition. Turkey under Mustafa Kemal fought back against the Allies, regaining control over Constantinople and all of Anatolia and eventually overturning and renegotiating the imposed Treaty of Sèvres. The United States, resolutely aloof from Europe's political affairs, pressed the Old World to relax the Versailles shackles on Germany, resist the Bolsheviks' blandishments, and also lower its expenditures on armaments. In November 1921, the United States unilaterally convened a naval disarmament conference in Washington to promote a model new order in the Far East.[1]

Postwar Europe was dominated by the victors through organs such as the Allied Supreme Council, the Conference of Ambassadors, and the Reparation Commission. Despite the hopes of its founders and its

1 Sally Marks, *The Illusion of Peace: International Relations in Europe, 1918–1933* (New York, 1976), 26–42; E. H. Carr, *International Relations Between the Two World Wars, 1919–1939* (New York, 1966), 25–78; and also Carole Fink, *The Genoa Conference: European Diplomacy, 1921–1922* (Chapel Hill and London, 1984), 3–30.

idealistic staff, the new League of Nations – lacking German, Russian, and American membership – was an institution essentially controlled by the Allies, if occasionally a forum for small-power expression and certain humanitarian functions. Blocs such as the Little Entente and the new Baltic states coalesced around certain common aims to uphold their rights and independence.[2] In sum, the victor states and their clients had acquired a vastly varied store of privileges, power, and problems from the peace treaties; but by 1921, their governments, parliaments, and press, recognizing the adverse consequences, began exploring the paths between strict observance and treaty revision.

The convocation of the Genoa Conference of 1922 was a major revisionist effort, falling neatly between the Washington Naval Conference and the Near-East Conference at Lausanne.[3] Its stated purpose was European reconstruction: to rebind the ties between capitalist Europe and Soviet Russia, to rebuild the productive capacity of Central and Eastern Europe, and to establish a viable European peace. Called by the Supreme Council, it included ex-enemy states and neutrals as well as non-European members of the British Empire. A thirty-four-nation summit loosely modeled on the Paris Peace Conference, it threatened to lessen the distinction among victors, vanquished, and neutrals to achieve the goal of "European pacification."[4]

Genoa's supporters included a broad range of statesmen. Its spiritual father was David Lloyd George, the wily, mercurial British prime minister, who sought to inherit Woodrow Wilson's mantle by forging a more liberal peace settlement and, by meliorating Britain's economic difficulties, to prolong his own stay in power. His partner, Aristide Briand, reluctantly agreed to a European summit conference to further France's goal of an Anglo–French pact. Italy's fragile coalition government promoted Rome's interests by choosing to work in concert with Britain, thereby hoping to reduce French influence, especially over the blocs that had formed in Eastern Europe. Inside the Allied camp, especially among conservative circles in Britain, France, Belgium, and Czechoslovakia, there were ominous warnings against tampering with

---

2 Jürgen Heideking, "Oberster Rat - Botschafterkonferenz - Völkerbund: Drei Formen multilateraler Diplomatie nach dem Ersten Weltkrieg," *HZ* 231 (1980):589–630; also F. P. Walters, *A History of the League of Nations* (London, 1952).
3 On the convocation of the Genoa Conference, see *DBFP*, 19:1–136; also Fink, *Genoa Conference*, 30–68.
4 Laurent to Poincaré, Berlin, Feb. 13, 1922, FMAE B 86.

the verdict of 1918. The League of Nations quietly mobilized against a rival form of organization.[5]

The other side – those states opposed to the peace settlement – responded cautiously to a grand European summit. In the face of widespread public fears and expectations, they weighed their internal vulnerability and the prospects of inadequate gains. When the replacement of Briand by Raymond Poincaré removed the reparations problem from Genoa's agenda, the Wirth–Rathenau government rightly despaired of improving Germany's position. When the Allies delayed the conference an entire month and prepared exigent terms for loans and recognition, Lenin had to pacify Bolshevik hardliners with promises that Soviet Russia would make "no further retreat." When the United States formally refused to attend, Berlin and Moscow glumly recognized that the main source of fresh capital had withdrawn. Even the neutrals, in trying to form their own bloc, fell into disarray over their willingness and capacity to aid German and Russian recovery. The press fanned fears of the military and economic consequences of a sterile European gathering.[6]

On the eve of the Genoa Conference, additional sources of friction had emerged over gaps in the treaties and the attempts to alter the status quo. There were radical attempts through military coups, such as D'Annunzio's seizure of Fiume in March 1922, emulating the example of Czechoslovakia's occupation of Teschen (1919) and Poland's seizure of Vilna (1920), if not Hungary's short-lived invasion of the Burgenland (1921).[7] Applied against "gray" (contested), ethnically mixed areas of the peace settlement, these adventures threatened to destabilize the new Europe. But if they were confined to southern and eastern Europe, if Great-Power interests were at least formally recognized, and

5 See Christoph Stamm, *Lloyd George zwischen Innen- und Aussenpolitik: Die britische Deutschlandpolitik 1921/22* (Cologne, 1977), 135–210; Georges Suarez, *Briand: sa vie, son oeuvre*, vol. 7 (Paris, 1941), 340–5; Ferdinand Siebert, *Aristide Briand: Staatsmann zwischen Frankreich und Europa* (Zurich and Stuttgart, 1973), 244–76; Matteo Pizzigallo, "L'Italia alla Conferenza di Washington, 1921–1922," *Storia e Politica* 14 (1975):308–48, 550–89; Danilo Veneruso, *La vigilia del fascismo: Il primo ministero Facta nella crisi dello stato liberale in Italia* (Bologna, 1968). On opposition, see Fink, *Genoa Conference*, 106–18.

6 Germany: Ernst Laubach, *Die Politik der Kabinette Wirth, 1921–1922* (Lübeck and Hamburg, 1968); David Felix, *Walther Rathenau and the Weimar Republic: The Politics of Reparations* (Baltimore and London, 1971). Russia: V. I. Lenin, *Collected Works* (Moscow, 1965–71), vol. 42: 390–3, 401–4, 410, 485–6; vol. 45: 443–4, 463, 469–70, 496, 506–13; Evgenin M. Chossudovsky, "Lenin and Chicherin: The Beginnings of Soviet Foreign Policy and Diplomacy," *Millenium* 3 (1974):1–16; also Richard Day, *Leon Trotsky and the Politics of Economic Isolation* (Cambridge, 1973).

7 See G. M. Gathorne-Hardy, *A Short History of International Affairs, 1920–1939*, 4th ed. (London, 1964), 83–4, 89–90, 95.

if there was some semblance of post hoc ratification by all parties involved, gray alterations could be tolerated.

More significant was the gradualist form of revisionism promoted by Lloyd George, Briand, and the leaders of Italy. It penetrated the major Allied councils that dealt with the complex postwar problems relating to Germany and its former allies, as well as to Turkey and Russia. But its strongest manifestation was displayed in individual initiatives, which in 1921 had led to the Anglo–Russian accord, the Franco–German Wiesbaden agreement, and France's and Italy's separate pacts with Turkey.[8] Step by step, the Allies jointly and singly had begun to fill gaps, mitigate shortcomings, and create new realities.

How were the victors to reconcile their political and economic requirements with a secure multilateral process of accommodation with their former enemies? The months preceding the Genoa Conference were not promising for the creation of an orderly path of revision. In the capitals of the Allies and their small client states, there was acute difficulty in coordinating national policies. Toward Germany on reparations and disarmament, and toward Russia on debts, credits, and recognition, the Allies emitted mixed signals of collective strictness and informal, individual leniency.[9]

If Genoa's daring design had its advocates, restraint had its as well. Rarely in history had a tattered, divided coalition of victors generously heeded the vanquished's complaints, however specific or justified, even of conditions damaging an entire continent. The guns of the Marne and the Somme, of Caporetto and Warsaw were still audible; Reich and Bolshevik atrocities were still fresh in mind; and few Allied statesmen were prepared to relinquish the economic and military advantages, however temporary, that they had obtained at an exorbitant price. And rarely had triumphant powers been able to curb the propensity of their small client states to profit from victory. The widespread dissatisfaction with the direction things had gone since 1919 could be appeased either by a fundamental alteration in Europe's postwar structure or by continued coups and piecemeal adjustments. The Genoa Conference was the crucible for revisionist diplomacy and beyond.

For six weeks in April and May 1922, Italy's port was a world capital,

---

8 Richard H. Ullman, *The Anglo-Soviet Accord* (Princeton, 1973); Jay L. Kaplan, "France's Road to Genoa: Strategic, Economic, and Ideological Factors in French Foreign Diplomacy, 1921–1922" (Ph.D. diss., Columbia University, 1974), 225–88; Salahi Ramsdan Sonyel, *Turkish Diplomacy, 1918–1923* (London and Beverly Hills, 1975), 113–43; *DBFP*, vol. 17, *passim*.
9 Fink, *Genoa Conference*, 69–142.

invaded by statesmen, journalists, businessmen, and spies, anticipating a major breakthrough.[10] After a few verbal fireworks during the opening session, the Allies and the Russians quickly came to a stalemate over their mutually irreconcilable demands. Playing his German card, Soviet Foreign Minister Chicherin lured Wirth and Rathenau into the separate Rapallo Treaty, signed on Easter Sunday, which was based on mutual recognition, complete waiver of debts and reparations, and full economic cooperation. This lopsided Soviet victory broke the capitalist front and menaced the new settlement in Eastern Europe. Germany, though gaining no relief from its immediate burdens, announced its independence, its crucial position in Central Europe, and its future *Vermittler* role between Moscow and the West.[11]

Frustrated by Rapallo, Lloyd George prodded his allies to forge their own agreement with Soviet Russia; but the West's pockets were empty and the only terms on which they could agree – full debt recognition and full restitution of private property – were unacceptable to Moscow. Bolstered by Rapallo, Lenin now preferred a negative outcome at Genoa to compromising his still-vulnerable regime. When Lloyd George – irritated by French and Belgian obstruction – threatened to make his own arrangements with Russia, he was stopped by his cabinet and by his own realization of the long list of joint problems facing the Entente *after* Genoa. Sapped of harmony but still welded together by habit and fear, the Allies reunited to give the Genoa Conference a decent burial. At the abortive follow-up conference at the Hague, Allied and Russian experts recited their disagreements over the past and the future.[12]

At the Genoa Conference, the Allies halted momentum toward either wholesale or piecemeal revision, and not only because of the audacious deed at Rapallo. The meeting's inadequate planning and coordination and the excessive press coverage and secrecy – predictable defects of conference diplomacy – thwarted the Allies' conciliatory ten-

10 First-hand descriptions in Harry Graf Kessler, *Tagebücher, 1918–1937* (Frankfurt/M., 1961), 288; Ernest Hemingway, in *Toronto Daily Star*, Apr. 24, 1922; Max Eastman, *Love and Revolution* (New York, 1964), 286–7; Louise Weiss, *Mémoires d'une européenne*, vol. 2 (Paris, 1969), 161.

11 Hemmer to Wever, Genoa, Apr. 22, 1922, Germ. AA T-120 K1946/5372/K505560-63. On Rapallo, see also Karl Dietrich Erdmann, "Deutschland, Rapallo und der Westen," *VfZG* 11 (1963):105–65; Ernst Laubach, "Maltzans Aufzeichnungen über die letzten Vorgänge vor dem Abschluss des Rapallo-Vertrags," *Jahrbücher für Geschichte Osteuropas* 22 (1975):556–79; Hartmut Pogge von Strandmann, "Rapallo – Strategy in Preventive Diplomacy: New Sources and New Interpretations," in Volker R. Berghahn and Martin Kitchen, eds., *Germany in the Age of Total War* (London, 1981), 123–46.

12 See Fink, *Genoa Conference*, 177–300.

dencies. The course of the negotiations underlined the Allies' fundamental disunity, their lack of confidence, authority, and leadership, and their inability to give substance to Genoa's conciliatory facade.

The conference nevertheless stimulated several initiatives by Lloyd George that called attention to dangers in the status quo. He introduced a security treaty; he publicly raised the question of Poland's eastern borders; and he supported the efforts of Austria to obtain financial relief, and of Hungary to breathe life into the Minority Treaties. The outcome reflected the current malaise and also foreshadowed future problems.

According to the draft security pact that Lloyd George presented at Genoa, all signatories were to pledge to refrain from aggression against their neighbors' territorial integrity and to use all means short of military action to mediate disputes.[13] Imitating the Four-Power agreement just signed in Washington, this bold proposal made no distinction between kinds of aggression, or kinds of response. Lloyd George's target was apparently not only the Paris Peace Treaties (whose enforcement at the next reparations deadline might involve armed action), but also Article 10 of the League Covenant, calling on members to protect each other against any form of aggression.[14]

If Germany and Russia at once recognized the value of this pact – that of curtailing the threat of punitive action against their misdeeds – France and its allies immediately perceived the danger. When Czechoslovak Foreign Minister Edouard Beneš sought to add teeth to the proposal – to include an enforcement apparatus as well as links to the peace treaties – Lloyd George backed off.[15] His peace pact was ultimately transformed into an anodyne nonaggression declaration (from which Germany was excluded), which remained in effect for only seven months following Genoa.[16]

One of history's curiosities (it was revived six years later, in a modified form, in the Kellogg-Briand Pact), Lloyd George's nonaggression pact represented his distinctive vision of European order. Believing that European security was unattainable through armaments and alliances, he sought primarily to prevent wars by accident. Even in the face of

13 *DBFP*, 19:571.
14 Crowe memo., Mar. 20, 1922, GB FO 371 C4543/458/62; Scialoja, Osservazioni, IMAE 52/34; "Gênes et le pacte européen," *L'Europe Nouvelle,* Apr. 16, 1922; "12th Meeting of League of Nations Representatives," Genoa, Apr. 26, 1922, LNA 40A/20136/20385.
15 Carole Fink, "European Politics and Security at the Genoa Conference of 1922," in Carole Fink, Isabel V. Hull, and MacGregor Knox, eds., *German Nationalism and the European, Response, 1890–1945* (Norman and London, 1985), 150–1.
16 Text in *DBFP*, 19:987.

treaty violations or of attacks on one's allies, or on a League of Nations member, he countenanced no automatic military response without consultation and negotiation. He was convinced that Europe must begin to shed its military burdens and blocs, and concentrate on the business of peaceful pursuits, where island Britain had much to contribute.[17]

Lloyd George's main partner on the continent viewed the problem more concretely from the point of view of treaty enforcement over a recalcitrant Germany. In Paris, Poincaré (who had refused to attend the Genoa Conference) cringed over reports from the Berlin press depicting the pact as an "innovation" that might enable the Reich to evade its treaty obligations. Insisting on the primacy of France's right to take sanctions, he ordered his deputy not to accept any derogation of France's rights.[18]

Beneš was more ambitious. In private conversations, he suggested that Lloyd George first sign the long-delayed guarantee pact with France and at least publicly "give his benediction" to the "survival and prosperity" of the Little Entente and Poland before promoting a generalized nonaggression pact.[19]

But it was not Lloyd George's purpose to enshrine the existing peace treaties or to create a new instrument of collective security; he in fact vetoed an Italian amendment to his pact that bound the signatories to hold consultations in the event of aggression.[20] The pact's revisionist impulse – well understood by Wirth, Rathenau, and Lenin – and its awkward timing just after Rapallo, triggered a frantic, poorly coordinated, but nonetheless effective French-led opposition that stopped it cold.[21]

Yet despite its ultimate demotion at the final session to a safely limited "moral engagement," the nonaggression pact left a bitter aftertaste. It gave Chicherin an opportunity to taunt the West and Japan for their hypocrisy over security and disarmament and for their armed intervention against the Soviet state.[22] In the face of long-term unquenched revisionist impulses, the Allies had manifested their seem-

17 Ibid., 148–9.
18 See, especially, Poincaré to Barthou, Paris, Apr. 22, 1922, FMAE Y 31; Apr. 25, ibid., B 95; Apr. 30, ibid., B 96.
19 Grigg, Notes of conversation with Beneš, Genoa, Apr. 21, 1922, Grigg Papers, reel 9; Lloyd George–Beneš conversation, Apr. 26, 1922, *DBFP*, 18: 565–71; Beneš to Lloyd George, n.d., Lloyd George Papers, F 199/3/5.
20 Schanzer to Lloyd George, n.d., IMAE 52/34.
21 Barthou to Poincaré, no. 279–81, Genoa, Apr. 28, 1922, FMAE B 95.
22 *DBFP*, 19:1035–6.

ingly unbridgeable disagreement over creating an instrument to refrain from the sword and to adjudicate quarrels peacefully.[23]

Another delicate open question involved Poland. By raising the prospect of a Western agreement with Russia, as well as of a general European nonaggression pact, the Genoa Conference had magnified the issue of Poland's unrecognized eastern borders. Article 87 of the Versailles Treaty (which had been reconfirmed at Spa) had established the Allies' authority to fix those frontiers not yet determined. In the meantime, the new Poland, in quest of its 1772 boundaries, had used armed power and local Polish patriots to make extensive territorial gains against its neighbors: In 1919 its armies had evicted the Ukrainian captors of East Galicia; in 1920 it recaptured Vilna from Lithuania; and after victory over the Red Army, it divided Belorussia, Podolia, and Volhynia with Soviet Russia in the 1921 Treaty of Riga.[24] The deliberations at Genoa over the consequences of Poland's eastward expansion revealed the extent of the Allies' ability and willingness to exercise or to modify their treaty rights and obligations.

Earlier, Allied statesmen had been reluctant to make de facto or de jure commitments in regard to regions of the former czarist empire, pending the outcome of the Russian Civil War as well as their initial probes of the durability and pliability of Lenin's regime. Also, dubious of Warsaw's strength and stability as well as the wisdom of its bloated eastern borders, they tended to impose restrictions on Poland's attempts to consolidate and legitimize its faits accomplis. Allied policies toward Warsaw were generally ill-coordinated, occasionally contradictory, and always linked to their strategies toward Russia, Germany, the other East European states, and each other.[25]

The oil-rich, former Habsburg province of East Galicia, which had been ceded to the Allies under Article 91 of the Treaty of St. Germain, provoked international concern over the repressive policies of the Poles toward the Ukrainian population; here were two people historically split by language, class, religion, and national goals.[26] From 1919 onward, Lloyd George, under pressure by liberal and pro-Ukrainian

23 See Poincaré to all missions, Paris, May 28, 1922, and, esp., responses by Allizie (Berne), May 30, Benoist (The Hague), May 30, Barrère (Rome), May 30, Couget (Prague), May 31, FMAE B 99.
24 R. F. Leslie, ed., *The History of Poland Since 1863* (Cambridge, 1980), 133–8.
25 Anna M. Cienciala and Titus Komarnicki, *From Versailles to Locarno: Keys to Polish Foreign Policy, 1919–1925* (Lawrence, Kan., 1984), chapter 1; also Piotr S. Wandycz, *France and Her Eastern Allies, 1919–1925* (Minneapolis, 1962).
26 Cienciala and Komarnicki, *Versailles to Locarno*, 151–81.

interests in Britain and Canada, had sporadically proposed solutions short of outright annexation, such as a twenty-five–year mandate supervised by the League, or some measure of autonomy for the Ukrainians. France, which at this time was strongly supporting Polish interests in Upper Silesia, urged restraint on its ally in the East. Beneš advocated an autonomous East Galicia, possibly linked commercially with Prague. From their opposite ideological viewpoints, the Moscow government and the remnants of the "West Ukrainian Republic" of East Galicia-in-exile both loudly complained of Poland's "colonizing" Galicia. But with the Allies distracted in the fall of 1921 by a host of major questions, Warsaw took advantage of the "indeterminate state of affairs" to proceed with the administrative annexation of East Galicia.[27]

Almost immediately afterward, in early 1922, Vilna's precarious autonomy was extinguished.[28] Poland, which had refused the League Council's proposals for a plebiscite, defied the Great Powers by calling elections for a Vilna *Sejm* and then acquiescing in the assembly's demand for incorporation. Lithuania, backed by Soviet Russia and Germany, was irreconcilable over the Polish coup.[29] By wavering too long over an alternative solution – a Polish–Lithuanian federation guaranteeing Lithuanian sovereignty – France and Britain had neither effectively restrained Warsaw nor won its confidence.

The frontier adjustments in the Treaty of Riga, adding almost 52,000 square miles to Poland's territory, had not been recognized by the Allies.[30] Indeed, the Riga Treaty placed Poland in the unique position of having virtually recognized Soviet Russia and the Soviet Ukraine, thus distancing itself from Britain and France, Czechoslovakia, and Romania; together with Latvia, Estonia, and Finland, Poland had also absolved itself from any Allied claim to imperial Russian debts. One of Poland's principal goals at Genoa was to obtain recognition, and prevent alteration, of the existing Russian treaties. But Paris and London held the key to Warsaw's ultimate security with the timing and nature of their acceptance of Riga.[31]

---

27 Muller to Gregory, Warsaw, Nov. 15, 1921, GB FO 371 6811/77/N13044/55. On Lloyd George's conception, see Grigg to Montpetit, Apr. 30, 1922, Grigg Papers, reel 10.
28 *DBFP*, vol. 23, no. 263. Background in Alfred Erich Senn, *The Great Powers, Lithuania, and the Vilna Question, 1920–1928* (Leiden, 1966).
29 A state of "cold war" existed between the two neighbors for fifteen years: no diplomatic relations, no direct communications, not even direct postal service. Cf. Anne M. Cienciala, *Poland and the Western Powers, 1938–39: A Study in the Interdependence of Eastern and Western Europe* (London and Toronto, 1968), 49–52.
30 Piotr S. Wandycz, *Soviet–Polish Relations, 1917–1921* (Cambridge, Mass., 1969), 250–90.
31 Laroche, note (for Poincaré) with additional notes by J. Laroche, Apr. 3, 1922, Peretti note, Apr. 10, Zamoyski notes, Apr. 6 and 10, Poincaré to Zamoyski, Apr. 19, FMAE Pologne, vol. 137; also *DBFP*, 19:295, 437, 447, 449.

On the eve of the Genoa Conference, the Allies, though distracted, were plainly displeased by the Vilna annexation as the climax of Warsaw's expansion.[32] The domestic as well as the diplomatic uproar over Vilna caused a reshuffling of the Polish cabinet. A former Lithuanian landowner, Konstanty Skirmunt, was named the new foreign minister, and he at once attempted to play a prominent role on his nation's behalf. He expressed warm support for Lloyd George's "pacification" efforts in Eastern Europe, making overtures to the Little Entente and offering himself as intermediary with Russia.[33]

The results were not promising. Beneš, suspecting a rival, assured Poland's exclusion from the Little Entente. Paris deplored Skirmunt's frenetic demarches, especially when Poland's meeting with the Baltic States triggered an intervention by Moscow that underlined Soviet dominance of the area. When Skirmunt journeyed to Paris and London on the eve of the Genoa Conference, his anxious queries over Poland's eastern frontiers encountered a cool reception from Poincaré and Lloyd George (a known opponent of Poland's territorial ambitions).[34]

At the Genoa Conference, Skirmunt found the limelight uncomfortable. Poland was given a seat on the important Political Sub-Commission; but the Rapallo Treaty was a grim reminder of Poland's vulnerability, however calmly Warsaw tried to react.[35] Beneš was a persistent opponent. During his private discussions with Lloyd George over the nonaggression pact, the Czech foreign minister adamantly opposed recognition of the present Polish–Soviet frontier, or of Polish control over Vilna and East Galicia.[36]

Lloyd George expressed his own opinion on the night of April 26, when he announced to a group of British and American journalists: "From the Baltic down to the Black Sea there is hardly a line . . . which

32 *DBFP*, 23:333. At the end of January, Curzon had warned Sapieha, the new Polish minister in London, that "annexation would be the final blow to Poland's international status," quoted in Cienciala and Komarnicki, *Versailles to Locarno*, 148.

33 See unsigned note, Paris, Feb. 23, 1922, FMAE B 107, on meeting in Berlin on Feb. 11 between Polish foreign ministry officials Juliusz Łukasiewicz and August Zaleski, and Soviet representatives Karl Radek and Nikolai Krestinsky.

34 Sergiusz Mikulicz, *Od Genui do Rapallo* (Warsaw, 1966), 49–79; Zygmunt J. Gasiorowski, "Polish-Czechoslovak Relations, 1918–1922," *Slavonic and East European Review* 35 (1956):172–93; notes, Apr. 3, 4, and 10, 1922, FMAE, Pologne, vol. 137; *DBFP*, 19:298–9, n. 3.

35 Muller to Curzon, Warsaw, Mar. 31, 1922, GB FO 371 C4903/458/62; Baraute to Poincaré, Warsaw, Apr. 13, FMAE Y 29; Apr. 20 and 26, ibid., B 117; Benndorf to AA, Warsaw, Apr. 29, Germ. AA T-120 L3094255/K096477-79; also tel. by Austrian Minister in Warsaw to Foreign Ministry in Vienna, May 8, AHHSt 180.

36 What was in Beneš's mind: perhaps to induce the British to trade a guarantee of support for France for London's abandonment of Poland's eastern claims; perhaps to create an East Galician "corridor" to facilitate Czechoslovak trade with Soviet Russia? *DBFP*, 19:565–70.

is not contested, and every one of those lines involves in itself the possibility of a terrible conflict in Europe." Scarcely reassuring to Poland, or France, was his depiction of a "racial lava surging right through the center of Europe" and his declaration that neither Germany nor Russia could be kept down permanently by any combination of powers.[37] Contrasting Romania's borders (which Britain, though not Russia, had already recognized) with Poland's, he termed Riga a "thoroughly bad treaty," the Lithuanian frontier still unsettled, and the East Galicia question still open.[38] As if to confirm the menacing wind from the east, Chicherin chastised Skirmunt for violating the Riga Treaty by signing the Allied protest against the Rapallo Treaty, and he criticized Poland's repressive policy in Vilna and East Galicia.[39]

In an acrimonious private meeting with Skirmunt, Lloyd George painted an even darker picture of the Soviet threat and Britain's irritation with its allies. The foreign minister pleaded for a prompt, orderly settlement of Poland's eastern frontiers. With the Russian negotiations foundering and his pact in ruins, Lloyd George impetuously decided to urge the delegates to discuss this delicate problem. But he then had to back off in the face of French and Italian coolness. Skirmunt seemed relieved to exit center stage and let the border question simmer a bit longer. But once more Chicherin took the opportunity during Genoa's closing session to underscore the uneven and unsettled conditions in Eastern Europe – the borders that were recognized by treaties and those contested frontiers established by force – where Russian and Allied interests would inevitably clash.[40]

Genoa's brief focus on Poland's vulnerable eastern boundaries had immediate repercussions. On his return to Warsaw, Skirmunt was attacked by the nationalists close to the militant Piłsudski because of the paltry results at Genoa. The cabinet soon fell, at least in part as a result of its inability to counter Lloyd George's bullying and Chicherin's taunts.[41] The Allies had not advanced positively or harmoniously on the recognition question; Italy had thrown its weight erratically, Beneš had

37 John Saxon Mills, *The Genoa Conference* (London, 1922), 117–19. That day, in private conferences with Barthou and with Jaspar and Schanzer, Lloyd George had worried out loud about Poland's being "crushed like an egg-shell," or "cracking like an egg" between neighbors Germany and Russia, *DBFP,* 19:574, 588.
38 *DBFP,* 19:588, 630–6, 677–9; also Barthou to Poincaré, May 3, 1922, FMAE, Pologne, vol. 137.
39 Chicherin to Skirmunt, Genoa, Apr. 24, 1922, *DVP SSSR,* 5:266–8.
40 *DBFP,* 19:741–6, 799–803; 23:483–4, 489–91.
41 Hoare to Curzon, Warsaw, May 18, June 1 and 7, 1922, GB FO 371 N4926/1876/55, N5454, N5644/5233/55; Panafieu to Poincaré, FMAE B 99, June 5, ibid., Y 37.

blocked solidarity among the East European states, and the Rapallo Treaty had raised the specter of a new partition of Poland.

Nine months later, on March 14, 1923, the Conference of Ambassadors finally recognized Poland's frontiers with Lithuania and Soviet Russia and its sovereignty over East Galicia.[42] By then, Lloyd George had fallen; the Allies, locked in the Ruhr crisis and the Memel dispute, bowed to Warsaw's faits accomplis. However, Poland's relief at this formal consecration of its borders was counterbalanced by the costs and conditions: Backed by Moscow and Berlin, Lithuania refused to accept the loss of its "capital" and for fifteen years maintained a state of "cold war" with Poland; Allied recognition of the Riga Treaty was accompanied by their renunciation of any responsibility to defend Poland against a Soviet attack; and, as foreshadowed by near civil war during the elections of September 1922 and by Ukrainian Communist party chief Christian Rakovsky's characterization of the union as an "act of violence," Poland's sovereignty over East Galicia was a mixed blessing at best. If the Genoa Conference had proved an inappropriate forum to deal with acts of force and complex ethnic and territorial questions involving great and small powers, the League of Nations had also been ominously bypassed.

Another example of hopes raised and dashed at Genoa involved Austria. Living largely on its accumulated capital, the new republic covered its expenses by printing extraordinary quantities of paper money to stave off bankruptcy.[43] Banned from *Anschluss* and constricted by its neighbors' tariff walls, the coalition government of Johann Schober had attempted to ease its isolation in late 1921 by concluding the controversial Treaty of Lany with Czechoslovakia, which traded credits for voluntary recognition of the Treaty of St. Germain. A long-term solution was essential to maintain Austria's survival and independence.[44]

Austria's rehabilitation touched the interests of all of its neighbors. Beneš sought to attenuate its Pan-German longings by bringing Austria within the orbit of the Little Entente. Italy sought to thwart this by tying its aid to Austria's strict neutrality, offering concessions in the

---

42 *Documents on Polish-Soviet Relations, 1939–1945,* vol. 1 (London, 1961), no. 4; also *League of Nations Treaty Series,* vol. 15 (Geneva, 1923), 260–5.

43 The cost of living multiplied twenty times between December 1921 and December 1922, cf. C. A. Macartney and A. W. Palmer, *Independent Eastern Europe* (New York, 1966), 200.

44 Rosenberg to AA, Vienna, Dec. 12, 1921, Germ. AA T-120 K362/3996/K115969-70; memo. from Austrian legation to Lloyd George, Jan. 25, 1922, Lloyd George Papers, F49/2/4; also K. W. Rothschild, *Austria's Economic Development between the Two Wars* (London, 1947), 14–32.

port of Trieste and dangling lures of joint ventures in Russia. While resting his principal hopes for rescue upon the League of Nations, Schober considered the Genoa Conference an important opportunity to plead his nation's dire financial straits and save his coalition government.[45]

Schober, like Skirmunt, initially found very limited interest and sympathy for his nation's troubles at the Genoa Conference. Italian Premier Luigi Facta was vague and noncommittal; Louis Barthou, the head of the French delegation (on instructions from Poincaré not to interfere in the League's work), was "glacial"; and Lloyd George, after delivering a tough lecture on the dangers of *Anschluss,* warmly praised Beneš's "statesmanship." In their private talks, the agile Czech foreign minister displayed an intense interest in Austrian politics and hinted at the prospect of another United States-backed loan.[46]

During the difficult days after Rapallo, Britain pulled another coup, by unexpectedly introducing the Austrian question in one of the technical commissions. On April 20, Chancellor of the Exchequer Sir Robert Horne called for a meeting the next day of countries "interested in Austria." Through this unexpected back door, Britain tried to revive Genoa's prospects, and Schober suddenly hoped for support – for an immediate renunciation by those states holding liens on all of Austria's assets, which would enable his government to apply for long-term credits and relief.[47]

But Austria's indebtedness was inextricable from its neighbors' financial burdens. Two of the successor states, Yugoslavia and Romania, refused to waive their claim to liens without relief from their "liberation payments," that proportion of the former Habsburg debt they had been forced to assume; although largely fictitious, these liberation payments did affect their own ability to secure credits – as Beneš eloquently insisted to the gathered diplomats. Faced with this obduracy, the British canceled their efforts. Schober, who had attempted to appeal to Europe's "conscience" as well as to its interests, returned empty-

45 "Programm für Genua," AHHSt 687; also Ackers-Douglas to FO, Vienna, Mar. 1, Apr. 6, 1922, GB FO 371 C3325/396/3, C5254/458/62; Pontalis to Poincaré, Vienna, Feb. 8, 1922, note, Vienna, Feb. 15, Poincaré to Min. Finance, Feb. 15, FMAE B 86; Pontalis to Poincaré, Mar. 25, ibid., B 90; Apr. 12, ibid., B 93; also Jung-Schuller conversations, IMAE 52/4.
46 Oppenheimer note, Nervi, Apr. 10, 1922, Bischoff Hausnotizen, Apr. 15 and 19, AHHSt 687.
47 Hennet to Schober, Nervi, Apr. 20, 1922, Schwartzwald to BMA, Genoa, Apr. 21, A Fin. Arch. 17; see also "Sixth meeting of League of Nations representatives," Genoa, Apr. 20, 1922, LNA 40A/20136/20226.

handed to Vienna where, at the end of May, he was forced by Pan-German rancor to resign.[48]

At Genoa, the successor states also refused to bow to outside pressures to attenuate their staunch protectionism. Beneš skillfully led his colleagues against British, Italian, and Austrian efforts to lower economic, currency, and transportation barriers. Bolstered by France, the Little Entente resisted any semblance of "reunifying" the Danubian area under the tutelage of one or more powers.[49]

Help came for Austria a full six months later, through a combination of private loans, government guarantees, political pledges, Austrian self-discipline, and the supervision and surveillance of the League of Nations.[50] But by then the right-wing cleric Ignaz Seipel was at the helm. A "saved" Austria had been neither integrated with its neighbors politically nor reconciled to its enforced independence from Germany. The powers that controlled Vienna's fate had been forced to prescribe elaborate stopgap remedies for the desperately ill patient without committing themselves to its ultimate survival.

A final example of frustrated treaty revisionism at Genoa concerned Hungary, which shared many of Austria's burdens – reduced frontiers, heavy reparations, dire economic straits, and exclusion from the League. Because of the Little Entente's militancy against the dangers of a Habsburg restoration, it was even more isolated. Budapest considered itself the spokesman for three million of its kin people who were now minorities in Czechoslovakia, Romania, and Yugoslavia, and it was therefore a strong advocate of activating the guarantees in the Minority Treaties.[51]

Before the Genoa Conference, the Hungarian premier, Count Istvan Bethlen, signaled his intention to use this opportunity to improve Hungary's international position, which had deteriorated still further over the Habsburg-restoration crisis. Italy gave measured support, but the

48 Schwartzwald to Ministry of Finance, Nervi, Apr. 21, 1922, A Fin. Arch.; Barthou to Poincaré, Genoa, May 11, 1922, FMAE B 97; Schonfeld to State Dept., Vienna, May 22, 1922, USDS 550 E1/330; Ackers-Douglas to FO, Vienna, May 19 and 26, 1922, GB FO 371 C7444, C7821/396/3.

49 Einstein to State Dept., Prague, Feb. 28, 1922, USDS 550 E1/124; Müller, Bericht, Apr. 25, 1922, Germ. AA T-120 K1946/5362/K505583; Barthou to MAE, Genoa, Apr. 25, 1922, FMAE B 95; Schwarzenberg to AA, Vienna, May 15, 1922, Germ. AA T-120 K362/3996/ K116049.

50 Peter E. Schmidt, "The Relief of Austria, 1919–1922" (Ph.D. diss., Case Western Reserve University, 1977), 427–521; also F. P. Walters, *League of Nations,* 206–10.

51 Hohler to FO, Budapest, Mar. 8, 1922, Germ. AA T-120, C3525/458/62.

Germans shied away from collaboration.[52] The Hungarian delegate used Genoa's opening session to read a lengthy statement recounting his neighbors' arbitrary measures that deliberately violated the personal and property rights guaranteed in the Minority Treaties.[53]

Beneš led the opposition, deeming the appeal outside the competence of the Genoa Conference, falling instead under the jurisdiction of the League of Nations. France and Poland supported the Little Entente. But desiring a "large" conference, which was not restricted to Russia alone, Britain and Italy had agreed in advance to admit the minorities question into Genoa's "political" deliberations. Hungary submitted a formal request to the Political Commission of the Genoa Conference. It proposed superseding the League's procedures with the appointment of commissions of enquiry to conduct on-the-spot investigations of minority conditions in the successor states.[54] While Genoa's principal actors were consumed with the Russian negotiations, Bethlen used his abbreviated stay to conduct private meetings with his neighbors; he found Beneš and Romanian Prime Minister Ionel Brătianu correct, but unsympathetic to his complaints over the treatment of Hungarians in Slovakia and Transylvania.[55]

When the Genoa Conference was about to end, a tired, irritable Lloyd George had to curb his concern for minority rights in Eastern Europe. Time constraints and realism forced him to acknowledge that the proper forum for such questions was Geneva.[56] This was a bittersweet victory for the League; its largely idle representatives clutched the handful of referred items from the prolonged summit conference as welcome confirmation of Genoa's ephemerality and Geneva's competence in dealing with Europe's knotty social, economic, and ethnic problems.

Postwar Hungary had for the first time taken part in a major diplomatic gathering, but, barred from all of Genoa's working subcommissions, only in a minor, ceremonial way. Afterward, it failed to obtain

52 Fürstenberg to AA, Budapest, Feb. 26, Mar. 2, 16, and 25, Apr. 4, 1922, Germ. AA T-120, L998/5412/L286550-51, 565-6, L999/5411/L285032-42, 340-51, 434; Simson, Aufzeichnung, Apr. 12, ibid., L795/5105/L233207-8.
53 Statement to the Political Commission, Apr. 11, 1922, *DBFP*, 19:360–1. At the time there was a complaint pending in the League against Romania over the treatment of its Hungarian minority, but also one directed against the Budapest government for having imposed a *numerus clausus* on its Jewish minority.
54 Text in *DBFP*, 19:836–7.
55 Ibid., 805–6; Doulcet to Poincaré, Budapest, May 2, 1922, FMAE B 98; John Balfour to Curzon, Budapest, Apr. 28, May 4, 1922, GB FO 371 C6423, C6741/458/62.
56 *DBFP*, 19:938–9.

British support in sponsoring its minorities appeal or in challenging the League's method of handling its "large and onerous burden" against the obstruction of the successor states.[57] But if the heady atmosphere of international conference diplomacy had solved no particular problem for Budapest, it had at least opened larger prospects for airing grievances and keeping minorities and border questions alive.[58]

By creating an environment in which unfulfilled and unfulfillable revisionist hopes were both ventilated and quashed and where the Allies had held together more in form than from commitment, the Genoa Conference produced short- and long-term repercussions. The momentum either for partial or comprehensive conciliation was checked, and Rapallo undoubtedly opened the road to the Ruhr. In the year after Genoa, the erratic fulfiller Rathenau was followed by the defter revisionist Gustav Stresemann, the exigent but wavering Poincaré was forced by financial exigency to curb France's insistence on strict enforcement, and the British Tories who succeeded Lloyd George promoted a precarious balance in Europe between treaty maintenance and selective revision. Japan moved farther away from collaboration with its European partners; and Italy's paltry rewards for its labors at Genoa undoubtedly facilitated the Fascists' seizure of power, resulting in an aggressive defiance of its former allies for its own nationalistic aims. Lenin's eclipse, coupled with the meager fruits of Genoa for Soviet Russia, aided the ascendancy of the hardliners and Moscow's increased alienation from the West. In Eastern Europe, the accommodating Schobers and Skirmunts were replaced by the stubborn Seipels and Piłsudski. In the new power balance that emerged after the Ruhr crisis and Germany's recovery, Beneš rapidly receded as a principal spokesman for the Allied camp.

Nevertheless, one side's *victoria mutilato* remained the other side's condition of "no, no never!" The "peaceful" twenties carried the heavy burden of Genoa's legacy of failure.

---

57 See Banffy to Gregory, London, June 9, 1922, GB FO 371 C8306/7925/211, also Crowe memo., June 30, Lampson to Tufton, July 7, Lampson minute, July 8, Drummond to Tufton, July 15, unsigned memo., July 20, Hurst to Lampson, July 31, Hohler to Lampson, Budapest, Aug. 25, ibid., C9534, C9694, C11024, C10921/7925/21, C12569/7965/21.

58 Hohler to Balfour, Budapest, June 2, 1922, GB FO 371 C8128/458/62. Despite its "implacable resentment against the territorial settlement," Hungary in the fall of 1922 was unanimously admitted to the League of Nations which, during the next two years, supervised its economic and financial restoration; until Germany's arrival in 1926, Hungary was the leading spokesman for minority rights and treaty revision, Walters, *League of Nations*, 211, 260–2, 288.

2

The Genoa Conference of 1922: Lloyd George and the Politics of Recognition

ANDREW WILLIAMS

It would be difficult to exaggerate the interest shown by historians and publicists in the period 1918–22. Lloyd George has been one of the most written about politicians in British contemporary history, barring Churchill. Until the 1960s or even 1970s most of this attention was negative, the degree of excoriation for his alleged "adventurism" in foreign affairs vying with that for his "duplicity" in domestic matters. A. J. P. Taylor's establishment of the Beaverbrook Library (now in the House of Lords) did much to remedy this tendency, as did the tireless writings of Kenneth Morgan.[1]

Until fairly recently, comment on the foreign policy pursued by the Lloyd George coalition usually was seen as subsidiary to that on domestic matters. We, of course, have Ullman's three-volume study of Anglo–Soviet relations until 1921, and Stephen White has contributed his *Britain and the Bolshevik Revolution* (1979) and, now, *The Origins of Detente* (1985)[2] on Genoa itself. Carole Fink's *The Genoa Conference* (1984) is the inspiration for this whole volume of essays and speaks for its own importance. Other works not of direct relevance are Michael Fry's *Lloyd George and Foreign Policy* (1977), which only goes up to 1916, and Michael Dockerill's contribution to Taylor's essay collection on Lloyd George's foreign policy, again only up to 1914. These books are at their strongest on the international diplomacy of the period,

---

1 Kenneth Morgan's *Consensus and Disunity: The Lloyd George Coalition Government, 1918–22* (Oxford, 1979) is the benchmark against which other accounts have to be measured. A. J. P. Taylor, ed., *Lloyd George: Twelve Essays* (London, 1971), brought together a group of young scholars, including Morgan, who have provoked something of a revision of the former prime minister's reputation.

2 Other books which touch on Anglo–Soviet relations in the period are Teddy J. Uldricks' *Ideology and Diplomacy* (Beverly Hills, 1979), and E. H. Carr's *The Bolshevik Revolution*, especially vol. 3 (London, 1966).

whereas White's *Origins of Detente* is perhaps weakest in its depiction of domestic context and discussion of attitudinal aspects.

This essay will therefore assume a background knowledge of the Genoa Conference itself and concentrate on 1) the state of Lloyd George's command over British politics and 2) the views of the "other side" (particularly the French and the Russians) held by key decision makers in Britain.

British hopes for fulfillment of Lloyd George's 1918 promise of a land "fit for heroes" had evaporated in the deepening economic and political crisis of the years that followed. By late 1921 unemployment had surged to over 25 percent of the insured working population, an unprecedented figure. Industrial unrest had almost reached the level of 1910–14, variously described as the "period of the Great Unrest" and the "Strange Death of Liberal England."[3] Lloyd George dominated a cabinet made up of Conservatives and Liberals who frequently had little in common. It has often been claimed that the compromises forced on Liberalism after the Lloyd George/Asquith split of 1916 led to its terminal decline and the rise of the Labour Party as that of both the working man and the disaffected working class.

Yet Morgan is probably right in saying that the coalition was the "only plausible inter-party government of national unity that modern Britain has known, other than in times of war."[4] The reasons for this are complex but lie at least partly in the need for nonpartisan politics in dealing with the immense international and socioeconomic disruption caused by war, which required a very adaptable policy. Ironically, the different parties that supported Lloyd George in the inevitable change of course that this entailed have pilloried him for being so "adaptable."

This was one of the few periods in this century, perhaps the last, when Britain was still able to influence its own destiny by manipulating that of others in Europe, much of which was prostrate. The Russians' initial desire to hold in London the meeting that later became the Genoa Conference reflected the continued importance of Britain as an actor in international politics.[5] Although Britain had a chance to exert its influence, it also needed Europe. If there was to be a trade revival, only Europe really provided a coherent market for British goods, especially manufactures from the smokestack industries. Lloyd George did

---

3 The origins of this phrase are, of course, in George Dangerfield's book of the same title, first published in New York in 1935.
4 Morgan, *Consensus and Disunity*, 1.   5 Cf. GB FO 371/C459/458/62, Jan. 1922.

not have the ability to apply deficit funding, although there is evidence his instincts went that way when even its inventor, Keynes, was still at heart a "sound money man."[6]

Russia was perceived as a key hope for the revitalization of markets for British exports and for those of the rest of Europe, but the British government could not go it alone in opening up the Russian market. It needed at least the good will of the Allies and that of the financial markets, especially the City of London. As Morgan says, "[it] made Millerand, Krassin, Rathenau, Poincaré and Kemal more decisive in shoring up or undermining Lloyd George's position than all the onslaughts of machine politicians or press lords at home."[7]

Another important factor in the situation was the *kind* of government Lloyd George practiced, which so annoyed his peers both at the time and since. He governed with a very small group of intimate advisors, the "Garden Cabinet," who often were not ministers at all. For example, when it suited him, he sidestepped the Foreign Office under Lord Curzon. His main advisor on Russia, especially during the 1921 trade talks, was E. F. Wise, who went on to be advisor to the Russian trade mission, ARCOS, and a Labour Member of Parliament.[8] Sir Edward Grigg, also not a minister, had his ear more consistently than Austen Chamberlain, by late 1921 leader of the Conservative Party. The archival evidence is full of complaints from Foreign Secretary Curzon that he had not been informed of key foreign policy decisions.

However, as both Morgan and White point out,[9] not too much should be made of these differences. A certain revisionism toward Germany, a dislike of France, and an agreement to keep the Empire strong were all widely felt to be good ideas. There were, evidently, differences over Turkey (the Chanak episode of 1922 showed this) and Russia, but the foreign secretary and his prime minister were not the ones to fall out. Not much personal love was lost, however, and it must be said that

---

6 Robert Skidelsky, among other radical elements, such as the Independent Labour Party and Liberal Party, did suggest what was later to be the basis of "Keynesianism." Cf. Robert Skidelsky, *Politicians and the Slump* (London, 1967) and *Oswald Mosley* (London, 1975) among other books. For a more recent discussion of this area see Peter Clarke, *The Keynesian Revolution in the Making, 1924–1936* (London, 1988).

7 Cf. Morgan, *Consensus and Disunity*, 110.

8 He also played an important role in the formal renewal of relations with Russia in 1929 and was constantly putting pressure on Ramsay MacDonald in and out of office. Cf. Andrew Williams, *Labour and Russia: The Attitude of the Labour Party to the Soviet Union, 1924–1934* (Manchester, 1989).

9 Cf. Stephen White, *The Origins of Detente: The Genoa Conference and Soviet–Western Relations, 1921–1922* (Cambridge, 1985), 13; and Morgan, *Consensus and Disunity*, 31, 114, where he says Curzon disliked Lloyd George's "protocol" not the "substance of his policies."

a lot of the later hostility toward Lloyd George derived more from his parvenu ancestry and difficult personal relationships than from his policies.[10] Nonetheless, he practiced a kind of government that still raises eyebrows in Britain, as when Mrs. Thatcher invited a nonelected economist to advise her in Downing Street.

Before elaborating where differences did exist, we should first look at the recent past of Anglo–Soviet contacts. The initial British reaction to the Bolshevik takeover had been a limited intervention, sanctioned largely by Winston Churchill as secretary of state for war. As Ullman makes abundantly clear, Lloyd George and the rest of the cabinet did not share Churchill's enthusiasm for the action and gave the approval they did out of a fear of losing Tory "diehard" support and having Churchill (ironically a Liberal) as a powerful voice in opposition. White shows that the government was looking for a way to disengage from conflict well before 1920 and that the Labour left has created a myth that it was their "Councils of Action" that prevented British support for Poland against the Bolsheviks in that year.[11]

Neither the Liberal/Conservative coalition nor indeed the Labour Party had much affection for the Bolsheviks, either initially or later. As I have shown elsewhere, the Labour leadership was always wary of Communist infiltration until at least 1939 and shared a view that there were "extremists" and "moderates" among the Bolsheviks, and that it was necessary to discourage the former group at the expense of the latter.[12] Arthur Henderson, at that time in Lloyd George's cabinet himself, was sent to Russia in June 1917 to bolster Kerensky. He saw the future rulers of Lenin's Russia as an "asiatic" menace come to life and summed this up as "Skin a Russian and Discover the Tartar."[13]

The wider principal concern about Russia lay in its destabilizing impact, especially in working-class circles and the Empire. The main fear was of "propaganda," which would be used in the Middle East and India to foment revolt.[14] But on February 10, 1920, Lloyd George

10 For a discussion of this see M. Bentley, *The Liberal Mind, 1914–1929* (Cambridge, 1977).
11 Cf. Stephen White, *Britain and the Bolshevik Revolution* (London, 1979), 43–51; Richard H. Ullman, *Intervention and the War* (Princeton, 1961) and *Britain and the Russian Civil War* (Princeton, 1968).
12 Cf. Williams, *Labour and Russia*, for more details.
13 Labour Party Archives, HEN/14/3, June 1917. See also J. M. Winter, "Arthur Henderson, the Russian Revolution and the Reconstruction of the Labour Party," *Historical Journal* 15 (1972):733–73.
14 One typical example is from the Viceroy of India to the Secretary of State for India, Nov. 11, 1919, GB CAB C.P. 148, Lloyd George Papers, F202.

admitted to Parliament what the Allied Supreme Council had already accepted in January: "Russia cannot be restored to sanity by force, as events have proved. Commerce has sobering as well as beneficial effects. The way to help Russia and Europe and Britain is by trade – that is, to fight anarchy, wherever it appears, by abundance."[15]

The next year was spent putting this pious hope into initial practice. The modalities of contact are significant because they illustrate the difficulty of later contacts, as at Genoa. Curzon expressed the hope that Litvinov, "this arch intriguer," would not be sent, and Krassin was the compromise candidate who, Morgan perceptively says, was seen by Lloyd George as a kind of Sir Eric Geddes, a businessman not a politician.[16] The first contacts were with members of Soviet cooperatives, not with the Bolsheviks. E. F. Wise was given the task of summarizing the pros and cons of trade, which were to be discussed at an Allied Supreme Council meeting at San Remo in late April 1920. Wise had met with members of the cooperatives on April 7 in Copenhagen, where he was "assisted" by O'Malley of the Foreign Office and R. W. Matthew of the Board of Trade, together with Monsieur du Halgouet of France. Wise felt that the group also represented the views of Belgium and Italy, somewhat naively perhaps as things turned out.

Wise decided that the Soviet system, if not communism, was permanent and that a trade agreement would be a first important step toward getting the Russians to behave properly in other areas, especially if they were given the hope of full recognition, either de facto or de jure.[17] On April 26, the Allied Supreme Council agreed to approach the negotiations cautiously by keeping them purely "economic," and Krassin arrived in London at the end of May. Wise warned just before he arrived that, to be successful, politics would *have* to be discussed at some point together with economics, but he was well aware that the main obstacle to this was the attitude of the other Allies, especially the Americans. The British would soon also have to decide where they stood on such thorny questions as the debts owed the Allies by the czarist regime. Wise had seen "indications that the Soviet Government is

---

15 Hansard, *Debates*, Feb. 10, 1920, quoted in Xenia Eudin and Harold Fisher, *Soviet Russia and the West, 1920–1927* (Stanford, 1957), 6. The best account of the trade discussions is Ullman's *The Anglo-Soviet Accord* (Princeton, 1973).

16 Morgan, *Consensus and Disunity,* 135. There is evidence that the Russians agreed, which is why they wanted Litvinov to give political purity to their position. See E. F. Wise, "Negotiations for Re-opening Trade with Soviet Russia," Apr. 18, 1920, Lloyd George Papers, F/202/3/3.

17 Ibid.

prepared to admit some claims as the price of peace but not otherwise."[18]

Even at this stage, however, it was clear that the French were going to prove the main obstacle to moving from the economic to the political. After discussions with Jules Cambon in late May 1920, Curzon reported that the French were not prepared to meet Krassin, even on the basis of the San Remo agreement, because to do so would imply some sort of recognition. Moreover, even the mild Krassin was seen by Cambon as "an extreme Bolshevist, imbued with their worst and most dangerous theories."[19] Although he "melted" a little toward the end of the interview, Cambon would go no further than promising to mention the discussion of a meeting to the French cabinet. Another reason the negotiations took so long to reach any satisfactory conclusion was the situation in Poland. The Poles eventually emerged triumphant in October, but the hostility of France proved a major obstacle to any real settlement of the Bolshevik problem.

In the Trade Agreement signed on March 16, 1921, Curzon got points promising to stop all "official" propaganda and to release nationals of both countries. The rest of the text was aimed at the modalities of a new trading arrangement, the debt question being left for a formal peace treaty to be signed later.[20] Curzon also clearly agreed with Lloyd George about the usefulness of the Trade Agreement for bringing the Russians into line: "In my judgment the Trading Agreement with Great Britain is of such supreme importance to them (for it is about the only thing that stands between them and collapse) that I can hardly imagine them not accepting our proposals [about propaganda and debts] without the least delay."[21] But it was not long before propaganda again appeared, and by August 1921 Curzon was complaining both about Lloyd George's handling of the Russians through the Board of Trade rather than the Foreign Office and about the "almost open warfare against us" in Asia Minor, Persia, and Afghanistan. Since a previous letter had said that "it is the Asian propaganda that is the real danger," clearly the Trade Agreement had not had Curzon's desired effect.[22]

The autumn of 1921 was dominated by the Washington Naval Con-

18 E. F. Wise, "Note on Economic Relations with Russia," May 21, 1920, Lloyd George Papers, F/202/3/5.
19 Curzon to Lloyd George, May 28, 1920, Lloyd George Papers, F/12/3/37.
20 *Trade Agreement between His Britannic Majesty's Government and the Government of the Russian Socialist Federal Soviet Republic,* GB Cmd. 1217, 1921.
21 Curzon to Lloyd George, Oct. 8, 1920, Lloyd George Papers, F/13/1/25.
22 Curzon to Lloyd George, Aug. 3, 1921, and Oct. 8, 1920, Lloyd George Papers, F/13/2/68 and F/13/1/25.

ference, which finally laid to rest the myth of the "Three Power Standard" so beloved of British admirals. This symbol of decline accompanied soaring unemployment and a growing feeling that recovery had to be European, not just British. Lloyd George responded with what has been described as his "swing to the left." He signed a treaty with Ireland, increased public spending to alleviate the plight of the unemployed, and sought the support of business for more ambitious measures to restore trade. As Morgan puts it, "it was external policy which offered a lifeline to the government now."[23]

Hence the government agreed to try to ameliorate the state of international relations by renewing contacts with France and Russia. The Trade Agreement of March 1921 had been only a first and imperfect step, but it did seem to encourage a new attitude in Russia – the New Economic Policy was greeted with great satisfaction in March 1921[24] – and Curzon's complaints about propaganda were more than drowned out by business interests (in a business-dominated Parliament) and by Lloyd George's optimism. This was encouraged by the government's knowledge of the appalling famine raging in Russia, which seems to have melted even Churchill's heart slightly.[25] Almost all cabinet references to Russia throughout 1921 concerned the famine, but the feeling grew that it was indeed driving the Bolsheviks to the negotiating table and that major concessions could be expected.[26]

However, major obstacles remained. Residual diehard distrust of Russia still existed in the cabinet, Churchill being its major spokesman. He had moderated his language since writing about a "Poison Peril from the East . . . a poisoned Russia, an infected Russia, a plague bearing Russia . . . [with] political doctrines which destroy the health and even the soul of nations," but he was still talking about having the "gravest objections" to helping the "tyrannic Government of these Jew Commissars."[27] The French were also going to be hard to persuade, as were

23 Morgan, *Consensus and Disunity*, 262.
24 Cf. White, *Britain and the Bolshevik Revolution*, 55–6.
25 One example of this knowledge came from an exchange of letters between a businessman in Odessa and his headquarters (International Harvester Co.) in Copenhagen, which Churchill passed to Lloyd George. The tone of these letters was that the situation was desperate and that there was a massive desire among the Bolsheviks to normalize conditions through trade. Lloyd George Papers, F/204/1/5, Dec. 30, 1921.
26 Cf. for example cabinet memoranda on Russia, Sept. 3, 17, and Oct. 11, 1921, and a letter from Lenin to a friend in Zurich, circulated to the cabinet by Curzon, "admitting failure of Bolshevistic theories," June 10, 1921, GB CAB 24/3283, 24/3321, and 24/3192.
27 Churchill to Curzon, Dec. 24, 1921, Curzon Papers, F/112/219, quoted by White in *Origins of Detente*, 43. The previous 1920 quote is from a Churchill editorial during the Soviet drive into Poland in 1920, Lloyd George Papers, F/204/3/2, no date, which probably appeared in the *Morning Post*.

the City and the bondholders, and even the editor of the *Times,* Wickham Steed, who was an ardent supporter of the French position. There could be no recognition until all these parties were placated. Hence Lloyd George used the next Allied Supreme Council meeting and private efforts to try to soothe these elements.

The British position on Russia, with exceptions such as Churchill, was therefore one of pragmatism in dealing with a probably "unclubable" interlocutor. There was general agreement that Soviet Russia was here to stay, a view disputed hotly by the Americans and the French. There was also a feeling that hostile actions of the Russians, such as propaganda in the Empire, could be stopped only by contact and what we would now call "confidence-building measures," of which some kind of de facto or de jure recognition and increased trading links were a first step. This did not mean, however, that the British had to *like* the Russians; rather it recognized a need to *civilize* them. This was the purpose of the 1921 Trade Agreement, and now of Genoa.

The Allied Supreme Council meeting in Cannes during early 1922 saw a rare harmony between Lloyd George and Briand, with agreement to resolve differences over German reparations, to draw up a defensive Anglo–French pact, and to convene a European economic conference to promote a resurgence of trade. The irony of the meeting at Cannes was that it achieved most of Lloyd George's aims and was wrecked by the political aftermath.

Lloyd George wrote to Austen Chamberlain from Cannes on January 10 to tell him that, apart from the "usual . . . unpleasant incidents with the French," he had obtained French agreement to all of his requests, including the presence of Germany at the economic conference that was to be held at Genoa. The problem is that one of the strangest incidents in recent history (that of the golf course) led to the fall of Briand as French premier and his replacement by Poincaré. As a supplementary omen, Lloyd George's car collided with Wickham Steed of the *Times* while at Cannes.[28]

Poincaré, acting true to form, objected to the Genoa venue as being in an unstable country and asked that the conference at least be postponed for several months. Curzon told the cabinet in early February that he had stopped that particular subterfuge,[29] but it was quite clear

28 Lloyd George to Chamberlain, Jan. 10, 1922, Lloyd George Papers, F/7/5/4, and Morgan, *Consensus and Disunity,* 238.
29 Meeting of Feb. 10, 1922, GB CAB 23/12/22.

that Lloyd George would have to try to get Poincaré himself to renew the promises made at Cannes. He did this in true Lloyd George fashion, going largely over Curzon's head through the wartime British ambassador in Paris, Lord Derby. Derby was instructed to arrange a secret meeting with Poincaré at one of the Channel ports (in the end Boulogne). Questions about the exact nature of the agreement reached at this meeting were to create disruption at Genoa, but it seems clear that the meeting was intended to be "informal" with no press present, "to clear up misconceptions and to facilitate business."[30] Curzon also put out parallel feelers for a meeting through the present ambassador to Paris, Lord Hardinge, but it is clear that Lloyd George was willing to make his own arrangements if necessary.[31]

The French were understandably cautious about any such meeting, and it was a difficult one, with Lloyd George asking would "the whole thing [Genoa] be frozen up until the French government were ready to thaw?" The interview with Poincaré was short and uncompromising, Lloyd George relating later that "I never spoke so strongly to any French statesman as I did to him."[32] As a result, Lloyd George formed a very low opinion of Poincaré, a judgment that gave him a dangerously low opinion of his "ally." But at least the two agreed that the Allied Commission of Experts should start to prepare for Genoa and compromised by postponing the start of the conference until the end of March.[33] Even the *Times* reported that "undoubtedly all difficulties have been swept away."[34]

The prime minister still had to make sure that the rest of the coalition government supported him. His efforts with Austen Chamberlain to ensure Tory support were particularly important. Lloyd George was well aware that the key to the City's heart lay through the Conservatives. He thus stressed to Chamberlain the strength of Britain's financial position and the weakness of its industry. The coalition had come under repeated attack from advocates of "Anti-waste" (i.e., lower government spending), which had led to grumblings of dissatisfaction

30 Derby to Lloyd George, Feb. 18, 1922, and Lloyd George to Derby, same date, with slightly different versions of the basis for discussion, Lloyd George Papers, F/14/5/38 and F/14/5/39.
31 White, in *Origins of Detente*, makes no mention of the Derby correspondence (a rare slip!) but does record the Hardinge–Curzon efforts, GB FO 371/7420, Feb. 20 and 21, 1922.
32 Lloyd George to C. P. Scott (editor of the *Manchester Guardian*), Mar. 2, 1922; cf. Trevor Wilson, ed., *The Political Diaries of C. P. Scott, 1911–1928* (London, 1970), 421.
33 For details of the meeting see White, *Origins of Detente*, 68–71.
34 *Times*, Feb. 27, 1922, quoted by White in *Origins of Detente*, 73.

from Conservatives about financial policy.[35] Genoa, he told Chamberlain, was "essential to create a spirit of reconciliation which will tend to create general confidence in the outlook. And confidence breeds business."[36] This did not, however, ensure that Chamberlain could, or indeed would want to, ask his supporters to forgive or forget Soviet debt. There were signs that British holders of czarist bonds feared a sellout.[37]

Lloyd George also had to keep the Liberal wing of his coalition happy. Genoa was just the kind of reconciliatory gesture that they loved, a radical foreign policy initiative. They were deeply unhappy about the prime minister's bowing to Tory idols and were vocal supporters of the Genoa initiative. Ironically of course, Churchill, still nominally a Liberal, was its greatest opponent.[38]

Chamberlain also told Lloyd George that the only real threat to harmony before Genoa was Winston Churchill. Philip Sassoon confirmed this, but it was clear from both of them that any explosion from that quarter would happen only if there was a real possibility of de jure recognition of the Soviet Union without all the outstanding problems being resolved. As Chamberlain rightly pointed out, "[t]he Cabinet had not really discussed Genoa," and the United States and the other powers were totally set against recognition. Sassoon, upon whom Lloyd George often relied for inside information about the mood of Parliament, allayed his fears about the Tories in general but confirmed that Churchill would resign over the recognition issue. Nonetheless, Sassoon did not think that other members would follow Churchill. He told Lloyd George that there was no "intense feeling on the subject of Recognition – I expect you will find more difficulty in the Cabinet than in the House of Commons."[39]

Lloyd George was finally forced to accept *in cabine* that de jure recognition could not be extended to Russia unless the Cannes Resolutions were satisfied.[40] Although Lloyd George expressed great anger at hav-

---

35 The "Geddes Case," allowing the passage of an extremely chauvinistic "Aliens Bill," only partly assuaged Tory bloodlust. Cf. Morgan, *Consensus and Disunity,* chapter 10, for details of this and "Anti-waste."

36 Lloyd George to Austen Chamberlain, Feb. 27, 1922, Lloyd George Papers, F/7/5/6.

37 Cf. Report of Special Meeting of the Association of British Creditors of Russia, Jan. 12, 1922, Lloyd George Papers, F/204/1/6.

38 Bentley, *The Liberal Mind;* Trevor Wilson, *The Downfall of the Liberal Party, 1914–1935* (London, 1966); and Trevor Wilson, ed., *The Political Diaries of C. P. Scott.*

39 Chamberlain to Lloyd George, Mar. 21, 1922, Lloyd George Papers, F/7/5/20, and Sassoon to Lloyd George, Mar. 24, 1922, F/45/1/11.

40 GB CAB 23/29, Mar. 27 and 28, 1922.

ing his hands tied in advance about the recognition question, he could not really have asked for more solid support in the circumstances. As it turned out, even Churchill behaved like a lamb in public, if not in private. During the conference he quipped to Lloyd George, "I would give a great deal for ten days painting along the Riviera."[41]

Having assured his lines of supply, Lloyd George now had to face the enemy. The French were just as troublesome as the Russians, perhaps even more so. Both Curzon ("The French will be the trouble") and the Italians communicated to Lloyd George their immense dissatisfaction with Paris. The Italians were very bitter and angry, ex-Prime Minister Nitti telling Curzon that there was "intense dislike and suspicion generally felt here in regard to France."[42] Albert Thomas of the International Labor Organization had warned Lloyd George through Thomas Jones, his cabinet secretary, that there was a very "bellicose spirit" in the French Chamber, that the Germans were now determined to take a tough line over reparations, and that there was no possibility of European reconstruction without American financial support.[43] Lloyd George had already decided, according to his intimate Lord Riddell, that "Poincaré is a fool!" and had rejected the latter's new proposals for an Anglo–French treaty after Cannes. The omens for Allied cooperation were very poor indeed.[44]

The Foreign Office reflected much of the foreign secretary's distaste for both the French and the Russians. The Russians' attempts to make discussion of recognition a preliminary to settling the debt problem were seen as prevarication – "[v]ery likely the Russian delegation at Genoa will attempt to raise all kinds of extraneous questions," such as the presence of all the Soviet republics. Such ideas were rejected as "ridiculous" by Gregory, Curzon's main assistant for matters to be raised at Genoa (and his effective representative there since ill health prevented him from attending). Reginald Leeper, head of the Russia desk, agreed, "[i]t's really rather funny," and Chicherin's requests were

41 Lloyd George to Chamberlain, Mar. 24, 1922, and Churchill to Lloyd George, Apr. 12, 1922, Lloyd George Papers, F/7/5/23 and F/10/2/63.
42 Curzon to Lloyd George, Apr. 6, 1922, Lloyd George Papers, F/13/3/15 and F/13/3/16, the last with an enclosure from Graham, British ambassador to Rome.
43 Thomas Jones, *Whitehall Diary*, vol. 1 (Oxford, 1969), 195.
44 Riddell, a divorcé elevated to the peerage in 1919, was never a cabinet minister and was somewhat of an outsider (like Lloyd George himself). His main importance to Lloyd George was as the proprietor of the *News of the World*. However, by 1922 the two men had become estranged over the prime minister's negative view of France. Cf. J. M. McEwen, ed., *The Riddell Diaries, 1908–1923* (London, 1986), 365 and "Introduction."

ignored. The Foreign Office's main concern was to balance the positive declarations of Russian "moderates," who evidently wished Genoa to succeed, and those of the "extremists," such as Trotsky, who did not.[45] Grove, one of the British diplomats in Moscow (Hodgson was *chargé d'affaires*), reflected a Foreign Office view that Lenin was in favor of "business" but was ill and could not be relied upon to save the day for moderation.

So the Foreign Office collaborated in the production of a draft treaty with the Soviet Union that could be used if all went well, but its officials were not optimistic that it would be produced for signature. They were perfectly aware that the French would object to any agreement and yet were loath to break with Paris. Leeper (Northern Department) summed up the dilemma perfectly: "It appears that at Genoa we shall be confronted with the choice of having the Bolsheviks as our friends for the immediate future, or the French. I prefer the latter and if sometime in the future we may have to part company with France I hope we shall not then insult her by saying that we prefer Moscow."[46]

As to what the Russians would actually ask, there were differences of opinion. In February, Gregory had to admit that the Russian attitude was far from certain. He was aware that both moderates and extremists would try to use Genoa for their own purposes: the latter to "make undertakings," the former for propaganda. The "inference from all this is that the Soviet leaders are merely throwing dust in the eyes of the Western world and that th[eir] real intentions . . . will be other than they profess." The Russians, he felt, were convinced that the Western powers were divided among themselves and weak ("singularly ill-informed," thought Gregory!). Gregory believed that all the Russians cared about was de jure recognition and postponement of substantive agreement on economic matters like debt until they were "in a better position to deal with the Powers and pursue their object of dividing them in order to triumph over the capitalist world."[47]

This rather pessimistic view was not universal. Wilton, the Foreign Office's man in Riga, told Gregory, just before the latter caught the boat at Dover, that "they will ask for many things but are ready in their hearts to make practically any concession provided they get de jure rec-

45 See, for example, Chicherin to Curzon, Feb. 28, 1922, and many dispatches in the same file about Lenin's speeches. GB FO 371/8186, N1908/646/38.
46 Leeper minute on report of conversation between Gregory and Seydoux (French Foreign Ministry), Mar. 29, 1922, GB FO 371/8187, N3075/646/38.
47 Memo. by Gregory on "The Soviet Government and Genoa," Feb. 12, 1922, GB FO 371/8189, N4293/646/38.

ognition, large credits, and, most important of all, retain their power." The Secret Intelligence Service alarmed the Foreign Office by saying that a key Russian demand would be that the Straits of Constantinople be given to them – Leeper showed his opinion of this by not forwarding it to Genoa. Maxse of the Northern Department compiled a list of what they were likely to ask, which proved at least partly incorrect. He believed, wrongly, that the Russians would *accept* their debts and only argue about how to pay them, but rightly, that they would make extravagant counterclaims. This report also cautiously agreed with the view that the primary Russian need was capital for reconstruction and that they would be flexible to a certain extent in assuring it.[48]

On April 3, Parliament gave Lloyd George a massive vote of confidence, 372 to 94 (the 94 including all members of the Labour Party, who were positive about Russia but distrusted the prime minister).[49] On that note, he left for Genoa, without Curzon but with E. F. Wise as a personal assistant (at the insistence of the Foreign Office, not allowed to sit in the conference proceedings), Gregory of the Foreign Office, the president of the Board of Trade, Sir Philipp Lloyd-Greame, and his assistant, Sir Sidney Chapman. There was one "participant" who was not supposed to be there, but who was on holiday in the vicinity of Genoa. F. E. Smith, the chancellor of the exchequer, a prewar diehard and intimate of Churchill, was used by Lloyd George both as a conduit to Tory reactions and to defuse Churchill's opposition. Although because of illness he was no longer the man he had been, he was a powerful support for the prime minister's position.[50]

Given this impressive lineup of doubters and outright opponents, it is surprising that Lloyd George invested so much hope in Genoa. But he hoped to cut through all the negative feelings with his vision of reconstruction. He felt that he *had* to succeed, telling Beaverbrook and Riddell, and many others, that "there is nothing else worth fighting for at the present moment," and that "he look[ed] to the Conference to restore his star to the summit."[51] He also looked upon it as the chance to push the revitalized liberalism of what turned out to be his last year

---

48 Cf. Wilton to Gregory, Apr. 3, 1922, Secret Intelligence Service to Curzon, Apr. 10, 1922, "The Attitude of the Soviet Government Towards the Genoa Conference," Apr. 5, 1922 (but written Mar. 15), GB FO 371/8187, N3130/646/38, N3381/646/38, and N3236/646/38.

49 House of Commons, *Debates*, 152:1883–1990.

50 Cf. John Campbell, *F. E. Smith, First Earl of Birkenhead* (London, 1986), 593–4. Apparently the area was a popular Tory holiday spot, Andrew Bonar Law also often being seen there.

51 Lloyd George to Beaverbrook, Mar. 23, 1922, Lloyd George Papers, F/4/6/10, and Lord Riddel recounting a conversation with Lloyd George in McEwen, *The Riddell Diaries*, 367.

in office – to boost the causes of peace, free trade, and, ultimately, individual effort.[52]

The detailed story of Genoa has been well told elsewhere, and this essay will not repeat the narrative. Rather, it will stress the relationships that existed between the different actors in the tragicomedy that unfolded.

The Rapallo Treaty between Russia and Germany came at such an early stage in the discussions that it left Lloyd George no time to use his powers of Welsh oratory to good effect. This "alters matters considerably," noted a Foreign Office official with typical British understatement.[53] In particular, it gave the French the upper hand. Because Russia had received de jure recognition by one Western power, albeit a defeated one, as well as effective annulment of debts, the goalposts of the negotiations had been moved. The moderates on the Russian side at Genoa and in Moscow (even given that such simplifications are rarely ever valid) simultaneously won a victory while reaching an impasse with the other states. This was not helped when Rathenau pretended to Lloyd George that he could not understand what all the fuss was about.[54]

Even before Rapallo, there had been problems for the Foreign Office. These arose principally from Lloyd George's often-mentioned propensity to sidestep his officials in favor of his unofficial advisors, on this occasion Wise. Gregory wrote a letter to Lampson in London that is the best single piece of evidence of this problem:

Of course the perennial problem still exists as regards Russia, namely the weakness of the Prime Minister for the infamous Wise, and as I write, he is closeted with the Prime Minister and Chicherin and Litvinoff. . . . For the moment they are only discussing the economic aspect of the Russian question, but I very much fear that it will be the same thing even when the political side comes to the fore . . . Lloyd Greame is the greatest ally we have got here and with his help I hope to be able to keep the F.O. end up. But I am not frightfully sanguine.

This extraordinary piece of evidence is also quite categorical about the Russians and French. The latter were "ferocious for the first two days, but after some very straight talking from the Prime Minister on Tues-

---

52 Cf. Wilson, *The Political Diaries of C. P. Scott,* 414–17, for a clear picture of this.
53 Note on Hodgson to Curzon, Apr. 17, 1922, GB FO 371/8187, N3556/646/38.
54 Gregory to Curzon, reporting the meeting, Apr. 20, 1922, GB FO 371/8187, N3745/646/38.

day, Barthou came to heel." On the Russians, Gregory was even more plain in his contempt:

You never saw anything like the appearance of the Bolsheviks. There were two who came to the plenary session, who looked for all the world as though they had stepped out of a Drury Lane Pantomime – real melodramatic cut-throats from the "Babes in the Wood" – ! Chicherin looks the degenerate he is, and of course except for himself and Krassin I fancy they are all Jews. It is very unpleasant to reflect that the main interest here is centred on the future relations between them and ourselves.[55]

However, Wise's "star appear[ed] to be slightly on the wane" even by the end of the above letter, probably because the Rapallo Treaty was signed on April 16 (possibly as Gregory was writing his postscript), and definitely because the other powers were as enraged by Lloyd George's personal style of diplomacy as was the Foreign Office. White makes clear that the Germans felt left out and trapped and fell into the Russians' arms to avoid being excluded from what seemed to them to be an impending Allied–Russian agreement. Lloyd George undoubtedly contributed to this Teutonic paranoia,[56] as did the French by their "bellicosity."

Rapallo convinced Curzon that Genoa was going to be a failure. He reminded Gregory that the political question of recognition could not be entertained until the Cannes Resolutions had been accepted in their entirety by Russia: "You will of course bear in mind the terms which were drawn up in London [by the Allied experts], and maintenance of which in integrity should be an indispensable condition of any form of recognition however restricted."[57] This, of course, also severely limited Lloyd George's flexibility of maneuver with both the French and his own diehards.

The memorandum presented by the Allies to the Russians as a final attempt to salvage the conference therefore had more of the hard French attitude than of the accommodating Lloyd George approach. A running battle between Lloyd George and Barthou developed in the First Commission, and some extremely hard words were exchanged. When Barthou complained about Soviet propaganda being distributed

---

55 Gregory to Lampson, Apr. 14, 1922, GB FO 371/8187, N3704/646/38.
56 For details see White, *Origins of Detente,* 155–60. Wise's absence from his hotel when the Germans tried to find out what Lloyd George was doing with the Russians in their private talks has also given rise to debate. Had he not been the "elusive Pimpernel," perhaps the Germans would not have been so precipitate. Cf. D'Abernon (Berlin) to Curzon, GB FO 371/8189, N4084/646/38.
57 Curzon to Gregory, Apr. 26, 1922, GB FO 371/8189, N40943/646/38.

in Genoa by members of the Russian delegation, Lloyd George sneered that the French had "seven little Rakowskys occupied solely with the issue of documents for the press."[58] When Barthou then returned to Paris for instructions, Lloyd George asked, "[d]id they, or did they not, sincerely desire to come to an agreement with Russia?"[59]

The sniping against France mainly reflected Lloyd George's realization that he had lost his battle, if not the war. In an effort to explain the defeat, he now looked for scapegoats. The Russians were the obvious ones. Lloyd George described the Soviet reply to the Allied memorandum as a very unsatisfactory production: "It was very provocative in form and had all the characteristics of Soviet diplomacy." The British were now said to believe that "while the Soviet Government was very anxious to come to a settlement it could not do so at that time." The problem was one of extremists in Russia, and "their difficulties were exactly the same as the difficulties of Western countries, due, not to practice, but to principle. Two antagonistic systems were confronting each other, and that was the cause of the present situation." They would be back when they fully realized the importance of "credits."[60]

The implication was clear: Lenin had his extremists to put up with, and so did the British – in their case the French. The Foreign Office was split in its allocation of blame. Foreign Office official O'Malley minuted the text of the memorandum handed to the Russians as only satisfying the "anti-Bolsheviks." By taking a middle ground between full recognition and "ostracism," it was "neither flesh nor fowl and it will render relations between ourselves and Russia more difficult than before." The only policy possible was one of "frankness and moderation" to bring Lenin back to "sanity" and to outflank the Comintern. Curzon agreed that there was a "great deal in Mr. Malley's argument." Sir Esmond Ovey, who was to become Britain's first ambassador to Moscow in 1929, was the only one who did not.[61] The British ambassador in Paris explicitly blamed the French for the impending failure of the conference.[62] By the bitterness of his attacks on the French, Lloyd George made it clear that he agreed.

---

58 International Economic Conference Papers, Apr. 23, 1922, Com. 1/2, Lloyd George Papers, F/144.
59 Ibid., Apr. 28, 1922, Com. 1/5.   60 Ibid., May 13, 1922, Com. 1/11.
61 Annotations on memo. sent to Russians, May 3, 1922, GB FO 371/8189, N4322/646/38. Of course, the Germans were also seen as blameworthy over Rapallo, especially with the suspected military (and secret) clauses of the treaty.
62 Hardinge to Curzon, May 5, 1922, GB FO 371/8190, N4346/646/38.

By the middle of May, Curzon was making suggestions for a venue for the next round with the Russians to iron out all the questions left unanswered at Genoa. Gregory's analysis of the Russian reply pointed out that they had ignored the loans issue, would not properly accept the propaganda clauses, and claimed that it was the West that had to come to terms with them because "her absence from the world market introduces disturbances that no artifice can remedy." Gregory felt that his grim realism had been vindicated, especially because the Russians said that they were still willing to discuss all points further, in the vaguest of ways.[63] The meeting at The Hague was finally settled upon as a place to resume conversation.

The Genoa Conference collapsed on May 19. Only one major British figure was delighted; Churchill, who had threatened to break with his friend the lord chancellor over his "treachery" at Genoa, probably mostly imagined, now saw his position vindicated.[64] The Americans made sure that they were seen to have been right to stay away. British Ambassador Sir Auckland Geddes had met Secretary of State Charles Evans Hughes, who had told him that the U.S. opinion was that before Genoa "Communism in Russia was dying of inanition." Genoa had served to give the Bolsheviks a breathing space and Hughes hoped no more would be afforded them.[65] The French were seen by the British as obstructionist to the last, initially at least denying Lloyd George's proposals for a Mixed Commission on the debt issue, although they later agreed to a lesser version of this. They also rejected his idea of a nonaggression pact and an agreement to abstain from propaganda.[66]

In his *Decline and Fall of Lloyd George,* Beaverbrook, a great admirer of the prime minister, commented that "Lloyd George had hoped for too much. He was receiving less than little – in fact nothing but disaster." For Beaverbrook, it was Poincaré who sank the conference because of his support for Belgium, "his dislike of Lloyd George," and "his hatred of Britain, an old French custom."[67] Stephen White uses a more sci-

63 Gregory to Curzon (from Genoa), May 11, 1922, GB FO 371/8190, N4322/646/38.
64 Campbell, *F. E. Smith,* 595–6.
65 Sir Auckland Geddes to British delegation, Genoa, dated May 17, 1922, GB FO 371/8192, N5353/646/38. This was confirmed by Lampson to Eyre Crowe who quoted a Mrs. Hamilton, an intimate of Hughes: "We should all thank God for what happened at Genoa. We had narrowly escaped an international catastrophe." May 24, 1922, GB FO 371/8191, N5053.
66 Gregory to Curzon, May 13 and 14, 1922, GB FO 371/8190, N4560 and N4675/646/38.
67 Lord Beaverbrook, *The Decline and Fall of Lloyd George* (London, 1963), 143.

entific analysis to conclude that the reasons for failure were more complex: insufficient preparation, especially because little was known about the conditions in Russia itself; the working methods of the conference; the lack of strength of the Allied governments vis-à-vis their own countries; and (most fundamentally) the divisions among the powers themselves, who had no common position for dealing with Russia. However, he also concedes that even these reasons might not have led to total failure had the "conference atmosphere" been different. Rapallo should also presumably figure in this list.[68]

The conference atmosphere is perhaps what Beaverbrook, the newspaperman, sensed better. There *were* significant dislikes between Lloyd George and the French government. Lloyd George's venom was all the more real as a former colleague of Clemenceau and Briand. For him, Poincaré was a minor figure who should know his place. Had not Signor Nitti called Lloyd George the "only first-class statesman in Europe"?[69] This arrogance cost him dearly in both international and domestic politics. He was revealed as a wizard with declining powers, and Genoa must have been instrumental in showing the Tories that they no longer needed him, as Austen Chamberlain discovered in October 1922 when he tried to get the Conservatives to "fuse" with the Liberals and they revolted, ditching him for Baldwin. The French refused to be bullied. And although Lloyd George continued to talk to the Russians in private (again through Wise), he was warned by Chamberlain that the coalition would not follow him. He had staked much, if not all, on Genoa, and although its failure was not his fault, he fell in its wake.[70]

Longer term, the Conservative government of November 1922 to December 1923 developed a growing hostility to Russia. The "Curzon Memorandum," a list of complaints sent in 1923, showed that relations had deteriorated. The Labour government of 1924 restored relations for the first time since the revolution of 1917 but had great problems in pursuing what were essentially Lloyd George's policies. Wise was by now a Labour Member of Parliament and played a key role both in 1924 and in 1929, when ambassadors were exchanged. (He was also British advisor to the Soviet trade office in London, ARCOS, from 1923 until his death in 1933.[71]) The Conservatives broke off diplomatic relations

68 White, *Origins of Detente*, 203–8.
69 Graham (Rome) to Curzon, Apr. 3, 1922, C4859, Lloyd George Papers F/13/3/16.
70 Cf. Morgan, *Consensus and Disunity*, 313–17, for another statement of this.
71 Cf. Williams, *Labour and Russia*, for details.

in 1927 and were generally anti-Soviet, with exceptions, until 1941.[72]
The Foreign Office retained its suspicious attitude toward Russia but
continued to reflect ambivalence about the usefulness of trade and contact in general.

72 Teddy J. Uldricks, "A. J. P. Taylor and the Russians," in Gordon Martel, ed., *The Origins of
the Second World War Reconsidered* (London, 1986), 162–86.

3

A Rainy Day, April 16, 1922: The Rapallo Treaty and the Cloudy Perspective for German Foreign Policy

PETER KRÜGER

Rapallo was by no means the dawn of a bright future for German foreign policy. The day when the widely discussed treaty between Soviet Russia and Germany was signed opened neither a new clear horizon nor a brilliant prospect for Germany's return to power. The German negotiators looked tense and exhausted, and immediately after the signing ceremonies, they had to explain, excuse, and defend what they had done.[1]

Rapallo became the catchword for sudden, shocking, and spectacular, as well as dangerous, agreements and forms of cooperation between Germany and Russia. It also gave a modern expression to and confirmation of deeper and older fears active until today. In the famous Adams-Jefferson correspondence, after the German Wars of Liberation in the summer of 1814, John Adams was troubled by the gloomy prospects of Russo-German dominance of Europe. "What may happen?" he asked. "Could Wellingtons or Bonapartes resist them?"[2] In May 1988, during the conflict over nuclear weapons in Europe, traditional

---

1 For the background of German foreign policy, the prevailing views, and the decisions that led to the signing of the treaty with the Russians at Rapallo, see Peter Krüger, *Die Aussenpolitik der Republik von Weimar* (Darmstadt, 1985), 151–83. In this essay I present some new findings from my recent research based primarily on the following sources: The files of the Politisches Archiv des Auswärtigen Amts, Bonn (Germ. PA AA), including not only the well-known central files and the files of the delegation sent to Genoa but also the reference files of leading officials (Haniel, Simson, Schubert, Dufour-Ferronce, etc.) and the files of German missions abroad (especially Rome) as well as private papers inside and outside the Archives of the German Foreign Office (in particular the Schubert Papers, still in possession of the family at Grünhaus in Germany); *ADAP*, series A, especially vols. 5 and 6 (Göttingen, 1987 and 1988); *Akten der Reichskanzlei, Weimarer Republik; Die Kabinette Wirth I und II* (Boppard, 1973); the memoirs and diaries of Wipert von Blücher, *Deutschlands Weg nach Rapallo* (Wiesbaden, 1951); Harry Graf Kessler, *Tagebücher 1918–1937* (Frankfurt/M., 1961); Friedrich von Prittwitz und Gaffron, *Zwischen Petersburg und Washington* (Munich, 1952); Werner Freiherr von Rheinbaben, *Viermal Deutschland* (Berlin, 1954); Moritz Schlesinger, *Erinnerungen eines Aussenseiters im auswärtigen Dienst* (Cologne, 1977); Ludwig Stein, *Aus dem Leben eines Optimisten* (Berlin, 1930).
2 Lester J. Cappon, ed., *The Adams–Jefferson Letters*, vol. 2 (Chapel Hill, 1959), 436 (July 16, 1814).

49

fears and suspicions were rekindled, and distinguished American and British journalists discovered signs of a new form of German *Drang nach Osten*. These signs conjured up the calamity of German history because the West Germans once more seemed to shake the European order. In a startling change of their foreign policy, the West Germans appeared to be working toward an alliance with Gorbachev's Russia in order to achieve reunification as well as the economic penetration and control of central and eastern Europe. These moves created a threatening vision of a powerful Russo-German combination in world affairs. Traces of all of this, on a smaller scale, had occurred in the Rapallo incident of 1922: German revisionism, power politics, the thwarting of the search for a new European order, the temptation of Eastern markets, and a strong economic as well as political position in the East, based on Russo-German cooperation.

Almost seven decades of open-ended debate about the Rapallo Treaty have produced an unusual wealth of information and interpretation. This partly controversial bulk of knowledge is well known; therefore I shall restrict my contribution to some new information and to some more general aspects. Moreover, I did not follow any sophisticated theoretical framework, but simply did what historians always do: I went to the sources and tried to discover new evidence, to explain what really happened that paved the way to Rapallo, and to draw some conclusions on German foreign policy and the situation of Europe. For that purpose, my analysis will proceed in three stages: 1) a more precise explanation, based on new sources, of what caused the trip to Rapallo to conclude the treaty negotiations with the Russian delegation; 2) some reflections on the conceptions and state of German foreign policy as revealed by the Genoa Conference; and 3) a short discussion of the German attitude within the wider framework of Europe, European reconstruction, and the European state system.

The Genoa Conference stood and fell with a minimum of European common sense. It was designed by Britian's prime minister, David Lloyd George, to arouse new interest in European problems and in solutions that would benefit each of the participating countries. There were numerous and difficult subjects to be dealt with at the conference: the economic reconstruction of Europe; steps toward political detente and reconciliation; joint agreements with Soviet Russia on financial claims, economic development, and diplomatic recognition; and security problems. Such an ambitious program necessitated a flexible organizational framework that included informal talks on specific questions and demanded caution and discipline as well as good nerves on the part of all the delegations. Each hour, unexpected things might happen. The success of the conference depended largely on common efforts, even though it could fail to produce common solutions in all controversies.

Despite some preliminary disagreements, the Genoa Conference marked the postwar return of Soviet Russia and Germany to an important conference on an equal footing with the other major powers. Not surprisingly, their actions attracted the most attention from contemporary observers and from subsequent historians as well. The Russian delegation was suspected of conspiring to harm the conference in order to exploit its chances to the utmost. But what caused the Germans to renounce the common effort of the Great Powers to reach a comprehensive agreement with Soviet Russia? Why did they conclude a separate treaty with the Soviet delegation, although knowing that they risked wrecking the conference by doing so?

It is generally recognized that Ago von Maltzan, the influential and shrewd assistant state secretary *(Ministerialdirektor)*, head of the Eastern Department of the German Foreign Office, and an intimate advisor to Chancellor Joseph Wirth, held a key position in planning German policy toward Russia and in preparing the Treaty of Rapallo.[3] However, there is still some disagreement about the extent of Maltzan's influence over the final decisions, as compared with that of Wirth and Foreign Minister Walther Rathenau. Moreover, it is well known that, up to now, nearly all important sources on the course of events that led to Rapallo can be traced back in one way or another to Maltzan. Because the hectic days before April 16 did not allow for detailed notes and reports, most of our knowledge is derived from the accounts presented soon after the event. The members of the German delegation responsible for the basic decisions were identical with those present at the crucial meetings, deliberations, and moments: Wirth, Rathenau, state secretary Ernst von Simson, Maltzan, and the legal advisor to the Foreign Office, Friedrich Gaus. All their statements afterward were made in defense of Rapallo. They all sat in the same boat and followed the phraseology of Maltzan, who set the tune with his detailed accounts. All other information, if available at all, seems to be secondhand or marginal. Up to the present day, this limited evidence has been accen-

---

3 Peter Krüger, *Schubert, Maltzan und die Neugestaltung der auswärtigen Politik in den 20er Jahren* (Auswärtiges Amt, Gedenkfeier für die Staatssekretäre Ago Freiherr von Maltzan und Dr. Carl von Schubert, 18. September 1987).

tuated by the fact that German historians in particular have been far more interested in Rapallo than in the Genoa Conference. A serious study of Genoa's causes and broader implications, however, might lead scholars to a more precise evaluation of German foreign policy in the early 1920s, and especially of the Rapallo Treaty.

It is indeed puzzling that no one has yet explored the remaining, albeit limited, opportunities for further research on the Rapallo Treaty. Obviously, this has something to do with the fact that the structure of the German foreign service, the internal disagreement on political strategy, and the missing political decisions on aims, priorities, and clear guidelines for Genoa have been neglected. As a result, historians have overlooked the strange role of the councillor of the German embassy in London, Albert Dufour-Feronce. Sent to Genoa after a last-minute decision and strongly supported by the head of Department III (Great Britain, the United States, etc.), Carl von Schubert,[4] Dufour was to keep in touch with the British delegation, but he was not officially a member of the German delegation, which lacked any high-ranking expert on Western affairs. After April 16, 1922, as is well known, Dufour helped reestablish good relations with the British. But until now, no one has asked what Dufour did at Genoa during the crucial phase, from April 12 to the morning of April 16.

Dufour's letters, which are not included in the German files of the Genoa Conference, reveal new details about the attitude of and the atmosphere within the oversized German delegation – the size being a consequence of political indecision and lack of clarity over ends and means, as well as an attempt simply to be prepared for all kinds of negotiations. They also reveal better than other sources the relationship between the British and the Germans, and they enable us to evaluate Maltzan's maneuvering more precisely.

After the establishment on April 11 of the highly important Political Subcommission that was to prepare proposals for the full Political Commission, the Germans felt satisfied because, with the strong support of Lloyd George, they participated in it. Thus, the principle was set up that the German delegation – and the Russian as well – should be entitled, like the Allies, to send two delegates to all commissions.[5] James Garvin, the editor of the *Observer,* who enjoyed good relations with Lloyd George, was "blissful," and he was convinced, as Dufour

4 Tel. no. 139 to London, Germ. PA AA, Büro Staatssekretär, Ye.
5 Carole Fink, *The Genoa Conference: European Diplomacy, 1921–1922* (Chapel Hill and London, 1984), 156–7.

(who met him on April 12) wrote, that this would be the beginning of a European League of Nations.[6] Although overly optimistic, Garvin's attitude revealed that one of Britain's aims for the conference was to give a fresh impetus to European cooperation.

However, the British made grave mistakes in the way they treated the German delegation. The Political Subcommission was adjourned, and on Lloyd George's proposal informal talks began between the Allies and the Russians. These talks were based on the notorious memorandum drawn up by the experts of the inviting powers on March 28.[7] The memorandum excluded German claims and interests, while reserving the provisions of Article 116 of the Treaty of Versailles in favor of Russia.

Since the autumn of 1921, Maltzan had stressed the dangers of the increased pressure of reparations, as well as those of a potential agreement between Soviet Russia and the Allies, particularly between the Soviet Union and France. Maltzan's main objective was to prevent the Western powers from jeopardizing the Russo-German relationship by their intervention.[8] This was exactly what seemed to be happening. Maltzan, who was undoubtedly the main figure in Germany's Eastern policy, aggravated the lurking fears and suspicions of the leading members of the German delegation, who became increasingly nervous and revived such traditional slogans as the policy of encirclement and of falling between two stools.[9]

The suspicion within the German delegation might have been heightened by the fact that, at the beginning of March, the Germans had already been informed about British intentions concerning the proposed course of the negotiations at Genoa. The opening addresses and plenary discussions were to be followed by a phase of informal meetings and private talks, in order to enable the delegates to get into close contact and to prepare the ground for detailed negotiations.[10] This was reasonable, and the Germans were supposed to participate in these talks. At Genoa, however, the situation seemed different. The Germans gained the impression that they were to be excluded from the informal meetings. Obviously, the British had underestimated the consequences

---

6 Dufour to Sthamer, Apr. 11–12, 1922, Schubert Papers, Politisches Tagebuch, vol. 9.
7 *DBFP*, first series, vol. 19, doc. no. 56. An earlier British draft came to the knowledge of the German Foreign Office: Dufour memo., Mar. 17, 1922, Germ. PA AA, Büro Staatssekretär, Ye.
8 Rheinbaben, *Viermal Deutschland*, 237–8. Rheinbaben and Maltzan were schoolmates.
9 Krüger, *Aussenpolitik*, 167; Dufour to Sthamer, May 6, 1922, Schubert Papers, vol. 10.
10 Dufour to Sthamer, Mar. 9, 1922, Schubert Papers, vol. 8.

of the London Memorandum and the reactions within the German delegation. They failed to discuss things intensively and on a higher level with the Germans, to reassure them and watch them closely in order to be informed of their deliberations and actions. They should have known how difficult and sometimes unpredictable German reactions were.

Nevertheless, it was Maltzan who was virtually responsible for creating a situation that made the Rapallo Treaty possible. From the very beginning of the conference he had prepared the ground: positively, by encouraging within the delegation the idea that it would be reasonable to conclude the prior negotiations with the Russians by signing a separate treaty;[11] and negatively, by augmenting the rumors that an agreement between the Allies and Soviet Russia was near, although he was soon informed that this was wrong.[12] Lacking any desire to reassure Rathenau or anybody else, Maltzan did a masterly job of leaving both the British and the German delegations in the dark, avoiding close contacts and clarifying discussions, while giving the impression of having nothing else in mind.

For all this, Dufour's letters offer new evidence. To mention only the most important point: What did Maltzan do from the morning of April 15 to convey to the British delegation the considerably increased fears of the Germans and their intention to enter into a treaty with the Russians? On the previous night, Francesco Giannini, an economic expert and one of the planners of the conference, had visited the leading German delegates on behalf of the Italian foreign minister, Carlo Schanzer, to inform them of the informal talks, with irritating and contradictory results. Afterward, in an attempt to justify the Rapallo Treaty, the Germans maintained that they had had the impression that an agreement between the Allies and Soviet Russia was imminent. Giannini wrote to Dufour to repudiate this claim. Outraged, he accused Maltzan of falsehood and protested vigorously against the bold statement of the Germans that they had made clear their intentions to "conclude with the Russians" under these circumstances.[13] But even the phrasing of the subsequent German announcements was ambiguous on this point.

---

11 Maltzan to Haniel, Apr. 10 and 13, 1922, Schubert Papers, vol. 9.
12 Ernst Schulin, "Noch etwas zur Entstehung des Rapallo-Vertrages," in Hartmut von Hentig and August Nitschke, eds., *Was die Wirklichkeit lehrt: Golo Mann zum 70. Geburtstag* (Frankfurt/M., 1979), 177–202. Schulin discovered a new source, a letter dated May 29, 1929, from the journalist Max Reiner to Harry Graf Kessler, the first important biographer of Rathenau.
13 Dufour to Sthamer, May 6, 1922, Schubert Papers, vol. 10; cf. Sthamer to Schubert on Sir William Tyrrell's judgment, Apr. 27, 1922, ibid., vol. 9.

Similarly embittered about the German assertions was Edward Wise, acting assistant secretary on the Board of Trade, who was the Briton most frequently in contact with Dufour and the German delegation. This point is crucial because of his much-cited meeting with Maltzan and Dufour late in the afternoon on April 15. Dufour, on his own initiative, had taken Wise by car to the German headquarters. The ensuing discussion was designed to furnish proof of Maltzan's statement that, having kept the British fully informed, he had then been free to go ahead with the Russians. Until now, Maltzan's memoranda have been the only sources available for this meeting.[14] But Dufour's letters reveal a different story. Maltzan's remarks to Wise were so equivocal that even Dufour, who was deliberately kept in the dark about what Maltzan had in mind, did not understand him.[15] It was clear that Maltzan needed proof, primarily for domestic purposes, that he had tried everything to keep the British informed and that they themselves, by their evasive actions, had forced the Germans to Rapallo.

Maltzan had to push the matter ahead simply because he could not be sure that there was no imminent danger of an agreement between the Allies and Soviet Russia. After meeting with Adolf Joffe and Christian Rakovsky on the morning of April 15, he was obviously informed by Joffe that evening that the Soviet delegation had broken off the negotiations at the Villa d'Albertis.[16]

Another turn now threatened: a joint agreement including the Germans and thus the end of all dreams of a special Russo-German relationship. Wise's telephone call the same day, April 15, at 11:00 p.m., asking Maltzan to formulate more precisely the four German objections to the Allied memorandum, was a hint in that direction. That night, there were preparations for the next morning's meeting with the Russians at Rapallo and the signing of the treaty that had been negotiated for months. Ernst Schulin's assumption that there must have first been a German call before the Russians phoned at 1:15 a.m. is now supported by new sources, which reveal that the Germans, not the Russians, took the initiative and speeded up the affair.[17] Moreover, we now know that it was Wirth, in full accord with Maltzan (a partnership that had begun

---

14 Ernst Laubach, "Maltzans Aufzeichnungen über die letzten Vorgänge vor dem Abschluss des Rapallo Vertrages," *Jahrbücher für Geschichte Osteuropas,* Neue Folge 22 (1974): 556–79; *ADAP,* A, vol. 6, docs. no. 56, 59, 60.

15 Dufour to Schubert (handwritten), Apr. 18, 1922, Schubert Papers, vol. 9; Dufour to Schubert, Apr. 29, and to Sthamer, May 6, 1922, Schubert Papers, vol. 10.

16 Schulin, "Entstehung," 186, 193–4.

17 Ibid., 194–7; Schubert memo., Apr. 24, 1922, Schubert Papers, vol. 9.

in October 1921), who pressed for signing the treaty, while Rathenau
had doubts up to the last minute. The foreign minister remains the
"violated" victim, in spite of his inclination toward an independent foreign policy, especially regarding Russia. On Sunday morning, April 16,
when Rathenau still hesitated, Wirth threatened to go to Rapallo himself to sign the treaty.[18]

The overall planning of German foreign policy was in a deplorable
state. The policy of fulfillment, the basic guideline of Wirth's moderate
center-left Weimar coalition cabinet, remained valid, but it had
become threadbare. Vigorous attempts to find new approaches, careless
in view of that delicate cloth, had torn holes in it. No one in the cabinet
or among the state secretaries had made an effort to find a new balance
or general orientation for the increasingly disparate parts of German
foreign policy or to set priorities. Wirth had tried to increase German
options and to evade the pressure of being bound into an Allies-domi-
nated European system by improving relations with the United States
and Soviet Russia.[19] Eastern and Western policies fell apart, the reparations policy began to lose its coherence and to become dubious as a
matter of rational consideration in the spring of 1922, and the fundamental question of whether an effort should be made to achieve European cooperation and understanding in vital economic and political
matters at the Genoa Conference was left unanswered. There was no
grand design born of a desperate situation in German foreign affairs, in
contrast to what Theodor Schieder, to whom we owe subtle insights
into this intriguing subject, once said.[20] The situation was anything but
desperate; on the contrary, there would have been promising prospects
if the German government had been willing to tackle the program of
Lloyd George's conference seriously and with a disciplined and considered strategy. German foreign policy really got into trouble as a consequence of Rapallo and the breakdown of the Genoa Conference. As
to the "grand design," it was merely a risky gamble that Germany
might substantially improve its international position by establishing a
special, intimate relationship with Soviet Russia, thereby continuously
threatening other European powers with a close Russo-German tie on
all levels and thus demonstrating for domestic as well as international
purposes a strong sense of national independence.

18 Schubert memo., Apr. 24, 1922, Schubert Papers, vol. 9; Blücher, *Weg,* 161.
19 Krüger, *Aussenpolitik,* 147–50.
20 Theodor Schieder, "Die Entstehungsgeschichte des Rapallo-Vertrags," *HZ* 204 (1967):558.

The domestic situation in Germany was more "desperate." Pressure was growing on Wirth's minority government from the ring-wing parties and from nationalists in all camps. Wirth himself, though a sincere democrat, was a nationalist. The advantages of inflation had become, at best, rather doubtful. The basis of foreign trade, vital to the German economy, had become shaky. All this threatened German stability and the social compromise upon which the Weimar Republic was based. A success in foreign policy was urgently needed, which would reduce the – exaggerated – pressure of the Allies and open new prospects of economic gains abroad.

Rathenau, an outsider in nearly every sense of the word, as well as a highly sensitive, self-reflective, complex, and imaginative man, felt this nationalist pressure extremely. He was under intense stress before and especially during the first weeks of the Genoa Conference.[21] He was convinced – like Wirth – that a more active, powerful, and independent German foreign policy was needed; the Foreign Office was too passive, and he felt incited "to put a new iron into the fire every day."[22] This made him nervous and impatient, and Maltzan knew how to exploit Rathenau's temper.

Such psychological preconditions also help to explain the decision to go to Rapallo, although the possible consequences were known in advance: The Genoa Conference might end in a complete failure; the British could be alienated and forced to align themselves again with France, although presumably without altering their fundamental policy; and the French could feel confirmed in their disapproving attitude toward this and similar conferences, and the occupation of the Ruhr would become an imminent danger. A Russo-German alliance was a nightmare to the Western powers, and to the French in particular.[23] Even the American press and the State Department were alarmed, suspecting German, and above all Stinnes's, intentions to monopolize the Russian market,[24] which added to America's already considerable objections to the Genoa Conference.

A German entente or alliance with Russia had long had its protagonists in Germany. It had been and remained attractive. Those who were attracted by this idea did not at all form a homogeneous group. On the contrary, the supporters of close relations with Russia were as diverse

---

21 Kessler, *Tagebücher,* 276–7; Prittwitz, *Petersburg,* 148.   22 Kessler, *Tagebücher,* 276.
23 Renata Bournazel, *Rapallo: naissance d'un mythe. La politique de la peur dans la France du Bloc National* (Paris, 1974), 117–41, 197–226.
24 Lang to Schubert, Mar. 17, 1922, Schubert Papers, vol. 9.

as were their motives: They were politicians, businessmen, and intellectuals, and what they were looking for was more influence and power in international affairs, a highly lucrative economic connection, and a sometimes sentimental devotion to Russian culture or to bolshevism. To some people this meant strong and rather one-sided bonds with Russia while most people were rather trying to balance Western ties, influence, or obligations in this way. Soviet Russia seemed to offer an outlet, a scope, or even a promised land for political and economic activity, and a threat to the Western powers as well.

After Versailles, the banker Paul von Schwabach, who was no "Easterner" and had close connections with the City of London, recommended balancing the influence of the United States and the Western powers by a cautious rapprochement with Russia.[25] This was only one voice in the pro-Russian chorus led by certain groups of German businessmen. More important were the Easterners in the German Foreign Office. Their diplomatic viewpoint was expressed in a statement by a future ambassador to Moscow, Rudolf Nadolny, in his memorandum on German-Russian relations on January 9, 1934: "The guideline of German policy has always been: static in the West, dynamic in the East."[26] The underlying characteristic of such attitudes and statements was the belief that in the East there was far more freedom for movement, for new and dynamic approaches, and for a more active German participation in international relations than in the West. As Wirth explained to Harry Count Kessler two days after Rapallo, the Germans were simply bound to become active again.[27]

But Rathenau had been explicitly warned about the French reaction to any German provocation. In his analysis of the information he had received concerning the apparently nervous mood of the French government, the acting head of the Western Department in the German Foreign Office, Gerhard von Mutius, had concluded that unilateral military actions, especially the occupation of the Ruhr, were imminent because they were the only measures the French could take without the consent of their Allies. This was a warning that such a dire consequence could be provoked if the Germans caused any serious trouble at the Genoa conference. As Mutius stated, for the French, "under the present circumstances, it would seem logical to thus obtain a surety, not so

---

25 Paul von Schwabach, *Aus meinen Akten* (private print, Berlin, 1927), 381–2.
26 *ADAP,* C, 2:316 ("Statik im Westen, Dynamik im Osten").
27 Kessler, *Tagebücher,* 300.

much in respect of Germany as of their Allies, which would subsequently have to be redeemed from the French in some form."[28]

Russo-German cooperation was obviously a nightmare not only because of German power but also because it might upset the entire region of central and eastern Europe between Soviet Russia and Germany. In this zone of insecurity and international sensitiveness, most of the states were politically unstable and suffered from economic imbalance, weak currencies, low productivity, and an insufficient amount of foreign trade. The Germans, cooperating with Soviet Russia, could exploit this situation.

Maltzan's great game sought primarily to gain freedom of action for Germany so that the government could seize every opportunity to improve its situation and pursue its interests with the fewest possible restraints. It was the old Great-Power ideal of the free hand in modern dress, taking into account postwar economic, political, and social changes. Therefore, as Maltzan stated more than once at Genoa, "We need the Russian cloud over Europe."[29] He knew that the Russians were far from making any agreement with the Allies, but the fear that they might do so was his strongest weapon.[30] Beginning in the autumn of 1921, he had made every effort to demonstrate the great danger to Germany of the negotiations between the Allies and Soviet Russia and especially of Article 116. Maltzan's decision to push the treaty through was political; it was pure power politics, notwithstanding the economic advantages. All explanations, however, emphasizing his impressive diplomatic abilities, his shrewdness, and his tactical calculation that the treaty must be concluded as long as there was a well-prepared pretext for it, are correct, but they do not reveal the driving force behind his efforts at Genoa. The first week must have been an ordeal for him; now he wanted to have a showdown concerning his conception. For at the very moment when the Allies failed to come to terms with Soviet Russia, the alternative, the chance to get a comprehensive agreement that included Germany, increased, and this would have put to an end any idea of freedom of action as he conceived it. In 1923 Maltzan had to realize that his conception had nevertheless failed, but he became a loyal supporter of a new political strategy.[31]

Such a new strategy was already at hand. The results of the phase of

28 *ADAP*, A, 6:86 (Apr. 6, 1922).
29 Germ. PA AA, Ritter Papers, "Rapallo," 4; cf. *ADAP*, B, 14:226.
30 Schulin, "Entstehung," 188.
31 Krüger, *Schubert, Maltzan*, 30.

reorganization and the career patterns revealed that Maltzan and Schubert were the "coming men" in the German Foreign Office. In spite of the fact that they were friends, Schubert, from the beginning, was highly skeptical of Maltzan's activities. He was by no means convinced of the dangers of Article 116, and news about pending Russo-French agreements he called "cock-and bull stories"; it was all French *"chantage"* and Russian "blackmail."[32]

Two points, corroborated by archival evidence, can be made about the events during the first two weeks of the Genoa Conference. The first is that the signing of the Rapallo Treaty was by no means certain from the beginning and depended on many unforeseeable circumstances. The second is that Rathenau, who was oriented principally toward the West, was not entirely convinced of the necessity of concluding an agreement with the Russians on that Easter Sunday in Rapallo. The Easterners in the German delegation were not as strong as historians have portrayed them. Perhaps the most outspoken and substantiated position against Rapallo within the German foreign service was that of Schubert. He was convinced that, for the time being, the German government could improve its international position, particularly toward France, only by close cooperation with Great Britain and on the basis of an intimate understanding between the British and French governments that would enable the British to bring to bear a moderating influence on the French, thus preparing the ground for a reasonable relationship among these three powers. This would strengthen Germany's position considerably.

Schubert's plans for Genoa were quite different from those of Wirth, Maltzan, and even Rathenau. After careful study of Lloyd George's policy and his schemes for the Genoa Conference, Schubert concluded that these offered the only real chance for a rapprochment of the European powers, including Germany.[33] Moreover, they were also a new start toward solving the reparations problem by agreement among Germany, France, and Britain and toward promoting the economic reconstruction of Europe. For that purpose, he recommended a conciliatory German policy to support Lloyd George. In particular, he tried to convince Rathenau – in vain – to avoid any provocative attitude in reparations problems, to react positively to signs of French willingness to propose a new scheme of a reparations provisorium, and to refrain from doing anything that might lead to a split in Anglo-French relations because good relations were the precondition for a moderating British

32 Schubert to Sthamer, Jan. 23 and Feb. 14, 1922, Schubert Papers, vols. 7 and 8.
33 Schubert memo., Jan. 19, 1922, Schubert Papers, vol. 7.

influence on France's policy toward Germany. When the French insisted on omitting reparations from Genoa's agenda, Schubert advised against any strenuous form of opposition, since reparations were bound to crop up in the discussions.[34] His conciliatory political line paralleled the attitude of the German financial experts at Genoa, who, like Schubert (who remained in Berlin), were horrified at the news of the separate treaty signed with the Russians at Rapallo.

The European context of Germany's foreign policy also presents a puzzling picture. The sources confirm the impression that the German government tried to participate and to have a say in all discussions dealing with the general topics and tasks of the Genoa Conference. Although prepared to present its own proposals, particularly in economic matters, it essentially adopted a wait-and-see attitude. The German government was somewhat noncommittal, although it had drafted interesting, possibly trend-setting ideas – for instance about first steps toward European economic integration by a customs union. To be sure, as a European solution of some of Germany's important economic difficulties and as an instrument to go beyond the Treaty of Versailles, the proposals concerning European cooperation, the removal of trade barriers, and the general acceptance of the most-favored-nation principle lay very much in Germany's interest. Nevertheless, they were reasonable, although perhaps politically premature.

What is more important, however, is the fact that the German government itself did not concentrate its efforts on these vital issues of European reconstruction. Even its planning was not consistent; it lacked the clear political determination to put different options side by side. Realistic suggestions on the preconditions and the necessary stages to achieve a European customs union – not really discussed at the conference – did not prevent deliberations on a partial customs union covering only Central Europe (the old *Mitteleuropa* idea) or even on a customs union with Austria alone as a beginning.[35] The German attitude was ambiguous toward plans for a kind of European reconstruction agency, the much-discussed international corporation. Belonging to the incentives of the Genoa Conference and in the beginning strongly supported by Rathenau, this most interesting project of a Central International Corporation was to be established by the governments of the

34 Sthamer to Schubert, Jan. 6, ibid.; Schubert memoranda, Feb. 27, Mar. 2 and 17, Schubert to Dufour, Feb. 27, and to Sthamer, Mar. 27, 1922, Schubert Papers, vol. 8.
35 Peter Krüger, "European Ideology and European Reality: European Unity and German Foreign Policy in the 1920s," in Peter M. R. Stirk, ed., *European Unity in Context: The Interwar Period* (London and New York, 1989), 90; *ADAP*, A, 6:59–62.

major European powers. Subject to their approval, the corporation was supposed to coordinate the formation of national corporations according to the agreed guidelines. In the protocol of February 25, 1922, which was also signed by representatives of the German government, it was agreed "that the main object of the corporation will be to examine the opportunities for undertaking work in connection with European reconstruction and to assist in the financing of such undertakings." Soviet Russia was to be given priority in joint reconstructive efforts. Other areas with alarming economic weaknesses were to be dealt with later.[36]

The same vagueness and hesitation characterized German thoughts on how to organize European security and cooperation. These were by no means enough to promote détente in Europe or a more stable and cooperative European states' system. The serious lack of a new European order came to public attention on the occasion of the Genoa Conference. The victors' alliances and global organization, the League of Nations, did not satisfy the urgent requirement of a more specific and precise European arrangement to establish a modern, durable European states' system. A new European consciousness was emerging, kindling hope that the Genoa Conference might advance European cooperation; this huge gathering was seen as a demonstration of Europe's identity, vibrancy, and will to survive. Pan-European sentiments expressed a common ground of shared problems and expectations.

Furthermore, the politicians grew disappointed with the weak performance of the League of Nations. Although criticism of the League was not fair, for it had existed for only two years and could not be held responsible for what the peacemakers had neglected, the disappointment was important because it furthered somewhat a return to the European idea. At Genoa, even the Czechoslovak foreign minister, Edouard Beneš, who was a sensitive and cautious politician as well as a staunch adherent of the League of Nations, agreed with Rathenau that a new League restricted to Europe was necessary. Yet all these hopes proved fruitless. Although other events also contributed to Genoa's failure, when the Germans decided to conclude the separate treaty with the Soviets at Rapallo, Lloyd George and his adherents had to bury their European plans and visions. Indeed, an important reason for the controversy over Rapallo inside the German delegation was precisely because of its adverse effect on European cooperation. Moreover,

36 Krüger, "European Ideology," 89–90.

Rapallo revealed the ambiguity of German foreign policy, despite the serious interest in European projects and mutual understanding.[37]

German intentions and approaches to European schemes had been stronger after the British-French conference in December 1921, which had laid the basis for the Genoa conference and to which Rathenau had been called in on specific points. Rathenau understood that governments must not only recognize the interdependence of postwar economic and political problems but also tackle these problems as a complex. This fresh stimulus, however, faded away for different reasons, which need not be discussed here again: the critical attitude of the French government after the change from Briand to Poincaré; the sharpening of the debate over reparations; the increasing nationalistic pressure in Germany; the stiffening political views of many governments; and the rising skepticism as to the outcome of the Genoa Conference in general and the attraction of the opportunities Soviet Russia seemed to offer, economically as well as politically, during the Russo-German treaty negotiations at Berlin.

When the Germans signed the Rapallo Treaty, it was obvious that an important prerequisite for this sudden decision was the lack of clear-cut aims, priorities, and tasks in the broad German program for the Genoa Conference. This lack provided the opportunity for the changing events and the atmosphere of the conference to exert a disproportionate influence on all deliberations, a phenomenon not unknown under the structural preconditions of modern conference diplomacy. This precarious situation then revealed the hidden priority when a decision had to be taken: After all, it was in the connection with the Russians. Therefore, the German delegation, in not giving priority to a policy of European understanding and in fact making possible quite the contrary at Rapallo, exerted a disruptive influence on the efforts to advance European cooperation. This happened even though many experienced people in Germany were convinced that European cooperation was desirable and was perhaps the only efficient remedy for Germany's troubles. At the time, however, this thinking in European categories and acting in favor of close European cooperation proved far less compelling than after World War II. Therefore, the preparations for the Genoa Conference and the conference itself produced only a new consciousness of European problems and a wave of publications on European unity.

37 Ibid., 90–1.

Actually, Rapallo was a firebell in the night for the European states' system. The political orientation and finally the fate of the Baltic states, of east-central Europe, and of the Balkans was at stake once Soviet Russia and Germany became strong. The Western powers were alarmed about their own immediate interests but less concerned about the vital interests of the smaller countries in eastern Europe. In the long run, a new constellation was able to arise in continental Europe, dominated by a possible Russo-German alliance, as in fact had been prepared for by the Munich Agreement of 1938 and consequently was concluded in August 1939.

4

Reparations in 1922

SALLY MARKS

Reparations in 1922 differed from reparations in 1921 chiefly in that the existing tension over the question only deepened as the 1921 settlement became progressively more unreal, not because it was necessarily unrealistic but because Germany refused to accept it.[1] Thus the year was dominated by the struggle to find temporary expedients that would replace or preserve the London Schedule of Payments of May 5, 1921,[2] and by the looming crisis as the gulf among the powers became unbridgeable just as time to bridge it ran out. The endless strife over reparations represented a fundamental power struggle, and the real question was who won World War I.

In dealing with a topic so fraught with technical complexity, deliberate misdirection, and mountains of paper as well as endless oratory, obfuscation, and political posturing, one must beware of truisms. These arose from several sources: from constant repetition at the time; from acceptance by public opinion in several states and by leaders who needed to believe their own rhetoric, perhaps because British and German documents were released well before those of other European states; and from the failure of some historians to pose hard questions. Above all, one must continually ask: Is this really so?

One truism that is undoubtedly true is that Germany did not accept the Treaty of Versailles. The treaty was based upon and reflected the military defeat of 1918. Germany rejected this defeat, and the victors did not insist on its acknowledgment. This German rejection of defeat, which was national, underlies the entire history of reparations and strongly affected its course. The political difficulties of Weimar gov-

---

1 Stephen A. Schuker, *American "Reparations" to Germany, 1919–1933: Implications for the Third-World Debt Crisis* (Princeton, 1988), 19.
2 For text, see Reparation Commission, *Official Documents Relative to the Amount of Payments to be Effected by Germany under Reparations Account,* 22 vols. (London, 1922–30), 1:4–9.

ernments in complying with even a modicum of fulfillment, their complaints about commands from the Reparation Commission, the perpetual efforts to gain negotiations (not only to reduce the bill but also to achieve diplomatic parity and so to erase the pattern of victor and vanquished), and the basic struggle over whether Germany would pay – all these reflected the national hatred of the treaty and determination to undo it, thereby eradicating and reversing the military verdict of 1918.

As France and Germany both understood, but Britain and America rarely seemed to, reparations constituted the primary battlefield in the continuing contest over who won the war and over whether Germany would again dominate the continent. Indeed, one German official termed this struggle "the continuation of war by other means."[3] Because Russia had effectively withdrawn from Europe, except briefly at Genoa, and the English-speaking powers were trying to do the same as rapidly as possible, the treaty did not reflect the underlying power equation of a fragmented continent. If reconstruction costs were transferred from the loser to the continental victors and added to their domestic and foreign war debts while Germany paid effectively nothing, as Britain and the United States seemed increasingly to intend, then the existing imbalance would be sharply accentuated and eventual German predominance would be virtually assured.[4] Thus the struggle over reparations started as the treaty took effect in January 1920 and lasted through the history of the Weimar Republic.

By 1922, reparations were established as the chief battleground of the postwar era, the focus of the power struggle between France and Germany over whether the Versailles Treaty was to be enforced or revised. The pattern was already well set of endless international conferences, some consisting of the Western Entente alone and some with German participation; of Allied demands and deadlines; of German defiance and appeals, especially to world opinion; and of mountains of paper and much propaganda, especially from the indefatigable Germans and the artful British. Thus far, Belgium, the junior partner of the Entente, had managed to engineer a series of last-minute compromises that generally gave France the form and Britain or Germany (or both) the substance.

By 1922 as well, most of the truisms were solidly established, thanks in part to inexhaustible German effort. There was endless talk, echoed by historians since, of the need for German reconstruction, though Germany had not been the battleground and it was not Germany's fac-

---

3 *Akten der Reichskanzlei, Weimarer Republik: Das Kabinett Cuno* (Boppard, 1968), 192.
4 Lasteyrie to Poincaré, Apr. 19, 1922, FMF, C.A.-4, 1A/387.

tories and mines that were in ruins. It became quickly accepted without much examination that reparations, which on the whole were not being paid, constituted the chief barrier to the economic recovery Europe sought and could not immediately find, even though (or possibly because) they had been designed in part to further the economic recovery and reconstruction of the devastated victors. Similarly, Weimar oratory successfully stressed Germany's feebleness, though this was clearly transitory and superficial. Germany remained potentially Europe's greatest power, its prospective dominance only heightened by the weakness of its new neighbors created from the collapse of the Habsburg and Romanov empires. There was an equally effective and careful confusion of Germany's undoubted financial disarray with economic weakness, which did not exist, to establish that Germany was too poor to pay. It was rarely noticed that Weimar governments generally had sufficient funds for whatever they wanted to do.[5]

By 1922, it had become a truism that Germany could not pay and that the London Schedule of Payments could not be executed. Never mind that in November 1921 Germany's foremost reparations expert told American leaders that Germany could pay 2.5 billion (American billion) gold marks a year, a figure somewhat below that of the London Schedule but far above what propaganda, policy, and truisms suggested was feasible. Many accepted the idea that Germany could pay only by an export drive that Britain deeply feared as potentially damaging to her already battered trade balances. In British eyes, Britain should do the exporting to Europe, not the reverse. To others, it became axiomatic that Germany could pay only through foreign loans, not from its own considerable assets.[6] Loans were attractive to Weimar politicians,

---

5 For example, for political reasons and in the hope of escaping reparations, in 1921 Germany voluntarily took on the Wiesbaden accord, although it was never executed. At Genoa and again in July 1922, German leaders considered accepting a costly agreement to redeem the 7 billion German marks left in Belgium in 1918 in order to gain reparations moratoria. *Akten der Reichskanzlei, Weimarer Republik: Die Kabinette Wirth I und II*, 2 vols. (Boppard, 1973), 2:738–9, 945. In 1925, there was sufficient money to attempt to use the mark question to regain Eupen and Malmédy, and in 1926 at Thoiry, Stresemann tried to buy Germany's way out of the territorial provisions of the Versailles Treaty. On the mark question and Eupen–Malmédy, see Manfred J. Enssle, *Stresemann's Territorial Revisionism: Germany, Belgium, and the Eupen-Malmédy Question, 1919–1929* (Wiesbaden, 1980).

6 Carl Bergmann, *Der Weg der Reparation* (Frankfurt/M., 1926), 141–5. Bergmann, who was visiting the United States, was no longer a civil servant but remained in close touch with the German government. He proposed payment of 10 billion gold marks over four years, the bulk of it in kind, the cash to be covered by an international loan. The German government, which did not accept his view that some concessions were necessary toward the larger end of a reparations write-down, did not endorse his scheme. British fear of a German export drive is clear in *Die Kabinette Wirth*, 1:381–2, and in a Federation of British Industries report enclosed in Moncheur to Jaspar, Dec. 9, 1921, BMAE, no. 5530/2027, Classement B, file 366V [hereafter B-366V]. For the other truisms, Logan to Hoover, Mar. 9, 1922, Logan Papers, file 2, is typical.

who shared some of the characteristics of politicians everywhere, for three reasons: Germany would not have to pay out of its own resources, the citizenry would not have to be taxed heavily, and the bankers would not approve the loans until the London Schedule was abolished and the total figure sharply cut.[7] This last was especially the point. German insistence that payment was possible only through loans was primarily designed to reduce the bill.

Through 1922, English and American financiers and those from Germany's neutral neighbors insisted that there be no loans until the final bill was set. It had been fixed in 1921, but thanks to German efforts, increasingly seconded by the British, the London Schedule lacked any aura of permanence. The bankers meant that it be revised sharply downward and set at a modest figure "for once and for all time," as J. P. Morgan, Jr., put it.[8] Curiously, the absence of any fixed sum except for the technical existence of the original very nominal and misleading figure of 132 billion gold marks was no impediment to a flood of loans from 1924 on. As in other aspects of reparations, the real concerns in 1922 were more political than purely economic, though some financiers probably persuaded themselves otherwise.

By this time, it was also axiomatic that reparations were causing the collapse of the mark, which in turn adducedly rendered impossible the financial reforms that the Reparation Commission demanded and Germany successfully resisted – with no intention of reform until reparations were written-down.[9] Dumping vast quantities of paper marks on the market was not the only way to gain foreign exchange to pay reparations in hard currencies, but it was the one that guaranteed the fall of the mark, thus supposedly "proving" that reparations were destroying the German currency. As Germany took this course in 1921,[10] it was a truism by 1922 that reparations were causing the German inflation,

---

7 *Die Kabinette Wirth,* 2:807.
8 Morgan made the remark (*Die Kabinette Wirth,* 2:859) during the June 1922 deliberations of the Bankers' Committee, which refused to consider a loan to Germany without reparations reduction and then rejected one with reparations reduction because the chief creditor, France, dissented.
9 Compte-rendu, Blackett-Loucheur talks, Dec. 8, 1921, FMF/B32254; German note to Committee of Guarantees, Mar. 8, 1922, note of Financial Service, French Embassy, Berlin, no. 214, Sept. 5, 1922, FMAE, Laurent Papers; de Gaiffier to Poincaré, Apr. 21, 1922, Poincaré Papers, vol. 16055; Logan to Hoover, Mar. 9, 1922, Boyden to A. A. Boyden, Nov. 21, 1921, Logan Papers; *Die Kabinette Wirth,* 2:863–7; Schuker, *American "Reparations,"* 21; Sergent to Tannery, May 16, 1922, FMF/B32266; Bergmann, *Der Weg,* 166.
10 Stephen A. Schuker, *The End of French Predominance in Europe* (Chapel Hill and London, 1976), 16; Belgian note of meetings with Fass, Dec. 2–3, 1921, Moncheur to Jaspar, Dec. 9, 1921, no. 5530/2027, BMAE, B-366V.

though little cash was being paid, and that reparations somehow caused the hyperinflation late in 1922, when no cash payments at all were being made. The French government and the intensely pro-German British Treasury thought otherwise, knowing that so few payments could not cause so much.[11] The relative ease with which Germany stabilized its currency in the dire circumstances of late 1923 leads one to ponder what could have been done in 1922 if the desire and will to act had then existed.

Through 1922, Weimar's leaders argued that they had done "the humanly possible" and that Germany could do no more, either to reform its finances or to pay.[12] They expected large rewards for any compliance at all and saw no point in making major efforts unless guaranteed a substantial reduction.[13] Meanwhile, the Wirth government continued to proclaim its policy of fulfillment. Described as "calculated inertia"[14] rather than outright resistance, this policy aimed both at preventing further punitive occupations of German territory and at demonstrating the impossibility of fulfillment.[15] Germany said incessantly that it could not meet its obligations, and the constant repetition had an effect. Further, British and American leaders tended to accept these statements without close examination, mainly because they did not wish to act to compel compliance. Thus, another truism was created, that both the London Schedule and the sharply reduced scheme of March 1922 were beyond German capacity to pay.

French leaders knew that the real question was not capacity to pay but willingness to do so.[16] They said so often, gaining only a truistic reputation for being vengeful and imperialistic. They were in fact neither, but rather very frightened. They understood the underlying power balance and the fact that by every yardstick, Germany was potentially far stronger than France, particularly if the fetters of Versailles were snapped. Because the French leaders had no more political courage than the Weimar politicians, they did not announce these realities,

---

11 Foreign Office memo., Nov. 23, 1922, GB FO 371/7487; de Gaiffier to Jaspar, Dec. 20, 1921, no. 12578/6048, BMAE B-366V; Financial Service, French Embassy, Berlin, Sept. 5, 1922, no. 214, FMAE, Laurent Papers.
12 *Die Kabinette Wirth,* 2:793.
13 *Die Kabinette Wirth,* 1:400, 404–5, 412; Bergmann, *Der Weg,* 141–5. Moderates in the *Auswärtiges Amt* and other government circles, such as Schubert and Bergmann, lacked much influence at this time.
14 Financial Service, French Embassy, Berlin, Sept. 5, 1922, no. 214, FMAE, Laurent Papers.
15 *Die Kabinette Wirth,* 2:817, 1:508.
16 Seydoux to Waterlow, Dec. 20, 1921, FMAE, Seydoux Papers, file 11; Financial Service, French Embassy, Berlin, Sept. 5, 1922, no. 214, FMAE, Laurent Papers.

nor did they put France's economic and financial house in order. Just as it was politically easier for German leaders not to tax or pay, it was politically easier for French leaders not to tax or reorganize industrially but to put their hopes in reparations, especially when the reconstruction bills came due in 1922.[17]

French leaders varied in tactics and style but were agreed in their appreciation that France had not won the war. Their concern was that France not be the loser, so they struggled to maintain the military verdict of 1918, but without the Allies who had made it. They managed to accept the departure of Russia and America but not that of Britain. Despite talk of perfidious Albion and hardheaded expert analysis,[18] they could not quite face the reality that their essential ally was no longer an ally. This was as true of Raymond Poincaré as of Aristide Briand, perhaps more so. Regarding both, truisms have misled the unwary. "Poincaré la guerre" was a timid procrastinator whose rigidity derived from dread of making decisions, whereas Briand, proclaimed as the apostle of peace, was devious, factually erratic, and devoid of much spine, but both saw Britain as France's salvation.

As the British moved steadily farther away from their wartime ally, the sole instrument left to a weakened France was the Versailles Treaty. Given German attitudes, enforcement of the treaty required Anglo–French agreement or coercion. When Britain resisted enforcement, French leaders pointed out that Allied unanimity always rendered force unnecessary, for Germany never resisted a united front.[19] This argument was accurate but unavailing, since Britain's real opposition was to reparations and to the treaty itself. Faced with the prospect of virtually unilateral coercion as the sole alternative to surrender, French leaders became niggling, legalistic, and very irritating in their desperation.[20] By 1922, Britain and France had reached an impasse, with each able to block the other's policy but neither able to prevail, while Belgium struggled to paper over the widening gap.

At the start of 1922, British leaders tried to lure the French away from treaty enforcement by the offer of a guarantee pact, which was intended as the prelude to a similar arrangement with Germany.[21] The

17 Pignerol to Lasteyrie, Jan. 27, 1922, FMF/B32266. So far, expenditures had amounted to 85 billion French francs, of which 28 billion had been paid by December 31, 1921.
18 Seydoux note, Dec. 17, 1921, FMAE, série Z, Allemagne, file 470 [hereafter Z/Alle/470].
19 Peretti note, May 27, 1922, FMAE, Z/Alle/236; Hardinge to Balfour, May 29, 1922, no. 1280, GB FO 371/7477.
20 R. S. Sayers, *The Bank of England, 1891–1944*, 3 vols. (Cambridge, 1976), 1:174, n. 1.
21 Curzon to Hardinge, Dec. 24, 1921, Curzon Papers F112/232; I.C.P. 211A, Dec. 21, 1921, GB CAB 29/24; A. Chamberlain to Curzon, Dec. 22, 1921, Chamberlain Papers 24/3/32.

French knew that the price of a British guarantee narrowly limited to French soil and without any military arrangements was abandonment of treaty enforcement, a large reduction of reparations, a sharp cut in the French military establishment, and other terms amounting to global surrender to British leadership.[22] It was to be a steep price for France and a big reward for Germany. Yet Briand was apparently much tempted, which was one reason for his fall in January 1922. Poincaré, who succeeded him, was equally concerned about French security against Germany and thus also eager for the British tie but not prepared to jettison the Versailles Treaty.

Indeed, Poincaré's policy through the spring of 1922 and at the Genoa Conference aimed at salvaging the treaty and what it represented. He was equally determined to keep the reparations question in the Reparation Commission where France had a preponderant position, thanks to its deciding vote in case of a tie and Britain's consistent tendency to offend Belgium.[23] Poincaré much feared the Genoa Conference, with reason, and looked for an excuse to torpedo it. On the other hand, his British counterpart was trying to circumvent the Versailles Treaty and to tackle a reparations reduction at Genoa where other states might overpower France's opposition to treaty revision that would benefit Germany.[24]

David Lloyd George had set postwar British policy on a nostalgic course. He yearned to return to the nineteenth century when Britain was the fulcrum of the balance of power, able to tip it as she chose. Thus he edged progressively away from France. His policy was dictated in part by a defective reading of the underlying power equation. Because Lloyd George focused on the short-term and superficial, he thought France strong and Germany weak, and so he hastened to redress the balance, as exemplified by his pact proposals so favorable to Germany and so costly to a frightened France. Britain rapidly ceased to fear Germany because it no longer possessed colonies or a navy of consequence, and thus could not strike at British concerns. Britain did fear France and sharply resisted France's attempts to restore its naval strength. Britain also turned against the Versailles Treaty, not least because it was not self-enforcing and Lloyd George did not want to enforce it. In part,

22 Waterlow to Seydoux, Dec. 6, 1921, Papers of Sir Edward Grigg, microfilm ed., Queen's University Library, Kingston, Ontario, reel 9; Seydoux note, Dec. 17, 1921, FMAE, Z/Alle/470; I.C.P. 220A, Jan. 4, 1922, GB CAB 29/94.

23 Poincaré to Barthou, May 1, 1922, tel. 24102, FMAE, Z/Alle/472; Poincaré to Barthou, May 6, 1922, tel. 330–1, FSHV, 6N82.

24 Sthamer to AA, Mar. 1, 1922, K. no. 4, Germ. AA, T-120, 4597H/2370/E188264–7, E188278–9, Mar. 2, 1922, K. no. 6, E188253– 6.

Britain lacked troops (particularly during the Irish troubles), and in part, British leaders were less convinced than the French that a united front would obviate the need for enforcement. Further, like Poincaré, British leaders understood that not acting was always easier and politically less risky than acting. Much influenced by historic rivalries, the British thus met French proposals for sanctions to compel enforcement by evasions and by muttering about French reversion to the policy of Louis XIV, and they seemed terrified of the shrinking army of a France trying to cling to British protection.[25] It became an Anglo–American truism that France was too powerful and threatened to dominate the continent. Thus it must be weakened – and building Germany up was the easiest way to accomplish this. Neither Lloyd George nor many Britons saw how far Britain had moved from the center of the power equation or what the long-term implications might be.

Lloyd George's economic policies were equally nostalgic. He hoped to revert to the halcyon prewar days when Germany was one of Britain's best customers, thereby curing Britain's persistent slump. He thought reparations were the chief impediment to German purchase of British goods, and so he wanted to do away with reparations. Again contemplating only the short run, he did not wish to enforce a settlement that he thought was against British interests. After all, if Germany paid three billion gold marks a year, which was unlikely, Britain's modest share would equal only half the value of her prewar export to Germany.[26] It became British policy to work constantly to reduce the reparations bill.[27] Once Britain sponsored and signed a lower arrangement, it worked to undermine and reduce that. But British efforts at treaty revision were always gradual, de facto, and indirect. Thus they never satisfied the Germans, who wanted a dramatic renunciation of the Versailles Treaty and negotiation of an entirely new settlement on the basis of equality and upon the premise that World War I had resulted in a draw.

British policy, like that of other states, arose from perceptions of national self-interest. However, Anglo-Saxon leaders, especially the English, had a talent that the French (except for Briand) conspicuously

25 Waterlow to Seydoux, Dec. 6, 1921. In reply, Seydoux doubted that Louis XIV would have put up with such a situation. Seydoux to Waterlow, Dec. 20, 1921, FMAE, Seydoux Papers, file 11. On British fears of the French army, Sthamer memo., Apr. 6, 1922, Germ. AA, T-120, 4597H/2370/E188139-45.
26 Montille to Briand, Nov. 26, 1921, no. 635, FMF/B32254; Seydoux memo., Dec. 5, 1921, FMAE, Z/Alle/469.
27 Seydoux memo., Dec. 17, 1921, FMAE, Z/Alle/470.

lacked. They knew how to present ordinary national selfishness in the most elevated and moral terms, and it has therefore become yet another truism that the British were wise, objective, and far-seeing, and pursued the only policies productive of permanent peace. This notion has lingered despite the impermanence of the peace that Lloyd George did so much to shape. In fact, British leaders, who tended toward basic agreement on major foreign policy issues, judged a question not on its merits but in terms of short-sighted national interest, just as politicians in other countries often did. Thus, British governmental and economic leaders set out to end reparations, saying that it was impossible for Germany to pay and important to make Germany a good market for British goods.[28]

In December 1921, Britain tried for a comprehensive settlement premised on an Anglo-French move to force debt cancellation on the United States. The effort failed because America simply would not cooperate in this respect.[29] Thereafter Britain aimed at a temporary arrangement for 1922, with the intent of using the year to gain a permanent settlement at its end.[30] This did not entirely accord with the German hope of a provisional settlement for several years,[31] but in general the Germans went along with Lloyd George, having learned in 1921 that Britain was their best hope of splitting the Entente and undoing the treaty.[32]

In December 1921 as well, Britain dangled the projected guarantee before France and hoped to come to an arrangement at Cannes. When that conference collapsed upon Briand's resignation, a temporary partial reparations moratorium was patched together for Germany in March 1922, with a May 31 deadline for reforms.[33] The one item settled at Cannes was the economic conference at Genoa, which Lloyd George intended to use for debt cancellation and drastic downward revision of reparations, despite nominal exclusion of reparations from

28 Moncheur to Jaspar, Dec. 16, 1921, no. 5634/2077, BMAE, B-366V.
29 Hoover to Harding, Dec. 16, 1921, Warren G. Harding Papers, microfilm ed., reel 234, frame 1018; Cheysson compte-rendu, Dec. 15, 1921, and encl., FMF/B32254; Seydoux note, Feb. 4, 1922, FMAE, Seydoux Papers, file 24; *Die Kabinette Wirth,* 1:481.
30 Maltzan memo., Mar. 2, 1922, Germ. AA, T-120, 4597H/2370/E188281-2.
31 Ibid.; *Die Kabinette Wirth,* 1:518.
32 *Die Kabinette Wirth,* 1:204, n., 238, 285. Again, there were disagreements in German policy-making circles that led to some alternation between cooperation with Britain and a harder line – and perhaps a general effort to have things both ways.
33 Thomas Jones, *Whitehall Diary,* ed. by Keith Middlemas (London, 1969), 196; Salter to German Delegation, Cannes, Jan. 12, 1922, Papers of the French Delegation to the Reparation Commission, FAN, AJ5/413; Reparation Commission to German Government, Mar. 21, 1922, AJ5/385.

the conference agenda at French insistence.[34] Further, his proposal for a toothless nonaggression pact was aimed primarily at preventing punitive action against German noncompliance.

As planning for Genoa proceeded in the early months of 1922, weighted down by the ever-present reparations problem, Anglo–German collaboration became intense. Already in December 1921, the British government had apparently prevented loans to Germany while simultaneously urging Germany to seek a moratorium, both moves intended to force Anglo–French talks on reparations aimed at sharp reductions.[35] After Cannes, in speaking to German representatives some British leaders preached a policy of catastrophe equally aimed at drastic reduction or the end of reparations, others hinted that resistance was safe as France was less strong than she seemed, and still others complained that Germany was too honest and should not worry about high Reparation Commission claims inasmuch as they would soon prove impossible of execution.[36] Germans were asked to provide arguments for Britons to use against France, and it was made clear that Britain was doing its utmost to reduce reparations.[37]

Despite this intensive preparatory collaboration, Lloyd George did not achieve any of his major goals at Genoa. A Franco–German reparations arrangement was under informal negotiation when the Rapallo Treaty offered Poincaré the excuse he sought to prevent treaty revision. Poincaré kept himself and the reparations question thereafter safely in Paris, steadily rejecting British calls for a meeting of Versailles Treaty signatories at Genoa before the dread May 31 deadline, refusing all talks until after the Reparation Commission had ruled, and implying that German noncompliance would be met with force, this last almost certainly intended to render its use unnecessary.[38] As negotiations continued after the end of the conference in Paris at the Reparation Commission, however, intensive British coaching produced a very reluctant German communication to the Reparation Commission on May 28

34 I.C.P. 236 revise, Feb. 25, 1922, GB CAB 29/95.

35 Seydoux note, Dec. 17, 1921, FMAE, Z/Alle/470; *Die Kabinette Wirth,* 1:464.

36 Schubert memo., Feb. 27, 1922, Maltzan memo., Mar. 2, 1922, Sthamer to AA, Feb. 16, 1922, A. 372, Sthamer memo., Apr. 6, 1922, Germ. AA, T-120, 4597H/2370/E188286-7, E188281-2, E188355, E188139-45.

37 Sthamer to AA, Feb. 25 and 27, 1922, A. 466, tel. 65, Germ. AA, T-120, 4597H/2370/ E188288-90, E188283.

38 Bergmann, *Der Weg,* 159–61. At Genoa, Bergmann was negotiating with Jacques Seydoux of the Quai d'Orsay. On Poincaré's policy: Poincaré to Barthou, Apr. 23, 1922, tel. 125–6, May 1, 1922, tel. 241–2, FMAE, Z/Alle/471; S.G. 18, Apr. 26, 1922, CAB 31/5; Poincaré to Barthou, Apr. 27, 1922, tel. 186–7, FMAE, Z/Alle/236; British delegation to Hardinge, May 28, 1922, tel. 4, Grigg Papers, 10; Poincaré to Barthou, May 6, 1922, tel. 330–1, FSHV, 6N82.

that seemed to meet many of the Reparation Commission's requirements and thus enabled France to save face. The partial moratorium was
therefore extended.[39]

Six weeks later Germany formally requested a full moratorium on
the remaining reduced cash payments for 1922 and for the next two
years.[40] Britain responded with a third effort toward a comprehensive
settlement, again trying to use the war-debt question. The Balfour
Note of August 1, designed to embarrass the United States into debt
cancellation, succeeded only in destroying Poincaré's plans for the
August reparations conference in London, which failed partly as a
result.[41] Although he rejected the Balfour Note, Poincaré was forced to
jettison his plans to use the chimerical C Bonds of the London Schedule
as a fig leaf to cover debt cancellation. He arrived instead with a hasty,
ill-prepared scheme to seize "productive pledges," such as German
state mines and forests, to insure that Germany would resume payment
at the expiry of the requested moratorium. Even the indefatigable Belgians soon realized that compromise was unattainable, and the conference adjourned without any resolution, the first purely Entente meeting to do so. Thereafter, formal German default was postponed by
accepting German six-month treasury bills in lieu of cash payments for
the remainder of 1922. Belgium, which was slated to receive the cash,
proposed this arrangement at British request, despite French protest,
and ultimately accepted the final scheme because the Bank of England
quietly guaranteed the German bills.[42]

This device provided a four-month respite that on the whole was not
devoted to facing the crisis looming at the end of the year, when there
must be a new arrangement or the London Schedule would resume
force and Germany would be in default. Britain, which would be crucial to any new settlement, was distracted by the Greco–Turkish con-

39 *Die Kabinette Wirth,* 2:759–841, *passim*; Reparation Commission annexes 1462a, May 28,
   1922, 1462c, May 30, 1922, 1470a and b, May 31, 1922, BMAE, B-366VI; Etienne Weill-
   Raynal, *Les Réparations allemandes et la France,* 3 vols. (Paris, 1947), 2:160–2; Bergmann, *Der
   Weg,* 165–7.
40 Foreign Office memo., July 15, 1922, GB FO 371/7480.
41 Cabinet 35 (22), June 16, 1922, 36 (22), June 30, 1922, 42 (22), July 25, 1922, GB CAB 23/
   30; Grigg to Lloyd George, July 29, 1922, Grigg Papers, 10; Foreign Office memo., Oct. 5,
   1922, GB FO 371/7685.
42 Reparation Commission to German Government, Aug. 31, 1922, GB FO 371/7484; Addison
   to Curzon, Sept. 19, 1922, no. 752, GB FO 371/7485. See also Great Britain, Parliament,
   Cmd. 2258, *Minutes of the London Conference on Reparations, August 1922* (London, 1924). The
   German government paid off all the bills on the due dates, primarily because of the British
   involvement, but ceased to pay interest on the outstanding bills after the onset of the Ruhr
   occupation. Photos of the bills are located in BMAE, B-366VI.

flict and the fall of Lloyd George. As a consequence, the British cabinet never discussed the reparations problem during the autumn of 1922. To a considerable degree, other countries waited on Britain, although France and Italy prepared schemes. As the conference necessary to resolve matters drew near, the British consulted Germany but not any of their erstwhile Allies, refusing Italian and Belgian requests for information.[43]

When the Allies convened in Paris on January 2, 1923, to face the problem at last, Britain attempted once again to trade war-debt relief, this time without reference to the United States, for British control of the reparations problem, with an eye to rapid reduction. But the complex British scheme, devised unilaterally by Treasury officials, was politically impossible for leaders of the continental receiver states, and they accordingly rejected it. Inasmuch as Britain would consider no other scheme, the conference promptly failed.[44]

Thereupon Poincaré, trapped between the British and the French right with no room left for maneuver, reluctantly launched the Ruhr occupation in a final effort to preserve the Versailles Treaty and the military verdict it embodied.[45] As a consequence, reparations in 1923 differed from reparations in 1922 in that the struggle reached its climax, if not its conclusion. As is well known, France won the battle but lost the war, thanks both to Poincaré's characteristic but costly hesitations and to the remarkable combination of erstwhile enemies and Allies arrayed against him. Thus, the ensuing years saw the progressive unraveling of both reparations and the Versailles Treaty. In the history of reparations, 1922 represented an intense but not entirely conclusive test of wills over a fundamental issue settled thereafter in ways more costly to Germany, France, and Europe.

43 Logan to Strong, Dec. 1 and 22, 1922, Logan Papers, file 2; *Das Kabinett Cuno*, 61; Le Tellier to Jaspar, Dec. 23, 1922, no. 4597/1917, de Gaiffier to Jaspar, Jan. 6, 1923, no. 209/98, BMAE, B-10.071; G. Grahame to Curzon, Jan. 7, 1923, tel. 6, GB FO 371/8626; *DDI*, settima serie, vol. 1, no. 261. Summaries of all the plans, including the German one never submitted to the conference, may be found in Bergmann, *Der Weg*.
44 For full texts of the complex Bradbury plan as well as those of France and Italy, and minutes of the debates, see Great Britain, Parliament, Cmd. 1812, *Inter-allied Conferences on Reparations and Inter-allied Debts Held in London and Paris, December 1922 and January 1923* (London, 1923) or France, Ministère des Affaires Etrangères, *Documents diplomatiques. Demande de moratorium du gouvernement allemande à la Commission des Réparations, 14 novembre 1922. Conférence de Londres, 9–11 décembre 1922, Conférence de Paris, 2–4 janvier 1923* (Paris, 1924).
45 Schuker, *French Predominance*, 24–5. On Poincaré's overtures to the British in an effort to escape the need for action, see Crowe memo., Dec. 27, 1922, GB FO 371/7491; Ryan to Lampson, Jan. 5, 1923, GB FO 371/8626; Hardinge to Poincaré, Dec. 20, 1922, Hardinge to Hermite, Apr. 14, 1924, Poincaré Papers, vol. 16003; Charles Hardinge, Baron Hardinge of Penshurst, *Old Diplomacy* (London, 1947), 276–7.

5

Germany and the United States: The Concept of World Economic Interdependence

MANFRED BERG

The foreign policy of the Weimar Republic was to a large extent preoccupied with the problem of reparations, a controversial issue for contemporaries as well as for later historians. What the Allies considered just compensation for damages and losses caused by German aggression, the Germans viewed as tribute imposed by relentless victors, which was designed to weaken their country permanently. Moreover, reparations involved more than money. In many ways, the issue raised the crucial question of enforcement or revision of the Treaty of Versailles. If the Germans successfully denounced Allied claims as unjust and absurd, they could hope to shatter the treaty as a whole. And if the Allies allowed Germany to default on reparations, who could guarantee that the Reich would still observe the treaty's other stipulations? The underlying challenge of who had won and who had lost World War I accounts for much of the intransigence on both sides.

Historians and economists have fought over reparations almost as fiercely as did the politicians of the 1920s.[1] After World War II, reparations were generally blamed for the ruin of the Weimar Republic;[2] but more recently, scholars have asserted that Germany's reparations policies, with only a few tactical modifications, actually consisted of continuous and successful obstruction.[3] To be sure, it is not surprising that neither the German people nor their governments ever accepted reparation payments as a moral obligation. However, this does not mean that all their efforts were directed exclusively toward sabotage.

---

1 For an account of the historiographical debate see the discussion in *Journal of Modern History* 51 (1979):1–85, and Peter Krüger, "Das Reparationsproblem der Weimarer Republik in fragwürdiger Sicht. Kritische Überlegungen zur neuesten Forschung," *VfZG* 29 (1981):21–47.
2 See, e.g., Ludwig Zimmermann, *Deutsche Aussenpolitik in der Ära der Weimarer Republik* (Göttingen, 1958).
3 See Sally Marks, "The Myths of Reparations," *Central European History* 11 (1978):231–55; Stephen Schuker, *American "Reparations" to Germany, 1919–1933* (Princeton, 1988).

Because the means and ends of German reparation policies varied significantly over time, the different political concepts behind them have to be analyzed carefully.

This chapter will emphasize the political concepts of two of the most prominent international statesmen of the Weimar Republic: Walther Rathenau and Gustav Stresemann.[4] Although both men were definitely revisionists, in the sense that they tried to overcome the consequences of the peace treaty and restore Germany's great-power status, their approach toward a change in the postwar order was moderate and cooperative, based on the logic of world economic interdependence and on close German–American relations. Since the latter consideration played such a key role in their concepts, the focus will also be on the United States and on the American response to European reconstruction before the Genoa Conference. Despite the preliminary failure in 1922 of revision through world economic interdependence, an analysis of this concept can contribute to a better understanding of German foreign policy in the so-called period of stabilization after 1923.

Notwithstanding their personal and political differences,[5] both Rathenau and Stresemann were exponents of a modern understanding of foreign policy that no longer defined international relations simply in terms of military power, but also emphasized the economic factor in world politics. Both men had made their way into German political life through business – Stresemann as a corporate lawyer for several industrial organizations, Rathenau as president of the Allgemeine Elektrizitätsgesellschaft, Germany's second largest electrical company[6] – and both had been articulate spokesmen for an export orientation of the Germany economy. According to people like Rathenau and Stresemann, the great-power status of the Reich depended on its position in the world market. Even during World War I, while noisily advocating an excessive war-aims program, Stresemann always maintained that Germany could not afford to retreat to an autarkic *Mitteleuropa* but had to carry on the struggle for the world market.[7] Although considerably

---

4 For a more detailed account, see my Ph.D. dissertation, "Gustav Stresemann und die Vereinigten Staaten von Amerika. Weltwirtschaftliche Verflechtung und Revisionspolitik, 1907–1929," Diss., Heidelberg, 1988; on Rathenau's role in Weimar foreign policy, see David Felix, *Walther Rathenau and the Weimar Republic: The Politics of Reparations* (Baltimore and London, 1971).

5 Rathenau and Stresemann were entirely different in origin and character, and as leading representatives of the two competing liberal parties, they were marked political rivals.

6 Cf. Berg, "Stresemann," 26–52; Felix, *Rathenau*, 42–4.

7 Stresemann's speech in the Reichstag in April 1916, *Verhandlungen des Reichstags. Stenographische Berichte*, 307:871; Berg, "Stresemann," 53–65.

more moderate, Rathenau did not fully escape the temptation to demand extensive territorial gains and high indemnities in case of victory, but he also admitted Germany's relatively strong dependence on foreign trade.[8] Regardless of the war's outcome, the world economy would remain an interdependent unity.

When the defeat of 1918 destroyed German military power, only its economic potential endured as a source of national strength. German politicians and businessmen believed that the peace treaty constituted the major impediment to economic reconstruction. But in the long run, even the victors would be forced to admit that an interdependent world economy could not exclude Germany as a consumer and supplier and that a revision of the Versailles Treaty was in their own interest, particularly under the looming menace of bolshevism. This, as Stresemann kept telling his audience, was Germany's chance to unleash its bid for revision.[9]

Both Rathenau and Stresemann, though personally shocked by Germany's defeat, rapidly adjusted themselves to the new situation. Whereas Rathenau concentrated mainly on the reorganization of domestic production, much along the lines of the state-run war economy he himself had earlier helped to create, Stresemann focused on Germany's reintegration into a liberal world economy.[10] Given the fact that Germany's access to world markets had been curbed by the Versailles Treaty, Stresemann's goal had a dual aspect, as both a revisionist end in itself and a precondition for wholesale change in the postwar order. Once Germany had recovered its leading economic position, the reestablishment of its political power would follow almost automatically. The problem was to convince its former enemies that their own economic fate depended on the restoration of Germany.

If the world economy was indeed an interdependent unity – entangled like "the interests of a family," as Rathenau once put it[11] – then

---

8 Walter Rathenau, *Probleme der Friedenswirtschaft. Gesammelte Schriften,* vol. 5 (Berlin, 1918), 61–93; Felix, *Rathenau,* 51.

9 See, e.g., the clippings of *Heidelberger Tageblatt,* Feb. 2, 1920, and *Vossische Zeitung,* Dec. 17, 1920, Gustav Stresemann Papers, vols. 216 and 222. Rathenau blamed the Entente for denying the "solidarity of world production" until its own lower classes would be fed up with "starving and freezing just like the vanquished." Walther Rathenau, *Was wird werden?* (Berlin, 1920), 22.

10 Cf. Rathenau, *Was wird werden?* and *Die demokratische Entwicklung* (Berlin, 1920). On Rathenau's work for the War Raw Materials Administration in 1915 and his activities in the Socialization Commission in 1920, see Felix, *Rathenau,* 52–3, 58–61; on Stresemann, see Berg, "Stresemann," 131–7.

11 Rathenau, *Was wird werden?* 34.

the Germans would also have to pay their share of reconstruction costs. Rathenau had always accepted the necessity of reparation payments and had argued this position against Hugo Stinnes at the Spa Conference in July 1920.[12] But Stresemann also, despite his nationalist background in the early Weimar years, had argued for partial fulfillment of the Allied claims within a few months after the signing of the Versailles Treaty.[13] It is generally acknowledged that the so-called fulfillment policy was never intended to adhere unconditionally to the London Schedule of Payments. However, it would be equally mistaken to view it simply as bad faith. When Rathenau took office as minister of reconstruction in June 1921, he told the Reichstag that fulfillment would undoubtedly raise the question of how deeply the other side would let the German people fall into misery.[14] But like Chancellor Joseph Wirth, he expressed his conviction that Germany had to extend itself to the utmost, because fulfillment was also a matter of national honor and world peace. According to its protagonists, fulfillment policy demonstrated the necessary German contribution to the reestablishment of a stable, prosperous world economy. The logic was simple: The constant pleading that the economic consequences of war and peace threatened to ruin victors and vanquished alike, and could be overcome not by force but only by overall cooperation, would not gain any credit unless Germany itself proved cooperative. As Rathenau emphasized at a meeting of the Reichsverband der Deutschen Industrie,[15] it was Germany's duty to contribute to the restoration of the world and avoid any talk of a possible default. The admission that the London Schedule was unfeasible had to come from the "world economy" (i.e., the Allies), and the minister of reconstruction was confident that this moment was no longer far away. To be sure, German leaders missed few opportunities to complain about the reparations burden and to demand revision. But it is important to make the distinction as to whether their underlying hope for revision was grounded in a fraudulent bankruptcy or in a strategy that required, at least in principle, the consent of the creditors.

Unburdened by governmental responsibility, Stresemann could, of course, utter "tougher" nationalist rhetoric than Rathenau. However, he basically agreed that there was no alternative to fulfillment and

---

12 Felix, *Rathenau*, 61, however, points out that the differences between Stinnes and Rathenau were not as serious as has often been alleged.

13 See his speech in the *Nationalversammlung* in October 1919, *Stenographische Berichte* 330:2917.

14 *Stenographische Berichte* 344:3744; see also Walther Rathenau, *Gesammelte Reden* (Berlin, 1924), 203–4.

15 Rathenau, *Gesammelte Reden*, 247–52.

international understanding.[16] Although he apparently was prepared even to accept the London Ultimatum, he could not prevail against the right wing of the German People's Party.[17] According to Stresemann, Germany's inferior position could be overcome only if it demonstrated a willingness to cooperate and consequently sought the support of the strongest power, the United States of America, which he regarded as the real winner of the war and which had undoubtedly emerged as the world's leading economic power.[18] Stresemann's concept of revision focused on the United States for three reasons: First, America commanded the almost inexhaustible financial and material resources that Europe needed, and it had to help because no one else could. Second, American industries, which were facing overproduction and unemployment, had a strong interest in the revival of German and European markets. And third, the United States, as a non-Versailles power and stronghold of liberal capitalism, seemed the most receptive to a plea for peaceful change and a businesslike solution to the reparations tangle.[19] Of course, Stresemann did not expect revision through world economic interdependence to develop smoothly. Britain was no longer able to perform its traditional role as the balancer of power; France seemed determined to dismember Germany without regard for the economic consequences; and the Americans would have to use their creditor power to force a change in French policies.[20] But much to Stresemann's disappointment, the United States showed no sign of taking a more active role in European politics.

Rathenau agreed that the ultimate key to a solution of the reparation problem lay with the United States, which he called "the general creditor of the world," while Germany was the "general debtor."[21] But he also recognized that the Americans, for the time being, were not inclined to accept any greater responsibility.[22] As minister of reconstruction, he could not wait for American intervention but had to seek a practical understanding with the Allies. Therefore fulfillment policy under Rathenau's guidance was aimed at three objectives: 1) agree-

---

16 See his speech in the Reichstag, April 28, 1921, *Stenographische Berichte* 344:3462–71.

17 Ernst Laubach, *Die Politik der Kabinette Wirth, 1921/22* (Lübeck and Hamburg, 1968), 18, n. 63.

18 Cf., e.g., his interviews with the *Chicago Tribune* and United Press, Feb. 27, 1920, Stresemann Papers, vols. 216 and 222.

19 Cf. Berg, *Stresemann,* 131–69.

20 See Stresemann to the former crown prince, May 14, 1922, Stresemann Papers, vol. 246.

21 Rathenau, *Gesammelte Reden,* 207–8, 215.

22 Speech at the DDP convention in November 1921, ibid., 355.

ments on deliveries in kind to satisfy French needs without straining Germany's currency reserves;[23] 2) cooperation with Britain to achieve a moratorium on reparation payments and an international loan for Germany;[24] and 3) German participation in the planned international consortium to revive trade with Eastern Europe and Russia.[25]

These objectives reflected the combination of revisionist and cooperative elements that characterized Germany's fulfillment policy in 1921–2. Rathenau's negotiations in November and December 1921 in London and in January 1922 in Cannes were, despite several minor differences, quite encouraging.[26] What seemed most important was that the German delegation had been received as an equal by the Reparation Commission and the Supreme Allied Council, and it had been given an opportunity to develop its viewpoint. Above all, the invitation to the grand economic conference originally to be held in Genoa in March promised to open up new revisionist perspectives if the reparation problem could be introduced under the topic of "economic reconstruction." Preparing to tell again their old story that European peace must be secured by a revision of the Versailles Treaty, the Germans planned to ask for the repeal of unilateral most-favored treatment for the Allies, the gradual removal of all trade restrictions, and an international loan to stabilize the mark.[27] It was hoped that the Genoa Conference might cause a breakthrough to German economic equality and treaty revision.

These hopes were quickly dashed, however, when the new French premier, Raymond Poincaré, who resented the whole idea of the Genoa Conference, succeeded not only in postponing the conference but also in excluding reparations from its agenda.[28] Rathenau, who in the meantime had become foreign minister in the Wirth cabinet, took pains to scale down Germany's expectations. He advised his emissaries abroad that even if Genoa did not yield immediate economic and financial results, Germany's interest still lay strongly in a conference of all European states.[29] Before the Reichstag's Committee on Foreign Affairs, Rathenau indicated that in case of failure Genoa might be succeeded by

23 On the Wiesbaden Agreement between Rathenau and Louis Loucheur, the French minister for liberated regions, see Felix, *Rathenau*, 75–8.
24 On his negotiations with the British government in London in November and December 1921, see his diary, Walther Rathenau, *Tagebuch, 1907–1922*, ed. by Hartmut Pogge von Strandmann (Düsseldorf, 1967), 265–73; Felix, *Rathenau*, 112–4.
25 Felix, *Rathenau*, 137.
26 See *ADAP*, A, 5:431–5, 479–87, 497–501; cf. Carole Fink, *The Genoa Conference: European Diplomacy, 1921–1922* (Chapel Hill and London, 1984), 37–43.
27 See memo., Jan. 27, 1922, Germ. PA AA, Büro Reichsminister 5h Genua, vol. 1.
28 Fink, *Genoa Conference*, 71–87.   29 *ADAP*, A, 5:597–8.

other meetings.[30] Indeed, a failure became more and more likely when the U.S. government's refusal to participate created the next setback for the idea of international cooperation. Without America, the prospects for a thoroughgoing solution of the reparation problem came close to nil.

The Reparation Commission's notes of March 21, 1922, which granted Germany a conditional moratorium but also demanded new taxes and far-reaching financial controls, provoked serious domestic opposition to continuing the policy of fulfillment.[31] Yet despite their political rivalry – it was an open secret that Stresemann wished to form his own cabinet – the foreign minister and the leader of the People's Party showed surprising agreement in the parliamentary debate.[32] Despite his charges that fulfillment had not yielded the expected fruits, Stresemann, like Rathenau, pleaded for continuing the policy of economic understanding. And similar to the government, the leader of the industrialists' People's Party now favored better relations with Soviet Russia in order to demonstrate greater freedom of action. This, however, could be no substitute for close cooperation with the United States. A long-term moratorium and an international loan, brought about by American intervention, remained the essential characteristics of Stresemann's blueprint for a reparation settlement:

The raising of such a loan necessitates the revision of the economic stipulations of the Versailles Treaty. . . . The attitude of the United States will be of crucial importance on the question of an international loan. I believe that it will be realized there that the old phrases after the war, "no European troubles," no interference with European confusions, will in the long run be impossible.[33]

And Walther Rathenau concluded his speech to the Reichstag by exclaiming:

Never before has a nation held the fate of a continent so inescapably in its hand as does America at this moment.[34]

Not only were German leaders constantly imploring America to come to the aid of a hopeless and destitute Europe. In his opening speech, the British prime minister, David Lloyd George, who had been the driving force behind the conference, stated that since a Genoese citizen had once discovered America, he hoped that this city might now

30 Felix, *Rathenau*, 130.
31 See Rathenau's telegram to the Embassy in London, *ADAP*, A, 6:55.
32 See speeches of Stresemann and Rathenau, Mar. 29, 1922, *Stenographische Berichte*, 354:6643–57.
33 Ibid., 6650.   34 Ibid., 6656.

rediscover *Europe* for the Americans.[35] To be sure, a conference on economic reconstruction without the world's largest industrial producer and major creditor did not seem to make very much sense. Yet all the dramatic appeals from Europe produced no response in Washington or in public opinion throughout the United States. According to the German *chargé d'affaires* in Washington, Germany's protests against the notes from the Reparation Commission and Rathenau's speech in the Reichstag had been widely ignored.[36] He reported with disappointment that the majority of Americans still believed in German war guilt and regarded Germany's present misery as a kind of punishment.

America's negative attitudes were by no means restricted to Germany but were also directed against any form of entanglement in European affairs. Press comments depicted the convocation of the Genoa Conference as a desperate maneuver of European governments that was doomed to failure because they lacked the courage to tackle the real problems.[37] And Congress, having just established the World War Foreign Debt Commission to secure the funding of Allied war debts, did not wish to see the United States drawn into discussions about debt cancellation.[38] U.S. Commissioner Ellis Loring Dresel told the Germans that it was not only domestic opposition that had prevented American participation at Genoa.[39] The administration, particularly Secretary of Commerce Herbert Hoover, did not expect anything from another conference of politicians but sought a comprehensive solution that combined reparations, war debts (on a more restricted scale), currency stabilization, and disarmament.[40] Obviously, the time for such a scheme had not yet arrived, so it seemed wiser to wait. The American ambassador in Italy, Richard W. Child, warned "that any enthusiasm for this conference is waning rapidly in Italy and in Europe. . . . Participation at this time . . . will lead to a situation where the United States will have to take a stand too definite and unpopular."[41]

These warnings appeared all the more justified after the notes of the

---

35 Copy of Lloyd George's speech in Germ. PA AA, Büro Reichsminister 5h Genua, vol. 2.
36 Tel. no. 47, Mar. 31, 1922, Germ. PA AA, Büro Reichsminister 27, vol. 1.
37 See, e.g., the article of Frank Simmonds in the *New York Herald,* clipping in Germ. PA AA, Büro Reichsminister 5h Genua, vol. 1.
38 Fink, *Genoa Conference,* 48–9; Felix, *Rathenau,* 127–8.
39 See memo. on Dresel's visit, Mar. 13, 1922, Germ. PA AA, Büro Reichsminister 5h Genua, vol. 1.
40 Werner Link, *Die amerikanische Stabilisierungspolitik in Deutschland, 1921–1932. Die Vereinigten Staaten und der Wiederaufstieg Deutschlands nach dem Ersten Weltkrieg* (Düsseldorf, 1970), 109–12.
41 See Child's report to Secretary of State Hughes, Jan. 30, 1922, *FRUS* 1922, 1:389–90.

Reparation Commission at the end of March revealed that conflict and not cooperation was on the European agenda. Dresel reported from Berlin that the French ambassador had announced "the most rigorous measures" in case of German resistance; meanwhile, his British colleague had called the Reparation Commission's demands "idiotic" and "preposterous."[42] The gloomy picture of disunity and strife, not just between the former enemies but also within the Allied camp, confirmed all too well the misgivings of those Americans who wanted to stay out.

In addition, American leaders strongly disapproved of British plans for the international consortium for trade with Russia as a violation of the open-door principle.[43] Their goal for European reconstruction was to promote the United States' trade, not to create a system of preferential commerce that would lead to closed markets. The Soviets' presence at the conference table made Genoa seem even more suspicious. Washington was unwilling to depart from its policy of nonrecognition so long as Moscow refused to acknowledge czarist debts and compensate foreign companies for the confiscation of their property.

Thus in his reply to the invitation from the Italian government, Secretary of State Charles Evans Hughes openly stated that the United States considered the forthcoming conference not an economic but a political one, in which it declined to be involved; the manner in which the Russian question would be handled was equally unacceptable.[44] This did not mean, however, that the United States took no interest in the Genoa Conference. Ambassador Child and Colonel James Logan, the assistant American representative on the Reparation Commission, went to the Italian Riviera as "unofficial observers" to keep their government informed.[45]

Of far greater interest to the U.S. government than European summit diplomacy was the meeting of the international bankers committee in Paris at the end of May to examine the conditions for a large reparation loan.[46] Although initiated by the Reparation Commission, these negotiations offered an opportunity to promote the American viewpoint of a "business-like" solution. Despite the exacerbation of tensions before the Genoa Conference, the chances for a breakthrough did not appear too bleak. Roland W. Boyden, who anticipated political and

42 Cf. Dresel's report, Mar. 23, 1922, USDS, RG. 59, 462.00 R29/1564.
43 Link, *Stabilisierungspolitik*, 112–14; see also Frank Costigliola, *Awkward Dominion: American Political, Economic, and Cultural Relations with Europe, 1919–1933* (Ithaca, N.Y., 1984).
44 *FRUS* 1922, 1:392–4. 45 Ibid., 394–6. 46 Cf. Link, *Stabilisierungspolitik*, 122–35.

business chaos in Germany as a result of the March notes, added that "one advantage is a decision likely to bring matters to a head, probably quickly."[47] The Reparation Commission now seemed prepared to appoint a committee of financial experts to study a German loan, and Boyden was convinced that such a committee would inevitably recommend a substantial reduction of reparations. Because the success of this initiative depended on the authority of the experts, he strongly recommended Benjamin Strong, the governor of the Federal Reserve Bank of New York, as the American appointee.[48] The French condition for creating the committee, that the London Schedule remain unimpaired, would no doubt become pointless if "world financial opinion" indicated that a large international loan was impossible unless Germany's obligations were reduced to its capacity to pay. Boyden intimated that even French officials had given their tacit agreement on condition that the loan produce substantial cash payments for France.

Washington welcomed the idea of a body of financial experts with an American member, but did not wish to be associated too closely with it. Secretary of State Hughes declined to approve Strong or to suggest an official nominee, since this might be construed as a formal commitment of the U.S. government.[49] But informally Hughes, Hoover, and Treasury Secretary Andrew Mellon agreed on J. P. Morgan, whose participation they deemed essential for the success of the enterprise.[50]

The leading Wall Street banker not only possessed an uncontested reputation as an expert but he also ensured the cooperation of the American financial community in the projected loan. Morgan, a friend of France since World War I, might use his authority to convince Paris to concede a reduction of reparation payments. The Wall Street magnate was nevertheless not out to flatter the French, but to talk business. Fully in accord with the administration, Morgan was determined not to settle for less than an overall solution of the reparation problem before raising a loan.[51] American and also British financiers felt no inclination to lend their money to Germany as long as an indefinite reparation burden and the ubiquitous menace of military sanctions rendered any investment extremely risky. But not even J. P. Morgan could obtain Raymond Poincaré's agreement to a long-term moratorium and a reduction of

---

47 See Boyden's report of Mar. 24, 1922, USDS, RG. 59, 462.00 R29/1565.
48 See his report of Apr. 5, 1922, USDS, RG. 59, 462.00 R29/1608.
49 Hughes's answer of Apr. 8, 1922, ibid.
50 Boyden was instructed to pass Morgan's name as his personal suggestion, Hughes to Boyden, Apr. 17, 1922, ibid.
51 Link, *Stabilisierungspolitik*, 132.

German obligations. The equally uncompromising French premier refused to surrender any of France's claims without in return receiving guarantees and a reduction of France's war debts. Thus, when the bankers stated that they could not report on any sound loan under their limited terms of reference (i.e., no changes in the London Schedule) and asked the Reparation Commission for an extension, a breakup of the loan committee became inevitable. The French delegate who vetoed the application found himself entirely isolated.[52] It was therefore not surprising that the loan committee's final report left no doubt that only a general revision of reparations could restore prosperity, but that its efforts had failed because of French intransigence:

They [i.e., the committee members] are deeply conscious of the immense assistance to the economic recovery of the whole world which would be afforded by the gradual conversion of the German obligation from a debt to Governments into a debt to private investors based like other public debts, not upon external sanctions, but upon the general credit of the debtor country. They believe, indeed, that the resumption of normal conditions of trade between countries and the stabilization of exchanges are impossible without a definite settlement of the Reparation payments as of other external public debts.[53]

Needless to say, the French member did not subscribe to these conclusions.

The loan committee's failure had no major impact on American self-confidence; for even without tangible results, the bankers' work appeared to have some beneficial effects. Colonel Logan commented from Paris that the committee had done a "good job" and clearly revealed "that the present policy is neither sensible nor business-like." "It is clear now," he concluded, "where the preponderance of world opinion lies, and this preponderance will finally have its effect."[54] A change in American policy seemed unnecessary. The next reparation crisis would inevitably occur and give the United States another chance to perform in its creditor position.

Seen from a long-term perspective, the reluctance of Washington and Wall Street to enter the reparations tangle in the spring of 1922 signified a final withdrawal from Europe. American political and business leaders basically shared the German view that the world economy constituted an indivisible unity that could not endure the permanent strangling of one of its most important links. At the Paris Peace Con-

52 See Boyden's report of June 7, 1922, USDS, RG. 59, 462.00 R29/1748.
53 See the report attached to Logan's dispatch of June 15, 1922, USDS, RG. 59, 862.51/1498.
54 Ibid.

ference the American delegation had struggled to limit reparation payments to Germany's capacity to pay, but had been forced to make numerous concessions.[55] Uninterested in collecting reparations for themselves, the Americans were primarily concerned with broader economic and financial issues. As expressed by the New York banker Paul M. Warburg a few months after the Paris Peace Conference: "Germany's solvency must be preserved, not only for her own sake but in the interest of her creditor countries, whose economic future depends so much upon that of her debtors."[56] To be sure, there was also a strong sentiment within American public opinion that considered reparations as due punishment for the aggressor and wanted to see the Germans pay to their utmost. However, among leading politicians and businessmen there existed a broad bipartisan consensus that reparations must not be the stumbling block to world economic recovery. In March 1921, Norman Davis, former undersecretary of state in the Wilson administration, wrote to the new Republican Secretary of State Hughes:

Through the highly industrial development of Europe prior to the war, Germany has become the axis, and the rehabilitation of Europe and its continued prosperity is most dependent upon that of Germany. Unless Germany is at work and prosperous, France cannot be so, and the prosperity of the entire world depends upon the capacity of industrial Europe to produce and to purchase.[57]

This was precisely the same reasoning that Germans like Rathenau and Stresemann tried to bring home to everybody who would listen. It is also interesting to note that even a well-informed observer like the American economic consul in Germany, Maurice Parmalee, did not question the honesty of the fulfillment policy. Although recognizing that the German government constantly exaggerated the costs of fulfillment while equally understating its own revenues, Parmalee blamed these inaccuracies not on bad faith but on "the confused state of German public finances and the more or less chaotic conditions in Germany at large."[58] Obviously, the two essential German points – that world prosperity required the economic restoration of the Reich and that the

---

55 See Klaus Schwabe, *Woodrow Wilson, Revolutionary Germany and Peacemaking, 1918–1919: Missionary Diplomacy and the Realities of Power* (Chapel Hill and London, 1985), 285–93.
56 See Warburg's memo., Oct. 20, 1919, USDS, RG. 59, 862.51/1232. Born a German, Paul Warburg was certainly not unbiased, but nonetheless his views were typical of the business community.
57 Quoted in Link, *Stabilisierungspolitik*, 56.
58 See Parmalee's report of Apr. 7, 1922, USDS, RG. 59, 862.51/1462. He had been sending this kind of report since June 1921; see USDS, RG. 59, 862.51/1370, 1382, 1430.

Germans were willing to cooperate in this process but were prevented from doing so by an unreasonably heavy reparation burden – had gained considerable credit among American policy makers. In his famous speech in New Haven in December 1922, Secretary of State Hughes came close to an official acknowledgment of this viewpoint when he asserted: "We do not wish to see a prostrate Germany. There can be no economic recuperation in Europe unless Germany recuperates."[59] The question was not whether the United States would intervene in the reparation problem, but when, and on what terms.

From the American perspective, the situation at the time of the Genoa Conference was not yet mature. European governments were not yet ready to settle their quarrels along the lines of American conceptions, nor was public opinion in Europe or the United States prepared. Under these circumstances, any premature action on Washington's part would only have threatened to dissipate American power and prestige. "It is easy to say," according to Child's explanation to President Harding of America's absence at Genoa, "that we stay out of Europe to save ourselves. I think I could demonstrate that we stay out of Europe to save Europe."[60] As things would inevitably get worse, the Americans felt strong enough to wait until the Europeans would readily accept their conditions. And much to German disappointment, they had plenty of time.

With the United States absent and reparations excluded, the Genoa Conference lost much of its appeal for German foreign policy. Still, before the opening, Rathenau proposed a meeting with Lloyd George on reparations.[61] The foreign minister was now determined to adopt a "firmer stance" and in the cabinet urged a rejection of the Reparation Commission's demands.[62] Fulfillment, he argued, had never meant compliance, and now the time had come to demonstrate these limits. With both Wirth and President Ebert's agreement that the prospects for Genoa were dim,[63] there seemed little need for further consideration. Rathenau summed up his expectations with the statement that he would be content if the delegation returned without any accident occurring.[64] At best, the conference would be an opportunity to present the German viewpoint on international economic distress in the pres-

---

59 *FRUS* 1922, 2:201.
60 Quoted in Costigliola, *Awkward Dominion*, 109.   61 *ADAP*, A, 6:76–7.
62 *Akten der Reichskanzlei. Weimarer Republik: Die Kabinette Wirth I und II* (Boppard, 1973), vol. 1, nos. 230 and 231.
63 Ibid., nos. 231, 234, 235; vol. 2, nos. 241a and 241b.   64 Ibid., no. 241a.

ence of world opinion and to establish better relations with the leading international statesmen.

There was no comprehensive concept for the Genoa negotiations. Instead, the crisis of fulfillment policy and the urgent desire for a foreign political "success" now induced the Germans to demonstrate their determination by playing the "Russian card" and concluding the Rapallo Treaty with the Soviets.[65] It may be argued that the meager results of the Genoa Conference only confirmed the pessimistic outlook of the Germans, and that the Rapallo Treaty was little more than a reasonable understanding over pending questions between Germany and Soviet Russia.[66] Yet there can also be no doubt that Rapallo contributed a great deal to spoiling the atmosphere at Genoa and nourishing doubts of German honesty and reliability. This displeasure was also felt by the Americans, even if the administration said nothing openly and pretended it disliked only the timing of the Russo–German agreement.[67] Germany, with its renunciation of all claims for compensation of expropriated private property, became the first major country to break the nonrecognition line of the capitalist states against Soviet Russia. The Rapallo Treaty undoubtedly contradicted the United States' policy on this point.[68] It certainly did not increase America's inclination to enter the reparations conflict on Germany's side.

After the failure of the Genoa Conference and the international loan committee, the reparations crisis reached a deadlock that was not broken until the adoption of the Dawes Plan two years later. In the meantime, all of Europe suffered from the economic and political consequences of the confrontation that followed Genoa. Germany had to undergo the Ruhr occupation, disastrous inflation, and dangerous unrest. France for the last time managed to demonstrate military superiority, but at very high financial and political costs.[69] Although the Anglo–American powers tried to remain neutral, there could be no doubt that British and American trade was badly hurt by the Ruhr conflict. Thus the solution of the crisis was largely due to the conclusion of American bankers that the United States' interests demanded action.[70]

65 See Peter Krüger, *Die Aussenpolitik der Republik von Weimar* (Darmstadt, 1985), 173–83.
66 See, e.g., Felix, *Rathenau*, 144–5.
67 See the report of *chargé d'affaires* Lang, Apr. 19, 1922, tel. no. 60, Germ. PA AA, Büro Reichs-minister 5h Genua, vol. 2.
68 See Link, *Stabilisierungspolitik*, 119–21.
69 See Stephen Schuker, *The End of French Predominance in Europe: The French Financial Crisis of 1924 and the Adoption of the Dawes Plan* (Chapel Hill and London, 1976).
70 On the American intervention in 1923–4, see Link, *Stabilisierungspolitik*, 201–17; see also Berg, "Stresemann," 196–218.

The appointment of "independent private experts" permitted Washington to stay aloof while at the same time giving European governments the chance to save face by agreeing to the proposals of an allegedly independent body of economic authorities. The Dawes Plan, which was finally adopted at the London Conference in August 1924, provided for both a reparation moratorium and an international loan; it worked out a new schedule of annuities and installed a control system that ensured protection for the German currency and guarantees for French claims.[71] As this system of surveillance was dominated by Americans, above all by the famous agent general for reparation payments S. Parker Gilbert, the United States, without any formal commitments, gained an influence in Germany that one author has characterized as a "penetrated system."[72]

For the historian, it is striking to see that all the major elements of the Dawes Plan had already been discussed in 1922. The Germans repeatedly urged the necessity of a moratorium and an international loan. The French insisted on "productive guarantees" for their demands. The Americans had always made it clear that the confidence of private investors could only be secured if reparations were removed from politics and decided by financial experts.[73] The control system Germany accepted in 1924 greatly exceeded the demands of the Reparation Commission in 1922. Finally, the basic concept of the Dawes Plan – the idea that the economic consequences of the war could not be overcome by a redistribution between the victors and vanquished, but only by general trade expansion and industrial growth – had already been the idea behind the Genoa Conference.

Therefore, why did this not work out two years earlier? Was it simply, as Hughes observed at the outset of the Ruhr crisis, that the Europeans had to undergo their "bit of chaos" before they would listen to reason?[74] From the American point of view this was obviously true. Without the disillusionment of the Ruhr crisis, neither the Germans nor the French would presumably have accepted a settlement so strongly dictated by American interests. The "wait and see" strategy advocated by the U.S. diplomats at the time of the Genoa Conference had evidently been a prudent one – at least from the American perspective of 1924. Whether the Genoa Conference might have suc-

---

71 *Die Sachverständigengutachten. Der Dawes- und McKenna Bericht. Mit Anlagen* (Frankfurt/M., 1924).
72 Link, *Stabilisierungspolitik*, 591–2. The term "penetrated system," however, appears much too strong considering the rapid decline of American influence after 1929.
73 See the final report of the loan committee, note 53.   74 *FRUS* 1923, 2:56.

ceeded had the United States been there obviously cannot be determined. Given all the flaws of postwar European politics, unless the United States had produced a comprehensive program of political commitments and material aid, it is rather unlikely. Something of the magnitude of the Marshall Plan, however, was totally inconceivable after World War I.[75] On the other hand, it is even more difficult to contemplate how the Genoa Conference might have succeeded *without* American participation.

Moreover, there was a significant change in German foreign policy after 1923, due not merely to different circumstances but also to different concepts. Although Rathenau and Stresemann manifestly shared the conviction that Germany's rehabilitation could be achieved only by economic and political cooperation with the Allies, particularly with the United States, the policy of fulfillment in 1922 still lacked consistency and coherency. Too fixed on short-term results, it considerably overestimated Germany's freedom of action. When the Germans finally realized that a substantial revision of the Versailles Treaty was impossible, they reacted with disappointment. The notes of the Reparation Commission at the end of March 1922, although harsh in tone, were by no means lacking in constructive elements, as German reparation experts pointed out.[76] But Wirth and Rathenau felt constrained to respond to public opinion and to demonstrate "firmness." The Genoa Conference, even before its opening, and before the preliminary decision to deal with the Soviets, was considered a failure.

When Stresemann took charge of German foreign policy, he adhered to a course of economic and political understanding regardless of domestic pressures that were certainly not less heavy than in 1922.[77] Under his leadership, Germany did indeed reemerge as a great power, even if this remarkable development was continually eclipsed by the exaggerated expectations of broad segments of German public opinion. Stresemann's achievements might, to some extent, have been due to his possessing greater political vigor than Rathenau, who, as a Jew and an intellectual, always remained an outsider in German politics. The former, in contrast, was a veritable *homo politicus* with a firm grounding in party politics and an unmistakable instinct for power. But more impor-

75 William McNeil, *American Money and the Weimar Republic: Economics and Politics in the Era of the Great Depression* (New York, 1986), 1, however, points out that the volume of private loans to Germany between 1925 and 1930 was more than twice as large as the amount of Marshall Plan aid.

76 See the discussions in the cabinet, notes 62 and 63.

77 For the following observations on Stresemann, see Berg, "Stresemann."

tant, Stresemann had comprehended that the concept of world economic interdependence required Germany's permanent integration into the West. With the support of the strongest power, the United States of America, this opened much better prospects for German resurgence than oscillation – *Schaukelpolitik* – between East and West.

Reparations, in Stresemann's scheme, played a secondary, instrumental role. First of all, reparation policy was clearly subordinated to such vital concerns as the preservation of the Reich's territorial integrity. "Our life and death," he proclaimed during the Ruhr crisis, "do not depend on paying one billion Gold Marks more or less . . . , but on the Rhine and Ruhr remaining German."[78] Later, reparations would even serve such ambitious goals as the revision of the territorial status quo established by the Versailles Treaty. Stresemann had understood that paying reparations, to a limited extent of course, bore considerable advantages for Germany. It secured foreign credit, improved the Reich's international reputation, and might even be rewarded with political concessions by the Allies. The evacuation of the Rhineland, which he traded shortly before his death for the Young Plan of 1929, marked the great success of his strategy of using reparations as a lever for peaceful revision. The close and successful German–American cooperation in the second half of the 1920s gives ample proof that Stresemann's constant references to world economic interdependence in 1921–2 were not merely rhetoric but expressions of a consistent foreign policy concept.

78 Quoted in Gustav Stresemann, *Vermächtnis,* 3 vols. (Berlin, 1932), 1:56.

6

American Policy Toward Debts and Reconstruction at Genoa, 1922

STEPHEN A. SCHUKER

The U.S. government considered the Genoa Conference a sideshow – a misconceived British conjuring trick to deal with the superficial features of trade depression on the Continent before agreement was reached on the political prerequisites for European economic reconstruction along sound lines. American policymakers perceived three such political prerequisites. The West European countries had to agree to write-down reparations to a figure that Germany could manage financially and accept without endangering political stability. The former Allies, chief among them Great Britain, had to fund their war debts to the United States on reasonable terms. Last, but not least, all European countries had to drastically reduce expenditures on land armaments along lines comparable to what the main sea powers had agreed to at the Washington Naval Conference. A realistic approach to international indebtedness and the transfer of military resources to civilian needs, so went the line in Washington, would promote balanced budgets, end inflationary excess, and foster respect for obligations at home and abroad. With comity among nations restored, trade would revive naturally, without hothouse schemes. The United States would provide adequate credit at market rates. Revived markets would create their own inducements.[1]

---

1 Carole Fink's standard monograph, *The Genoa Conference: European Diplomacy, 1921–1922* (Chapel Hill and London, 1984), covers U.S. policy as well as European aspects of the conference itself. For the wider context of American foreign policy, particularly toward Europe, in the postwar years, see among other works Denise Artaud, *La Question des dettes interalliées et la reconstruction de l'Europe (1917–1929)*, 2 vols. (Lille and Paris, 1978); Joseph Brandes, *Herbert Hoover and Economic Diplomacy: Department of Commerce Policy, 1921–1928* (Pittsburgh, 1962); Peter H. Buckingham, *International Normalcy: The Open Door Peace with the Former Central Powers, 1921–1929* (Wilmington, Del., 1983); Frank Costigliola, *Awkward Dominion: American Political, Economic, and Cultural Relations with Europe, 1919–1933* (Ithaca, N.Y., 1985); L. Ethan Ellis, *Republican Foreign Policy, 1921–1933* (New Brunswick, N.J., 1968); Dieter B. Gescher,

Of all foreign-policy issues facing the Harding administration, the Allied war debts had the greatest domestic resonance. At the start of the 1921 fiscal year, the gross domestic debt of the federal government totaled $25.3 billion. Over $10 billion of that sum had been incurred to finance loans to foreign governments associated with the United States in the prosecution of the World War. The Washington authorities had not generally employed their creditor position as leverage to extract political concessions from the European Allies, either during or after the hostilities.[2] Paradoxically, however, the belief by most Americans that their leaders had not indulged in the sort of crude power politics so abhorrent to Wilsonian idealists reinforced the popular notion that monetary obligations ought to be collectable in a straightforward businesslike manner. Moreover, with the enthusiasms of 1917–18 now a receding memory, the U.S. taxpayer demanded relief. The Treasury had resisted the frequent postwar calls to sell off foreign obligations to the public in order to reduce the Liberty Bond debt and lower taxes. In 1920, outgoing Secretary David F. Houston had denounced the "specious attempt to delude the present generation into the belief that it can avoid the pains and penalties incident to the war by some kind of finan-

---

Die Vereinigten Staaten von Nordamerika und die Reparationen 1920–1924 (Bonn, 1956); Michael J. Hogan, *Informal Entente: The Private Structure of Cooperation in Anglo-American Economic Diplomacy, 1918–1928* (Columbia, Mo., 1977); Melvyn P. Leffler, *The Elusive Quest: America's Pursuit of European Stability and French Security, 1919–1933* (Chapel Hill, 1979); Werner Link, *Die amerikanische Stabilisierungspolitik in Deutschland, 1921–1932* (Düsseldorf, 1970); Robert K. Murray, *The Harding Era: Warren G. Harding and His Administration* (Minneapolis, 1969); Carl P. Parrini, *Heir to Empire: United States Economic Diplomacy, 1916–1923* (Pittsburgh, 1969); Benjamin Rhodes, "The United States and the War Debt Question, 1917–1934," Ph.D. diss., University of Colorado, 1965; Dan P. Silverman, *Reconstructing Europe after the Great War* (Cambridge, Mass., 1982); Marc Trachtenberg, *Reparation in World Politics* (New York, 1980); Robert H. Van Meter, Jr., "The United States and European Recovery, 1918–1923," Ph.D. diss., University of Wisconsin, 1971; and Joan Hoff Wilson, *American Business and Foreign Policy, 1921–1933* (Lexington, Ky., 1971). References to the relevant literature in article form appear in Richard Dean Burns, ed., *Guide to American Foreign Relations since 1700* (Santa Barbara, 1983). Biographies or autobiographies of the major players include Richard Washburn Child, *A Diplomat Looks at Europe* (New York, 1925); Herbert Hoover, *The Memoirs of Herbert Hoover*, 3 vols. (New York, 1952); Betty Glad, *Charles Evans Hughes and the Illusions of Innocence: A Study in American Diplomacy* (Urbana, Ill., 1966); Merlo J. Pusey, *Charles Evans Hughes*, 2 vols. (New York, 1951); David E. Koskoff, *The Mellons: The Chronicle of America's Richest Family* (New York, 1978); and Lester Chandler, *Benjamin Strong: Central Banker* (Washington, D.C., 1958). Significantly, David J. Danelski and Joseph H. Tulchin, eds., *The Autobiographical Notes of Charles Evans Hughes* (Cambridge, Mass., 1973), does not even mention Genoa.

2 As Kathleen Burk shows in *Britain, America, and the Sinews of War, 1914–1919* (Winchester, Mass., 1985), the Wilson administration imposed petty and often vexatious restrictions on the use of its loans by Great Britain, but it did not take advantage of those loans to change the political balance between the two nations, as the Roosevelt and Truman administrations would do a generation later. (On American use of economic power to force political concessions in 1944–5, see Richard N. Gardner, *Sterling-Dollar Diplomacy in Current Perspective* [New York, 1980].)

cial magic."[3] The Treasury had also succeeded in providing the Allies with a three-year respite in the payment of interest on what they owed. But the moratorium would expire in October 1922. By that time, the Treasury sought to have refunding schedules firmly in hand.

Although some of the Continental nations suffered from manifest liquidity problems immediately after the war, no one doubted that the British, with their huge portfolio of foreign assets, could pay as promised if only they wished to pay. Assistant Treasury Secretary Albert Rathbone conducted intermittent discussions with his opposite number in Whitehall, Sir Basil Blackett, during the first part of 1920. Blackett had appeared ready to fund the debt on a normal commercial basis in twelve series of publicly marketable bonds, at an interest rate of 5 percent, and with maturity dates running (as specified in the Liberty and Victory loan acts) from 1938 to 1947.[4] Then Prime Minister David Lloyd George had veered away for political reasons and twice sought to embarrass the United States into unilateral cancellation.

The outgoing Democratic point men at Treasury and State, Russell C. Leffingwell and Norman Davis, made clear to the retiring British *chargé d'affaires* in January 1921 that personally they "hated these debts" and were "inclined to think it would be in the ultimate interest of America . . . that they be cancelled." Nevertheless, both men warned unambiguously, "public opinion would not contemplate such a solution and it simply was not practical politics to talk about it. . . . Proposals and manoeuvres tending to suggest [cancellation] merely defeat their own object."[5] After the change of administrations, the fresh Republican team in Washington, Secretary of the Treasury Andrew Mellon, his assistant, Eliot Wadsworth, and Secretary of State Charles Evans Hughes, reiterated this line. Mellon waved away British references to the grave political and economic disorders troubling parts of the Continent. Mellon anticipated the early return of prosperity and

---

3 D. F. Houston to the President, July 14, 1920, box 95 (Bonds of Foreign Governments file), Office of the Assistant Secretary of the Treasury for Fiscal Affairs, 63A 659, Paperwork Management Branch, USTD.

4 For a retrospective file on these negotiations, see Sir Auckland Geddes no. 476, May 14, 1921, GB FO 371/5661: A3778/247/45; also Foreign Office memo., "Inter-Allied Indebtedness and Attitude of the United States," Apr. 4, 1922, GB FO 371/5662: A7885/247/45. The key American records on the Rathbone–Blackett talks are in box 120, RG. 39, Treasury–Bureau of Accounts; also box 233, Assistant Secretary for Foreign Loans Albert Rathbone files, RG. 56, USTD NA.

5 Ronald C. Lindsay memo. for Sir William Tyrrell, Jan. 4, 1921, GB FO 371/5661: A247/247/45.

trade expansion, and he invited the British to send a funding mission without reference to the debts of the Continental nations.[6]

All the same, the U.S. Treasury sought to retain maximum latitude to settle the war debts in a practical fashion without interference from an importunate Congress. At the request of the president, Senator Boies Penrose in June 1921 introduced a bill drafted in the Treasury authorizing it to extend the time of payment on both principal and interest as it saw fit, and also to accept the obligations of the contracting nation or other foreign governments in exchange for the original war debts. That would have made it possible for the Treasury to have accepted domestic obligations of the Allied debtors, or even German reparation bonds, in exchange for the war debts.[7]

But the Penrose bill encountered heavy weather almost immediately. Senator Kenneth McKellar of Tennessee discerned a scheme to make the American people pay, aside from some "little driblets," some $10 billion of the German war indemnity. "A more unwise, a more impolitic, a more unfair, or a more unjust, a more un-American measure . . . could not have been devised," he fulminated. "It would have been better for us to have just handed over to Germany $10,000,000,000 in the beginning, and dropped it there, without going into the war, than to take such a step as this." Senator J. Thomas Heflin of Alabama, referring to the draft bonus legislation also circulating in Congress, trilled: "Let us be just to the American soldier . . . before we display charity and generosity toward the nations that borrowed from us ten billions of American money." And Senator Henry F. Ashurst of Arizona, not to be outdone, advised Europe peremptorily to "go to work." "We saved Europe and our Christian civilization," he modestly observed, "but that does not imply, now that the peril is past, that we should feed the Europeans and allow them in their great cities to live in idleness and sometimes in luxury."[8]

Mellon met with a skeptical reception when he journeyed to Capitol Hill for Finance Committee hearings on the bill. He was forced to

6 Geddes no. 294 of May 3, 1921, GB FO 371/5661: A3098/247/45. Assistant Secretary Wadsworth nurtured some private doubts. He wrote to a friend on diplomatic assignment in Berlin: "It is sometimes puzzling to see just how we can collect $500,000,000 of interest from Europe in its present condition, not to speak of the principal. However, we keep going on the general principle that it will be collected some day, somehow, and by somebody." Yet publicly Wadsworth too hewed to the official line. See Eliot Wadsworth to Ellis Loring Dresel, Aug. 15, 1921, folder 421, Dresel Papers.
7 Geddes no. 437 of June 24, 1921, GB FO 371/5662: A4598/247/45.
8 *Congressional Record,* June 24, 1921, 3015–16, 3021–8.

make the damaging admission that the British government had twice solicited all-around war-debt cancellation.[9] Nevertheless, Penrose finally managed to have the bill reported out to the full Senate with only minor restrictions on the secretary's authority. A bipartisan group of six irreconcilables, headed by Senator Robert M. La Follette, Sr., which sought to bar the Treasury from offering more favorable terms than those specified in the Liberty Loan Acts, did not initially prevail.[10] The British ambassador derided the opposition as a manifestation of "Irish influence" and of no real importance.[11]

Opposition in the House of Representatives Ways and Means Committee, however, gathered steam in the fall. Mellon, after consulting with the president, had to acquiesce in a redrafting of the bill that placed authority in the hands of a five-member commission.[12] The bill that passed the House on October 24, 1921, also barred the commission from accepting the bonds of any foreign government in lieu of those of another (thus closing off the option of the European Allies assigning their German reparation revenues to the United States in payment of debt). The Treasury took solace in the fact that the bill still left the commission free to convert the inter-Allied demand obligations on such terms, rates of interest, and dates of maturity as it judged fitting.[13]

Before the Ways and Means Committee, Mellon, to ward off further restrictions, had taken the confident line that the British, the French, and even the Belgians and Italians were sure to pay eventually: "We think that it will all work out. Those countries are becoming rehabilitated; they are at work, and a new generation is growing up. . . . I have not any doubt that all the debts of those leading countries will become very substantial securities that will be available to this country."[14]

Yet other forces belied that confidence. Reginald McKenna, former

9 *Refunding of Obligations of Foreign Governments,* Hearings before the Committee on Finance, United States Senate, 67th Congress, 1st Session, on S. 2135, pp. 49–53.

10 *Refunding of Obligations of Foreign Governments,* Senate, 67th Congress, 1st Session, report no. 264, Aug. 19, 1921.

11 Geddes no. 595 of Sept. 9, 1921, GB FO 371/5662: A6631/247/45.

12 Geddes no. 677 of Oct. 17, 1921, GB FO 371/5662: A7591/247/45. On reflection, Treasury strategists came to see the advantage of a broadly based commission that could take the heat for deferring interest payments when that proved politically or economically advisable. "If the secretary did it alone," wrote Assistant Secretary Wadsworth privately, "the position would not be so satisfactory as it would appear that he had decided to take such action on his own judgment" (Wadsworth to Ellis Loring Dresel, Oct. 29, 1921, folder 421, Dresel Papers).

13 *Refunding Foreign Obligations,* Report by Mr. Fordney, from the Committee on Ways and Means, to Accompany H.R. 8762, 67th Congress, 1st Session, House of Representatives, report no. 421, Oct. 20, 1921.

14 *Refunding Foreign Obligations,* Hearings before the Committee on Ways and Means, House of Representatives, on H.R. 7359, Thursday, Oct. 6, 1921, p. 21.

chancellor of the exchequer and the chairman of the Joint City and Midland Bank, made what his own embassy called a "deplorable" impression when he frankly urged cancellation during a transatlantic speaking tour in early November 1921.[15] Just two weeks later, Minister of Liberated Regions Louis Loucheur, Aristide Briand's right-hand man in the French cabinet, made a heavy-footed appeal through Belgium for an economic conference that would convene in Washington as soon as the Naval Disarmament Conference came to an end. Briand, who always relied more on personal instinct than on careful study of his briefing books, returned to Paris from the naval negotiations convinced that the Americans might agree at such an assemblage to write-down the war debts radically. The British stood aghast at the naïveté of the French notion that they could trumpet their refusal to disarm on land or sea and at the same time engineer a conference at which the Americans unilaterally granted debt remission. "M. Briand must have been singularly misinformed if he brought back such an impression," minuted Sir William Tyrrell at the Foreign Office. "I believe it to be a 'terminological inexactitude' propagated by M. Loucheur for stockjobbing purposes."[16] Tyrrell proved all too prescient about the prevailing temper on Capitol Hill. The war-debt legislation as revised by the Senate Finance Committee in December 1921 – against the backdrop of the Washington Naval Conference – required confirmation by the upper house of the prospective appointees to the World War Foreign Debt Commission. Even more alarming, this draft specified that new funding agreements should run for no more than twenty-five years and carry a minimum interest rate of 5 percent.[17]

In January 1922, after vigorous lobbying, the Treasury managed to get the minimum 5 percent rate reduced to 4¼ percent and the provision for rigid semiannual interest payments stricken from the bill. Still, Mellon remained on the defensive throughout. The Democratic opposition made much political capital out of the administration's refusal to earmark war-debt revenues for a veterans' bonus. The legislation passed the Senate in final form on January 31, 1922, against solid Democratic opposition. On the Republican side of the aisle, Senators William E. Borah, Robert M. La Follette, Sr., and George W. Norris joined in the

---

15 Geddes no. 742 of Nov. 8, 1921, GB FO 371/5662: A8357/247/45.
16 Tyrrell minute, Dec. 22, 1921; also Sir G. Grahame no. 199, Dec. 21, 1921, GB FO 371/5662: A9553/247/45.
17 Geddes nos. 802, 814, 815, 818, Dec. 13–17, 1921, GB FO 371/5662: A9275/A9361/A9369/A9375/247/45.

view that the law as enacted did not go far enough to mandate debt collection.[18] The views of the Congressional opposition found considerable reflection also in the press, particularly after Loucheur indiscreetly told a *Baltimore Sun* reporter on February 16 that France would never be able to pay a sou to America. The *Washington Post,* which often mirrored official sentiment, pointedly complained a few days later that much of the money that European governments were wasting on excessive armies, oil schemes, airplane plants, arms factories, and submarine shipyards rightfully belonged to the American taxpayer.[19] This was the political backdrop against which the U.S. government weighed the issue of participation in the Genoa Conference.

American diplomats were surprisingly ill-informed at this time about the details of European politics. Washington never obtained a comprehensive report on the Loucheur–Lloyd George discussions that took place in November and December 1921. The administration remained unaware of the specifics in the offensive that the two leaders discussed to force debt cancellation on the United States as the chief plank of a prospective plan for European economic reconstruction. Loucheur probably should have known better from the start. Had not Maurice Casenave, on the basis of his long-time service with the French economic mission in America, warned in July 1921 that, for Congress, war debts had quickly become "like the clerical question used to be" in the French Chamber – a matter certain to be dragged into everything, whether the ostensible issue under discussion was tariff revision, tax reduction, or the soldiers' bonus?[20] Although Loucheur indulged in a certain amount of wishful thinking (for example, the fantasy that "America" might intervene to reconstitute the German gold reserve in case of monetary stabilization there), he was probably misled in this case at first by his British interlocutors. Sir Basil Blackett of H.M. Treasury gave his French contacts on December 8 the idea that Great Britain might well take the lead, waive the British share of German reparations, and unilaterally cancel the Continental war debts owed to London without awaiting an American quid pro quo. When it turned out that Prime Minister Lloyd George would not proceed an inch without

18 *Refunding of Obligations of Foreign Governments,* 67th Congress, 2nd Session, Senate, calendar no. 408, report no. 400, Jan. 16, 1922; also Geddes nos. 65, 82, 91, and 126, Jan. 15–Feb. 22, 1922, GB FO 371/7281: A751/A880/A1135/A1292/236/45.
19 *Washington Post,* Feb. 22, 1922.
20 Maurice Casenave to M. Vignon, *chef de cabinet* to the president of the republic, July 21, 1921, box 5, folder 8, Louis Loucheur Papers.

cancellation of war debts by the United States, the grand schemes nurtured at the subordinate level for recasting the reparations schedule collapsed like a house of cards. Lloyd George then proceeded with his nebulously conceived plan for an economic conference – with the implicit purpose of forcing all-around debt cancellation on America never absent from his calculations.[21]

The American ambassador to London, the erstwhile journalist and sometime inebriate George Harvey, had few connections and little standing with the government to which he was accredited.[22] Reduced to reading Philip Kerr's *Daily Chronicle* in his efforts to comprehend the British official mind, Harvey nevertheless caught the drift of Lloyd George's strategy. The prime minister, he reported on December 13, 1921, wanted President Harding to take the initiative in calling an economic and financial conference in order to "put the United States under tacit obligations to make pecuniary sacrifices through cancellation of debts in full or in part. . . . While unquestionably sincere in his expressed desire to stabilize Europe, his underlying purpose is to obtain great reduction of English indebtedness to the United States through [a] voluntary campaign or proposal of our government, thus while talking loudly of England's determination to pay in full, saving both face and money." With a grasp of English prose style that only his friend Harding could fully savor, Harvey added: "to suggest sitting tight is doubtless superrogative."[23]

Back in Washington, Secretary of Commerce Herbert Hoover picked up intelligence through his own channels about the nature of an emerging Lloyd George–Loucheur deal. The prime minister and "Loucher" (as Hoover slyly called him) planned to invite the United States to call an economic conference and then to spring a plan entailing the elimination of pensions from the reparations bill and the reduction

---

21 Note Loucheur, "La politique financière á imposer á l'Allemagne," Nov. 30, 1921, box 5, folder 11; note Cheysson, "Conversation avec M. Basil Blackett," Dec. 8, 1921, box 5, folder 6; "London Negotiations," Dec. 8–9, 1921, box 7, folder 4; "Reparations Negotiations," Dec. 18–20, 1921, box 5, folders 11 and 13, Loucheur Papers.
22 Harvey was not merely "out of the loop"; despite his crucial position he had actually become a figure of fun. Governor Montagu Norman of the Bank of England provided this intelligence about the Cannes Conference, the preliminary to Genoa, to his fellow central banker, Benjamin Strong of the New York Fed: "There was only one morning at Cannes when everybody looked hopeful and happy: a rumour was going around that your Colonel H. had been damaged in a motor accident and people hurried out of town to look at his corpse. But in a couple of days he was about again and everybody was again looking hopeless and dejected!" (Norman to Strong, Feb. 6, 1922, Benjamin Strong Papers, 1116.3.)
23 Harvey to State, Dec. 13, 1921, USDS, RG. 550.E1/–.

of French claims against Germany by one-half. Having made these gestures to enlightened opinion, the two statesmen would then demand, as a quid pro quo, the abandonment of war debts all around. Hoover sent an urgent warning to the president. A conference at which the British and French made such proposals would create "an impossible situation" for the administration. Harding needed no further prompting. "The feeler outlined," he replied, ". . . is doubtless a very promising one for Europe, but it is not possible to consider it in the United States."[24]

In these circumstances, the notion that the United States should await events with a vigilant passivity commended itself to most of Washington officialdom. West European experts in the State Department who monitored the progress of the German inflation had worried since the early fall of 1921 that the financial situation there could spiral out of control.[25] Yet when Roland Boyden and James A. Logan, unofficial American delegates to the Reparation Commission, proposed to take the lead in suggesting a revision of the London Schedule of Payments on a "more conciliatory and businesslike basis," the State Department had mandated caution. The department limited itself obscurely to expressing "interest" in the plans of its Paris representatives. Approving an initiative was "a little too final," Assistant Secretary Fred Dearing had ruled.[26] Noting that "our Allied friends . . . regard the position of their American loans with more and more mirth," Logan in September suggested privately to his friend and former housemate, Under Secretary Henry P. Fletcher, that the United States offer to accept the relatively secure reparation B-bonds in war-debt payments both as a way to collect something and as a means to enhance American influence on a subsequent European economic settlement. "We would like to follow a policy of European isolation but as yet no formula has been developed the application of which would have the effect of protecting us from the workings of normal universal economic laws," Logan reminded his superiors at home. In making this argument, however, Logan demonstrated that he was out of touch politically. The activist view had no appeal to Congress. Similar urgings for linking war

24 Hoover to Harding, Dec. 15, 1921; Harding to Hoover, Dec. 16, 1921, box 70, Secretary of Commerce–Personal files, USHHPL.
25 William R. Castle (Chief of the Western European Division) memo., Sept. 2, 1921, USDS 462.00R29/932.
26 James A. Logan to Under Secretary Henry P. Fletcher, Aug. 29 and Sept. 2, 1921; Assistant Secretary Fred Dearing minute, Sept. 24, 1921, USDS 462.00R29/1026 and 1043.

debts with reparations got nowhere in Washington for the rest of the fall.[27]

It is noteworthy that the American observers at Reparation Commission headquarters in the Hotel Astoria had few illusions about German strategy and little sympathy for that country's plight. Roland Boyden, after visiting Berlin with the commission in November 1921, reported that Chancellor Joseph Wirth seemed lacking in firmness and frankness, afraid of his own cabinet, and unwilling to stand up to the industrialists.[28] State Department analysts similarly disliked the idea of letting Germany off "scot-free" for a number of years except for deliveries in kind. They suspected that Berlin had "put one over on [Sir John] Bradbury" – the chief British proponent of a complete moratorium plan. Still, they did not feel sure enough of their ground to take a firm position. In the end they evaded a substantive judgment and merely instructed American delegates in Paris to insist narrowly on the payment of accumulated U.S. army costs in any moratorium arrangement.[29]

Nor did the State Department position on reparations change markedly after the Cannes Conference fiasco at the beginning of the new year and the subsequent fall of French Premier Briand. In late January 1922, while preparations for Genoa went forward, the French once again sought to inveigle the United States into supporting the Reparation Commission rather than the Supreme Council as the key decision-making body regarding reparations. They also invited the United States to place an unofficial member on a subcommittee appointed to consider fluctuation of the German exchange. After a series of top-level meetings, the State Department characteristically declined to take a position. The French, minuted Assistant Secretary Leland Harrison, were "fishing." Secretary Hughes, who by temperament as well as judi-

---

27 Logan to "Prather" Fletcher, Sept. 9, 1921, USDS 462.00R29/1043; Fletcher to Logan, reporting Assistant Treasury Secretary Wadsworth's response, Sept. 21, 1921, USDS 462.00R29/1046; also Leland Harrison memo. for Dearing and Fletcher on Montagu Norman's proposal for linking reparations and debts and the Treasury refusal to respond, Nov. 28, 1921, USDS 462.00R29/1492.

28 Boyden to Hughes, Nov. 22, 1921, USDS 462.00R29/1307.

29 Castle memo. for Arthur N. Young, Dec. 3; and State to Boyden, Dec. 6, 1921, USDS 462.00R29/1285. The American official opposition to a complete moratorium should not be seen as an anti-German position. It is noteworthy that even some key German officials thought that, with a modest foreign advance for currency stabilization, the Reich could get by without a full moratorium and could indeed continue to pay 2.5 billion gold marks yearly (the precise figure for the standard annuity later recommended by the Dawes Committee). See Castle "Memorandum of Conversation with Mr. Carl Bergmann" [of the *Kriegslastenkommission*], Dec. 5, 1921, USDS 862.51/1453.

cial training liked to decide matters on the most circumscribed possible grounds and to avoid bold initiatives until the time was ripe for them, declared that he was "not ready to take up the reparations question." To ask the Senate to confirm appointment of an unofficial delegate to a committee on exchange would open a Pandora's box. "The process of confirmation might start a number of things."[30]

In short, the American government in early 1922 considered Lloyd George's grand scheme for European reconstruction premature at best. With the congressional majority darkly suspicious of European intentions, and the British and French giving ample reason to nurture such mistrust, the State Department refined temporization into a high art. The wonder is that the administration did not turn down the idea of participation in the Genoa Conference out of hand.

Within their own frame of reference, President Harding and his chief cabinet officers – Hoover, Mellon, and Hughes – thought of themselves as internationally minded. And given the disillusionment with all things European prevailing in the country at large, undoubtedly they were right in relative terms. Hoover, however, of the three dominant department heads, had the least sympathy for France and Great Britain, in part precisely because he had come to know those countries so well. During his wartime service overseas, Hoover had reacted strongly against the lack of idealism that he professed to find in French and British political culture. His loathing for European methods of haggling grew almost to obsessive proportions, and he declined to return to the old Continent thereafter for close to twenty years.[31]

Although charged with a heretofore minor portfolio, Hoover had a towering public reputation and did not feel called upon to observe the customary departmental boundaries.[32] His rivals in the struggle for bureaucratic turf joked maliciously that the so-called Great Humanitarian served as "secretary of commerce and under secretary of all other departments."[33] Yet owing to his boundless energy and the extraordinary competence of his staff, Hoover could frequently exercise his

---

30 A. N. Young, Dearing, Harrison memoranda, Jan. 30–Feb. 21, 1921, USDS 462.00R29/1450.
31 Arthur M. Schlesinger, Jr., *The Crisis of the Old Order, 1919–1933* (Boston, 1957), 80–1.
32 For a shrewd newsman's description of Hoover's bureaucratic ambitions at the beginning of the Harding administration, see John Callan O'Laughlin to Ellis Loring Dresel, Mar. 11, 1921, folder 305, Dresel Papers.
33 Schlesinger, *Crisis of the Old Order*, 84. The sally is widely attributed to Under Secretary of the Treasury S. Parker Gilbert.

sharp elbows without encountering open resistance. Harding, who recognized the limits of his own intellectual talents, stood in awe of all three cabinet luminaries. But Hoover in particular had his ear.

As official Washington straggled back from the 1922 New Year's holiday, Secretary Hoover sent Harding and Hughes a strategy memorandum regarding Genoa. His approach, he claimed (with characteristic anti-French bias), "would meet with a welcome in every country in Europe except one and even in that country . . . would be welcomed by the saner economists and business people." As Hoover saw it, the notion that the world needed stabilized exchange, currency reform, or lowered trade barriers on some global level represented a superficial analysis of the problem. The main challenge, he held, was to make an economic peace between France and Germany. "Currencies cannot be stabilized until inflation has stopped, and inflation cannot be stopped until government budgets are balanced, and [the] government budgets of Europe cannot be balanced until there is a proper settlement of reparations and until there is a reduction of expenditures including armament. Before these reforms can be carried into any other part of the Continent they must first be obtained in France and Germany, for chaos here is defeat everywhere."[34]

As he did so often, Hoover combined sound economic analysis with impractical political prescription. He proposed that the German and French governments both simply face the music. The Germans as a whole, he recognized, had profited enormously from inflation so far. They had avoided taxation, enjoyed subsidies on everything from food to freight rates, and unloaded depreciated paper marks on gullible foreign speculators. Yet the path followed heretofore led to "bankruptcy and social chaos" in the end. If the German government would resolutely "force the issue upon her citizens," stopping the inflation and the import of luxury goods, that country, he believed, could pay an up-front indemnity of $1 billion from assets secreted abroad and thereafter transfer some $300 to $400 million (about half the current schedule) in reparation annually. The French, in his view, had likewise gained enormously in economic productivity since the war even though government finances remained in "complete chaos." If France mustered the courage to increase taxes to the maximum and to "rigidly slaughter

---

34 Hoover to Harding, Jan. 4, 1922, and attached "Memorandum on the Major Questions before the Proposed Economic Conference in Europe," box 235, Secretary of Commerce–Official files, USHHPL; copy of memo. for Secretary Hughes in USDS 550.E1/3.

expenditure" – slashing the military budget by 80 percent and reconstruction subsidies by 90 percent – the budget could be instantly balanced. Indeed, a $150 million surplus would appear forthwith to make a start on paying off foreign liabilities. Moreover, if France disarmed to save resources, Hoover predicted that Poland, Czechoslovakia, Romania, Yugoslavia, Greece, Italy, and Belgium would follow suit, until "the Europe mind [sic] predicates its future in terms of peace and not in war." Even if the parties reached a satisfactory reparations settlement, he concluded, ending the European arms buildup became "the second question that must antecede the real constructive work of economic upbuilding."

Getting down to specifics, Hoover sketched out an interim deal that might justify additional sacrifice by the American taxpayer. The Allies would have to accept a five-year partial moratorium on reparations. They would have to scale down the Rhineland occupation armies to a token 25,000 men. On the other side, the Germans would eliminate subsidies, impose serious taxes, and stabilize the mark by dint of their own efforts. All Europe would cut land armaments by one-half. The main Central Banks, with some assistance from the New York Fed, would help reorganize the currencies of east central Europe and set the Habsburg successor states on their feet. Together, these measures would save the Continent from social unrest, curb artificial dumping by nations with depreciated currencies, and improve foreign markets for U.S. goods. As a counterpart, the administration might then feel warranted in providing a five-year moratorium on war debts to all countries except Great Britain.

The Hoover program thus called for substantial moral regeneration from the embattled Europeans and offered in return a quite modest reward. As a practical matter, the commerce secretary did not really expect the nations preparing for Genoa to embrace his brand of religion. In private, Hoover expressed a degree of outrage that did not show through the modulated cadences of his official memoranda. During the war, he grumbled, ignorant U.S. Treasury officials, mostly lawyers without "a day's experience in business," had handed out money "like drunken sailors." They had enabled overseas governments to "extend their investments at the American taxpayer's expense." Could any self-respecting European state now dare to ask for external-debt remission? Surely not, for the commercial fabric of the world could not stand "the shock of refusal to pay obligations honestly entered upon."

The Europeans, moreover, would have to recognize that "the whole mass of armaments must come down in steps or they will come down in a second world crash." The American people held no responsibility for the "degeneration" that had brought about unbalanced budgets, currency inflation, and demoralization of exchange on the other side of the ocean. To the contrary, they had asked for nothing and given everything. They had "poured out literally billions" to stem the tide of famine after the war. They had already contributed "generously, even royally," to the recovery of European agriculture and industry. In short, if the European governments failed to submit to the "surgical operations" he proposed, no one could fairly describe this as a failure of American statesmanship.[35]

No other cabinet officer put up a formal paper for Genoa challenging the Hoover approach. But this did not mean that State or Treasury was prepared to accept a lead from the upstart Commerce Department. It was no accident that Commerce still occupied a broken-down building at 19th Street and Pennsylvania Avenue, symbolically as well as spatially removed from the locus of executive power around the White House. Moreover, the frequent differences in outlook between State and Treasury on the one hand and Commerce on the other involved a personal as well as a policy dimension. The main officials at the State and Treasury Departments, mostly scions of the East Coast upper class who had known each other since preparatory school, came from a wholly different social milieu than did the second-generation Jews and Middle-American scholarship boys whom Hoover recruited through his academic contacts in the fields of statistical economics and engineering to head the bureaus and divisions of the Commerce Department.[36]

The conflict started, but did not end, at the top. Secretary of the Treasury Mellon had little use for Hoover and no confidence in his judgment. Hoover's tendency to elaborate a precise written solution for every problem, replete with figures and statistics, annoyed him so much that he ultimately stopped reading his colleague's reports. Engineers like Hoover, he thought, got so caught up in scientific formulae that

---

35 Hoover to Joseph H. Defrees of the U.S. Chamber of Commerce, Jan. 11, 1922, box 21, Secretary of Commerce–Personal files; also Hoover to Russell C. Leffingwell, Nov. 17, 1921, box 51, Secretary of Commerce–Personal files, USHHPL.
36 On Hoover's recruitment of his staff, see particularly his correspondence with Professors Edwin F. Gay of Harvard, E. R. A. Seligman of Columbia, and A. A. Young of Cornell in boxes 25 and 336, Secretary of Commerce–Official files, USHHPL.

they neglected the human element so important in business affairs. "In all my business enterprises," Mellon philosophized in the middle 1920s, "I never once put an engineer in charge."[37] While Mellon bristled at Hoover's style, Under Secretary S. Parker Gilbert disliked his substantive views. On the World War Foreign Debt Commission, Gilbert found Hoover so "extreme" and "disagreeable," so rooted in "his own personal prejudices and his own preconceived ideas," that he later apprehended "real danger to our foreign policy" should the commerce secretary succeed to the presidency.[38]

Over at the State Department, Secretary Hughes maintained relations of wary mutual respect with Hoover, but the impersonal civility that Hughes employed to shield himself from unpleasant encounters did not set a model for his staff.[39] Throughout the winter and spring of 1922, functionaries on both sides feuded over the responsibility and the credit for configuring a commercial treaty with Germany. William R. Castle, chief of Western European affairs, complained to Ambassador Houghton in Berlin: "The secretary of commerce himself is not averse to advertising and the various Jews who run the different divisions of his department love it."[40] The problem, as Castle and like-minded diplomatists saw it, was not simply that Hoover appeared "insanely ambitious for personal power" and that his Jewish retainers took "every opportunity to put across people of their own race." Castle also suspected that his Commerce interlocutors, owing to relations with their German coreligionists, might wish to see the Reich let down easily from its reparation obligations. Castle dilated frequently to his foreign-service cronies on the subject. A few years later, he went so far as to circulate approvingly a business contact's observation that senior Commerce officials failed to defend American interests consistently and instead worked "hand in glove with the whole Jew outfit in Frankfurt." It would indeed be interesting, Castle suggested, to know how

37 Confidential Mellon remarks to Garrard B. Winston, his under secretary from 1923 to 1926, cited in Burton J. Hendrick notes of an interview with Garrard B. Winston, Apr. 7, 1942, Hendrick Papers.
38 See Gilbert to Mellon, May 7, 1928, along with Mellon's appreciative reply, May 24, 1928, copies in box 6, David E. Finley Papers.
39 On the Hoover–Hughes relationship, see boxes 280–1, Secretary of Commerce–Official files; and box 47, Secretary of Commerce–Personal files, USHHPL. Despite the lack of personal warmth and the many frosty letters that the two men exchanged over the years, Hoover continued to respect Hughes and offered to reappoint him secretary of state in 1929 (Hoover to Hughes, Nov. 9, 1928; Allan Hoover to Dr. Franz G. Lassner of the Hoover Library, May 23, 1966, General Accession 71, Hoover Presidential Papers, USHHPL).
40 Castle to Ellis Loring Dresel, Mar. 6, 1922; Castle to Alanson B. Houghton, July 13 and Aug. 21, 1922, box 4, William R. Castle Papers.

much "some of the Commerce people like Klein, Chalmers, and Domeratzky have to do with the great Jewish banking institutions."[41]

Though generally not as articulate as their Commerce confrères and apt to leave less of a paper trail, the second-tier officials at State and Treasury who performed the real labor on European affairs not only worked harmoniously together, but frequently lived together. A surprisingly large number held membership in "The Family," a bachelor house at 1718 H Street, a stone's throw from the White House. A mere forty-five individuals became members of The Family from its founding in 1907 through its dissolution in 1954, and of these only twenty-four had won acceptance by the mid-1920s. But this select group included, at the time of the Genoa Conference, Under Secretary of State "Prather" Fletcher, Assistant Secretary of State "Nemo" Harrison, Assistant Secretary of the Treasury "Waddy" Wadsworth, Governor "Ben" Strong of the New York Fed, James A. ("Logie") Logan of the unofficial delegation to the Reparation Commission, the vice-president of the U.S. Chamber of Commerce, the American representative on the International Chamber of Commerce, the counselors of embassies in London and Berlin, and the ministers to the Netherlands and Switzerland.[42] This close-knit circle of friends corresponded assiduously about the problems of European reconstruction.

Nor did these informal connections stop at the working level. President Harding dropped in for dinner at The Family, and Secretary Hughes held off-the-record meetings with foreign diplomats there. In 1921–2, both Assistant Secretary Harrison and Assistant Secretary Wadsworth lived at The Family full-time. In the spring of 1921, Harrison had arranged to have himself appointed "liaison with the Treasury Department" in connection with war debts, indemnities, restitu-

---

41 Castle to Ambassador Alanson B. Houghton, Jan. 7 and May 12, 1926, box 2; Castle to Ambassador Myron T. Herrick, June 8, 1926, box 3, Castle Papers; also Col. T. Bentley Mott to Myron T. Herrick, Sept. 2, 1922, folder 2, container 2, Myron T. Herrick Papers. (Julius Klein, Louis Domeratzky, and Henry Chalmers, the three chief objects of Castle's ire, served, respectively, as director and assistant director of the Bureau of Foreign and Domestic Commerce and as chief of the Foreign Tariffs Division. The Hoover Commerce Department files do not indicate that any of these men maintained independent contacts with the New York Jewish banking community, although Hoover's closest friend on Wall Street was indeed Lewis Strauss of Kuhn Loeb & Co. [Strauss and Paul Warburg correspondence in boxes 82 and 311, Secretary of Commerce–Personal files, USHHPL]).

42 See George V. Allen, "Notes on the Family," in Richard Fyfe Boyce, *Diplomatic and Consular Officers, Retired, Inc.: A History*, typescript in the Harvard College Library (n.p., 1969), 98–112; also "The Family" file, box 5, Leland Harrison Papers. Membership in The Family included four of the five under secretaries of state who held office in the 1920s, fifteen additional diplomats who over the years held the rank of minister, ambassador, and assistant or under secretary, three assistant secretaries of the treasury, and eight army generals. Not a single official of the Commerce Department joined. Nor did a single Jew.

tions, and reparations. When Wadsworth asked to see all the cables from the Reparation Commission relating to foreign loans, the higher-ups at State agreed that "anything we think Treasury may wish to have will be sent – this without any *arrière pensée.*" In practice, "Waddy" and "Nemo" would discuss all pertinent matters at breakfast or in a lunch-time turn about Lafayette Park and then send parallel memoranda up to their superiors.[43] By contrast, when Hoover asked to see reparations cables, Hughes dispatched a testy reply, addressed to "Dear Mr. Secretary." He would send over paraphrases of "those portions of messages regarding reparations which will serve you in working out commercial policies." But the State Department reserved the right to determine what information appeared pertinent to the work of the Commerce Department, and it would have to withhold confidential material bearing on foreign relations.[44]

Very likely, President Harding paid little attention to the squabbling over nuances and the jockeying for position among his foreign policy advisers. As the Teapot Dome scandal would later reveal, the genial and indolent chief executive remained pleasantly oblivious to far worse skulduggery in the nether depths of his administration. Apprehending the world as he did from the standpoint of Marion, Ohio, Harding rarely thought it necessary to concentrate his energies on the fine points of foreign economic policy. Harding's preoccupation in the foreign field lay in pursuing disarmament as a pathway to peace, economic stability, and popular esteem. On this subject the president saw eye to eye with Hoover. Since the beginning of his term in office, Harding had periodically expressed interest in Hoover's pet scheme for banning loans to foreign countries undertaking to increase their armaments. (Although the governor of the New York Fed warned against interfering with market forces and underscored the administrative impracticality of the idea, Hoover, with Harding's blessing, continued to pursue it with quasi-theological zeal.)[45] Hoover's approach to the Genoa Con-

---

43 Harrison memo., Apr. 18, 1921; Wadsworth to Harrison, Aug. 31, 1921; Harrison to Wadsworth, Sept. 2, 1921, boxes 11 (Treasury file) and 12 (Wadsworth file), Harrison Papers.

44 Hoover to Hughes, Dec. 6 and Dec. 15, 1921; Hughes to Hoover, Dec. 13 and Dec. 16, 1921, box 47, Secretary of Commerce–Personal files, USHHPL.

45 For the exchanges between Harding and Hoover on disarmament generally and the idea of using foreign loans as a lever in particular, see Hoover to Harding, May 11, 1921; Harding to Hoover, May 14, 1921; Hoover to Harding, Dec. 31, 1921; Harding to Hughes, Jan. 12, 1922, all in box 235, Secretary of Commerce–Official file, USHHPL. For the debate between Hoover and Governor Strong about the practicality of the idea, with Hughes as usual playing the referee, see Strong memo. on foreign loans, Apr. 14, 1922; Strong to Hughes, Apr. 20 and June 9, 1922; Hoover to Hughes, Apr. 19, 1922; Hughes to Strong, June 29, 1922; copies in box 375, Secretary of Commerce–Official file, USHHPL, and in Strong Papers, 0111.1(1).

ference thus coincided perfectly with Harding's visceral convictions about world affairs. Without getting into the details, Harding cheerfully endorsed the main lines of the Hoover analysis. The president intimated to the *New York Times* on January 6, 1922, that national prosperity must come from within. The European nations themselves should therefore take the initiative in solving European problems. The United States would neither call an economic conference nor permit Allied debts to the United States to be discussed at one. Whether or not this country participated would depend on whether the Europeans promised to get to "the root of the problem" – namely the burden of land armaments.[46]

These cautious comments led to the usual public divisions. The Wilsonian *New York World* urged the government to forget its narrow "obsession" with war debts and to send Hoover to Genoa with a broad mandate to "put the influence of the United States back of a general European settlement."[47] The *New York Commercial* similarly argued that both agricultural and industrial profits often depended on the 10 percent margin provided by the export trade, and that the country had little to lose in making another effort to hasten European recovery.[48] The *Washington Post*, by contrast, contended that the tendency of European policy was "obnoxious to the United States." The former Allies were developing "a well-defined plan to place the burden of Europe's losses upon the backs of the United States and Russia." They sought to get the United States to cancel war loans, to underwrite Germany's debts, and to acquiesce in the exploitation of Russia. These ill-disguised schemes should "make the United States more than ever determined to beware of entanglements."[49] The *Post* editorial probably represented average opinion in the country at large better than did the New York press. Enlarging on familiar nationalist themes, two prominent Republican senators, Henry Cabot Lodge and Frank Brandegee, called at the White House on January 8 to rehearse the familiar arguments for the United States staying away from Genoa.[50] U.S. diplomats abroad also reinforced the message. Ambassador Richard Child's cable from Rome on January 13 was typical: "Prudence alone would appear clearly against any participation not absolutely dictated by moral duty. It is well recognized that vast banking interests, anxious for more transactions and middleman profit, will use all influence to involve us. . . . The

46 *New York Times,* Jan. 6, 1922.	47 *New York World,* Jan. 12, 1922.
48 *New York Commercial,* Jan. 12, 1922.	49 *Washington Post,* Jan. 6, 1922.
50 See *Congressional Record,* Jan. 24, 1922, 1833–4.

United States holds all the chips, [the] European group of nations all the cards. Participation by us will probably mean [the] common interest of all participants in one group while the United States stands alone."[51]

Despite the cool tenor of public opinion and the skeptical assessments of its diplomats abroad, the administration decided to await the elaboration of the Genoa agenda before committing itself one way or the other. By the last week in January, the Commerce and State Departments had put aside their quarrels for the moment. Opinion at both departments turned sharply negative toward Genoa. Hoover, after reconsidering his memorandum of January 4, urged the president not to send a delegation. While he did not think that America should turn its back on an "honest-to-God economic conference," he foresaw nothing of the sort taking place at Genoa. The meeting there promised to be "purely political and merely a move and manoeuvre in the great game." The danger nonetheless loomed that the conference might embarrass the United States by "seeming to promise a solution of economic ills." Hoover hoped that the conference could be postponed six months. In that case it would not be necessary for Washington to decline formally. Six months hence, the French people might become disillusioned about the possibility of collecting reparations, and the American people might undergo a similar process of disillusionment. Then one could "look forward to better sailing."[52] William R. Castle, head of the Western European Division at State, came around to a roughly similar view. The British and French positions stood so far apart, Castle informed the secretary on January 25, that holding the conference had become inopportune. Moreover, an economic conference that excluded from its purview reparations, domestic financial policies, and foreign loans would have "very little to discuss." With most of the essential subjects ruled off the agenda, the principal topic left, as Castle wryly noted, would be "the discussion of Russia, with Mr. Lenine as the principal performer."[53]

At the working level of the Treasury and Commerce Departments, a few unregenerate internationalists fought a rearguard action against the emerging consensus. Yet even some of these professional Euro-

---

51 Child to State, Jan. 13, 1922, USDS 550.E1/6; also Child to State, Jan. 30, 1922, USDS 550.E1/23; similar warnings in Lewis Einstein (Prague) to State, Jan. 18, 1922, USDS 550.E1/11; Harvey (London) to State, Feb. 6, 1922, USDS 550.E1/31.

52 Hoover to Harding, Jan. 23, 1922, box 21, Secretary of Commerce–Personal files, HHPL; also Assistant Secretary Dearing, memo. of conversation with Mr. Hoover, Jan. 23, 1922, USDS 550.E1/75.

53 Castle memo. for Hughes, Jan. 25, 1922, USDS 550.E1/72.

peanists lost interest as concrete plans for the conference took shape. At the Commerce Department, the food expert and statistician E. Dana Durand, chief of the East European Division, argued at first that Genoa might at least smoke out the intentions of the Bolshevik leadership and preserve the Open Door for American trade and investment in case the revolutionary régime in Russia adopted a "more or less normal economic policy." Only gradually, from February through early April, did the reports arriving from the U.S. trade commissioner in London serve to change Durand's mind.[54] Durand had gotten to know Edward F. Wise, the chief British technical planner for Genoa, on the Interallied Food Council during the war. Durand reminded Hoover that they had both come to despise Wise as "an idealist not much inclined to take account of hard realities" and as a close-minded socialist with an "excessive faith in what governments could do." Wise had particularly offended them by pushing a scheme that would have enabled European countries to fix the prices for American farm products.[55] Eventually, Durand concluded that Wise's latest hot-air balloon would not get off the ground. Hence America need not fear a missed opportunity. While the British and the Germans engaged in flatulent talk about helping Russia to recover, the Europeans all blithely assumed that the United States would "foot the bills." And this was not in the cards. In fact, Durand felt confident, anything less than a comprehensive scheme for rehabilitating the Soviet Union would fail. The unavailability of raw materials, the inadequacy of transport, the absence of markets, and the quasi-religious fanaticism of the Bolshevik leadership all posed insurmountable obstacles.[56]

Even into February, Treasury Under Secretary S. Parker Gilbert, a holdover from the Wilson administration, argued that final passage of the debt funding law and the palpable success of the Naval Disarmament Conference made it feasible for the United States to take part in Genoa after all. Gilbert recommended postponing the conference somewhat to see what could be done on the reparations front. And the agenda had to be narrowed to exclude inter-Allied debt. If these things were accomplished, Gilbert maintained, the United States might be

54 Durand memo. for Julius Klein, Bureau of Foreign and Domestic Commerce, Feb. 2, 1922, box 91; Durand memo. for Hoover, Feb. 16 and Feb. 28, box 91; Durand memo. for Hoover, Apr. 15, 1922, box 259, Secretary of Commerce–Official files, USHHPL.
55 Durand memo. for Hoover, May 11, 1922, box 141; Durand memo. for Hoover, Feb. 16 and Feb. 28, 1922, box 91, Secretary of Commerce–Official files, USHHPL.
56 Durand memo., "General Economic Situation in Russia," Apr. 15, 1922, box 259, Secretary of Commerce–Official files, USHHPL.

able to accomplish a good deal toward international financial and economic recovery without endangering its own position. With the establishment of the World War Foreign Debt Commission, Gilbert thought it safe for the United States to "announce a broad-minded funding policy, leaving actual negotiations with the governments concerned to follow later in Washington." Gilbert, however, came to represent a distinctly minority view, and, although Secretary Mellon thought of him like a son, he had no independent political clout.[57]

Even Governor Strong of the Federal Reserve Bank of New York, who monitored the progress of a scheme for a new gold-exchange standard to be launched at Genoa, did not dare to argue for American participation. Strong had won a reputation as the internationalist outrider in the foreign-policy establishment; for that very reason, he had to remain circumspect. Strong had good reason to suspect that Hoover considered him a "mental annex to Europe."[58] And he received all too frequent reminders that his critics in Congress perceived the Federal Reserve System as "the arch enemy of the agricultural class." Faced with determined hostility from an ignorant Congress, he explained to Montagu Norman of the Bank of England, the Fed had to avoid independent action that would "embarrass this administration, which includes our best friends."[59] Norman, in any case, advised Strong that Genoa figured as a mistimed, "largely political" project that could not yield more than marginal benefits from a Central Banking point of view. He considered the notion of stabilizing exchange impracticable before the leading nations had adjusted debts and reparations and reestablished free gold markets. "And is it not true," he asked rhetorically, "that when these things shall have happened stability in the Exchanges will be looking after itself in the old-fashioned way and artificial stability will hardly be necessary?"[60] Strong seconded the notion. The wisest course, he informed Norman, was to postpone broad discussion of economic matters until after the midterm Congressional elections in November 1922. If by that time the principal Allies had granted a reparations moratorium to Germany and begun negotiations with the World War Foreign Debt Commission, and if in addition Britain had restored sterling to parity with the dollar on a gold basis, constructive

57 Gilbert memo. for the secretary, Feb. 3, 1922, box 95 (Genoa Conference file), 63A 659, Office of the Assistant Secretary for Fiscal Affairs, USTD.
58 Hoover, *The Memoirs of Herbert Hoover*, 3:9.
59 Strong to Norman, Feb. 18, 1922, Strong Papers, 1116.3.
60 Norman to Strong, Feb. 23 and 27, Mar. 8 and 22, 1922, ibid.

discussion on a range of institutional problems could follow. His Washington friends, Strong reported after visiting The Family in early March, looked upon Genoa "as the qualifying round for a real match to be played later."[61]

Secretary Hughes, after surveying the views of his cabinet colleagues and State Department subordinates, characteristically outdid all of them in caution. Upon reflection, Hughes decided not even to approach the British about postponing the conference, since that might commit the United States ultimately to attending if its stated desiderata were met. Instead, he would say as little as possible. On March 8, Hughes announced America's refusal to participate formally on the simple ground that Genoa would be a conference of a "political character" from which questions had been excluded without satisfactory determination of what constituted the "chief causes of economic disturbance."[62] In order to keep informed, Washington instructed Ambassador Child to sit in as an observer, and also directed James A. Logan of the U.S. unofficial delegation to the Reparation Commission to vacation in the area during the proceedings for his health.

Policymakers in Washington had little reason to regret not sending an official delegation to Genoa. From the Rome embassy, Child sent a steady stream of messages telling the State Department how right their decision had been. He suggested that European statesmen planning for Genoa sought mostly to shore up their domestic political fortunes by appealing to "internal avarice or fears." The United States, he advised, should bide its time. It should quietly await the development of a bloc of European opinion prepared to stand against "imperialistic intrigue and purely political programs and in favor of liberal economic cooperation." In the meantime, it should refuse to "rush in as a volunteer adjuster or to be dragged in as an easily hoodwinked creditor who innocently goes afield to meetings of his debtors."[63] From Genoa itself, Child reported with a hint of *Schadenfreude* that the conference droned on "in great confusion" and that nothing constructive would emerge from it. The imprecise plans for European reconstruction, he claimed, had turned out to be largely "a device of the British Department of Overseas Trade" for getting other nations to chip in for credits that

61 Strong to Norman, Feb. 2, 18, and 21, Mar. 4, 1922, ibid.
62 Hughes to Italian ambassador in Washington, Mar. 8, 1922, *FRUS* 1922, 1:384–96.
63 Child to State, Mar. 16, 1922, USDS 550.E1/108.

would enable countries with depreciated currencies to purchase British supplies and machinery.[64]

Logan, reporting on his "health" vacation on the North Italian coast, agreed that the U.S. government had proved "extremely wise and far-sighted" in refusing to participate. Logan did not endorse the common American impression that Genoa was a "cess-pool of political intrigues" and "Machiavellian machinations." But he considered its accomplishments in the fields of finance and economics to be "highly academic in character." He was not particularly worried by the Rapallo Treaty between Germany and Russia; he accepted the evaluation of Carl Bergmann, his highly regarded interlocutor on the *Kriegslasten-kommission,* who blamed it all on Rathenau – "a man with exaggerated ego and exalted conceit." But clearly the treaty had poisoned the atmosphere at Genoa. Constructive action on reparations would have to proceed under the auspices of the Reparation Commission in Paris.[65] The one innovative proposal endorsed by Child – for an international credit organization that might promote investment by facilitating the recycling of idle capital and gold surpluses – won no favor in Washington. Foreign Trade Adviser Arthur N. Young minuted that the idea recalled the now-discredited ter Meulen plan launched at the 1920 Brussels Financial Conference. The problem, held Young, was not lack of credit, but the fact that such a "distressingly large portion" of previous credits had been devoted to nonproductive uses, including most notably luxury imports, deficit finance, and military expenditure. It had become evident that "no plan of international credits is a fundamental remedy for the ills of Europe." The nations there had to take constructive action to help themselves.[66] The Western European Division did not wait for the conference to end before writing its obituary. The Genoa recom-

---

64 Child to State, Apr. 29, 1922, USDS 550.E1/226.
65 Logan to State, Apr. 28, 1922, USDS 550.E1/293. Rathenau was widely despised for appearing to be what he was not, and his behavior at Genoa came as no surprise to initiates. Emile Francqui of the Société Générale had sent to Belgian Ambassador de Cartier in Washington the following characterization some months earlier: "Rathenau, we must keep reminding ourselves, is one of the best-tempered of German swords. He has the talents of his race, the gift of flattery, the knowledge of how to allay distrust. He has used these gifts in the past and will use them again in the future, but when he thinks he has succeeded in his purposes, he will raise his head again to dominate those whom he will have conquered." De Cartier thought the description so fine that he circulated it to his American friends. See Francqui to Emile de Cartier de Marchienne, Feb. 11, 1922, in de Cartier to Lamont, Mar. 12, 1922, box 84/3, Thomas W. Lamont Papers.
66 Child to State, May 1, 1922; Foreign Trade Adviser Arthur N. Young memo., "Outline of International Credit Plan proposed by Ambassador Child," May 1922, USDS 550.E1/228; similar position taken by Economic Adviser Arthur C. Millspaugh, USDS 550.E1/307.

mendations for currency stabilization, balanced budgets, central-bank cooperation, and a new gold-exchange standard were "not likely to cure Europe until the major illnesses, reparations and armaments, have been attended."[67]

Washington showed little further interest in Genoa or its successor conference at The Hague. Before the delegates had scattered, attention quickly shifted back to the pivotal issues of reparations and war debts. The State Department put pressure on J. P. Morgan to join the Bankers' Committee sitting in Paris to pass on conditions for a German loan.[68] His mandate, as Morgan partner Dwight Morrow expressed it so well, was to find a way "to make France recede from an indefensible position with regard to reparations which will be compatible with the dignity of a great nation which contributed so much to the winning of the war and which bore so much of the suffering of the war."[69] For the moment, the task proved impossible. Premier Raymond Poincaré, Briand's successor, refused to accept the finding of the Bankers' Committee that Germany would have to be accorded a reparations moratorium before it received a stabilization loan. J. P. Morgan, the leading interpreter of U.S. investment markets, had no intention of twisting arms in Paris. Morgan found Poincaré a prickly customer. Yet as regards substance he confessed privately that he did not know which way to advise the French. If they preferred security to reparations, they were "entirely within their rights." All the same, they could not "talk one way and act another." And they certainly could not expect American investors to lend money to Germany until they had made up their minds.[70] The dilemma would take time to resolve. Events moved steadily toward the application of sanctions under the Versailles Treaty and a test of wills between Germany and France.

The U.S. Treasury, meanwhile, offered a variety of blandishments to the British to begin negotiations for funding their war debt. Assistant Secretary Wadsworth made no bones about his wish to secure Britain's "courageous meeting of the situation . . . as a precedent for the other

---

67 Western European Division, "The Reconstruction of Europe," Apr. 18, 1922, USDS 550.E1/ 370.
68 From Paris, Boyden had suggested that Governor Benjamin Strong of the Federal Reserve Bank of New York be asked to serve. Mellon vetoed the idea of sending someone who might be perceived as a government representative. Through the State Department, he directed Boyden to propose J. P. Morgan as his "personal suggestion" instead (Boyden to State, Apr. 5, 1922; Hughes to Boyden, Apr. 8, 1922, USDS 462.00R29/1608).
69 Dwight Morrow to Thomas W. Lamont, May 1, 1922, Lamont Papers, 113/14.
70 J. P. Morgan to Herman Harjes (his Paris partner), Nov. 23, 1922, box 176, J. P. Morgan Papers.

governments."[71] The British, however, still attempted for some months to wriggle off the hook. Chancellor of the Exchequer Sir Robert Horne admitted in the privacy of the cabinet that Britain could now make remittance without any exchange difficulty. "The problem is not how to find the dollars, but simply how to persuade our own people to pay the taxation involved in the transfer of the dollars to the Exchequer's control." As a purely economic proposition, Horne argued, Britain would actually draw advantage from funding its debt. To do so would help bring America into Europe, promote economic growth on the Continent, and thereby help solve the lingering problem of British unemployment and trade depression. "We have more to gain by the restoration of Europe than we have to lose by paying our real debt to the United States government, even if (which I do not believe) there is any real chance of our being let off in whole or in part."[72]

Horne's analysis coincided excactly with expert opinion at the Bank of England and with the convictions of the broadest-gauged thinkers in the City.[73] Lloyd George, however, refused to accept this reasoning. Not only did the wily Welshman dislike America intensely, but he focused his concern on the political balance in the House of Commons far more than on the balance of payments. At Westminster and in significant parts of the higher civil service as well, many considered the American demand for funding, as the permanent under secretary of the Foreign Office put it, "incredibly mean and contemptible."[74] Lloyd George thus drew on a deep well of sentiment as he initiated the tortuous cabinet discussions that led to promulgation of the Balfour Note. Ostensibly, that note committed Whitehall to seek no more in German reparations and payments from its Allied debtors combined than proved necessary to fund the British debt to America. The subtext, however, gave out a different signal. In practice, the note figured as a crude attempt to embarrass the United States into unilateral cancellation – as

---

71 Lamont to Sir Basil Blackett, reporting conversation with Wadsworth, June 8, 1922, Lamont Papers, 80/15.
72 Chancellor of the Exchequer memo. [actually drafted by Blackett], "British Debt to the United States," June 8, 1922, C.P. 4020, GB CAB 24/137.
73 Montagu Norman to Benjamin Strong, Feb. 25, June 13 and 19, July 26, and Aug. 17, 1922, Strong Papers, 1116.3.
74 Sir Eyre A. Crowe minute, May 18, 1922, GB FO 371/8191: N4766/646/38. Crowe and other policymakers perceived at least an implicit link between the capacity of Britain to lead in Russia's rehabilitation and its success in deflecting America's funding demands. Indeed, Crowe's outburst came in reaction to a May 13 editorial in the *Chicago Tribune*, which noted sourly that, if the Europeans made loans to Russia as a consequence of Genoa and The Hague, they would be "lending our money."

the prime minister's own private secretary put it, "shamming bankrupt in order to put [America] in the dock, demeaning ourselves in order to blacken her and defraud her of her debt."[75] The stratagem merely led to an exchange of verbal salvos across the Atlantic and to hardened attitudes on the American side. Herbert Hoover wrote bitterly to a friend: "Europe has no realization of the necessity to meet certain primary questions on her own responsibility, and before this realization comes . . . they will probably need to go deeper into the ditch than they are now. . . . The propaganda systematically put across by our British friends . . . contributes nothing to the situation except extreme irritation to the American people."[76]

Hoover himself returned the irritation in kind with slashing declarations against the British in a notable speech early in the fall. And Mellon too, according to the standards of the Morgan partners, appeared "rather hard-boiled."[77] As Thomas Lamont wrote to the head of the firm, Mellon "apparently thinks that in some mysterious way all the indebtedness will finally be paid. He is the watchdog of the Treasury, and naturally considers it his duty to see that the Treasury gets every penny out of its debtors. . . . He seems to think, too, that if we keep alive all these notes owing to us from dinky little countries all over Europe, the fact that we are holding the notes will give us a sort of stranglehold politically on some of those countries and enable us to tell them what they shall or shall not do. Herbert Hoover has that same benevolent idea."[78]

Gradually, moderates in both Washington and London moved toward an accommodation. Secretary of State Hughes later revealed that he had planned to propose an initiative on reparations just prior to the Balfour Note, but that the note had spoiled the atmosphere and compelled him to rest on his oars.[79] In the fall of 1922, Hughes was again moving slowly toward a new proposal for an Expert Committee

75 Sir Edward Grigg to Lloyd George, "Our Debt to the U.S.A. and the European Position," July 6, 1922, box 19, 1st Baron Altrincham Papers (in private hands), London.
76 Hoover to Frederic R. Coudert, Aug. 28, 1922, copy in Lamont Papers, 141/20.
77 Lamont to E. C. Grenfell, Oct. 19, 1922, ibid., 111/14.
78 Lamont to J. P. Morgan, Oct. 6, 1922, ibid., 108/13.
79 Ibid. Roland Boyden, U.S. unofficial delegate on the Reparation Commission, excitedly reported to his contacts at Morgans in August 1922 that Hughes had "in general" endorsed his scheme to reconvene the Bankers' Committee with a broad mandate to give "independent advice on Germany's capacity to pay" and to propose methods for that country's financial rehabilitation. But the secretary had no choice but to hold the matter in abeyance when an "antagonistic" public attitude developed as a result of the Balfour Note (George Whitney to J. P. Morgan, Aug. 21, 1922, box 176, J. P. Morgan Papers).

to look into reparations. Given the expressed will of Congress, Hughes felt, a reparations revision had to precede and not follow any review of debts to the United States. Until congressional sentiment changed, Hughes argued in his usual cautious way, the Debt Commission's hands remained essentially tied. It was imperative, therefore, for the British to "come across" in order to dispel antagonism toward London and to foster more flexibility in public opinion on the general question of inter-Allied indebtedness.[80] Eventually, London got the message. In January 1923, a British Debt Funding Mission headed by the practical-minded Stanley Baldwin arrived and rapidly reached a compromise with the Americans. But by then the Germans had openly revolted against the Versailles Treaty. The French had occupied the Ruhr. The notion of a worldwide conference to discuss European reconstruction would have to await the outcome of the Franco–German test of strength.

In retrospect, American policymakers had no reason to rue their decision not to participate in the Genoa Conference. Events had ratified the administration view that Europe's basic problems were political rather than economic. Experience had shown that the essential reparations and war-debts settlements had to precede technical agreements looking to global economic recovery. The cost of delay was admittedly high, but probably unavoidable. Whatever Lloyd George might profess to believe, opening the Russian market could not under the best of circumstances solve the fundamental problems of Western Europe. And the stakes in the conflict between France and Germany made it impossible for either country to yield on reparations without a protracted struggle.

As the Genoa Conference wound down, Secretary Hughes assessed its outcome as "positively harmful." Beforehand, he insisted, communism had given signs of "dying of inanition." By exaggerating the immediate importance of trade with a stripped and starving Russia, however, the Western powers at Genoa had played "straight into the hands of the Bolshevik oligarchy" and given it a new lease on life.[81] Ambassador Child, Washington's man on the spot, did not take anything about the conference so seriously. Child found most of the leaders of Europe, whom he had observed at close range, to be "stupid, . . . selfish and . . . lacking in directness and brevity and sincerity." He felt the

---

80 Lamont to J. P. Morgan, Oct. 6, 1922, Lamont Papers, 108/13.
81 Geddes no. 1 to British Delegation, Genoa, May 17, 1922, GB FO 371/8192: N5353/646/38.

usual shock of the American innocent at the "intrigues, undisclosed purposes, suspicions, hatred and complete self-seeking" that character- ized European diplomacy. He tossed the "mimeographed nothings" of the expert subcommittees into the corner unread. In fact, from his arri- val through "terrible railway tunnels filled with smothering gases," through the constant rainstorms that accentuated the dreary physical appearance of the host city, to the "lying tongues acclaiming the con- ference a great success" at the end, Child found the whole experience an aesthetic trial and a diplomatic bore.[82] In any event, a conference designed primarily to meet the exigencies of British domestic politics, and that failed to consider American political requirements at all, stood no chance of clearing away the obstacles to world economic revival.

82 Child, *A Diplomat Looks at Europe,* 26, 32, 35, 40–1, 52–3.

Oil Fields near Baku, 1920s

English Unemployed Queuing outside a Labor Exchange, 1924

"Genoa: Europe Lay Waste and Deserted—But the Conferences Were still in Session," *Simplicissimus,* April 12, 1922

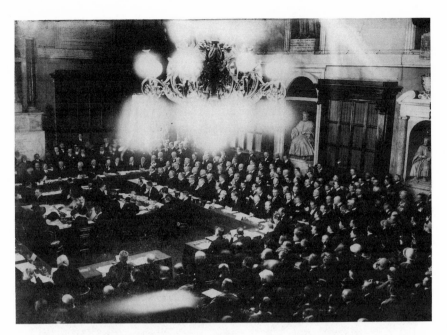

Opening Session of the Genoa Conference

"Opening Session of the International Conference at Genoa: Silence on Disarmament! Don't Speak about the Treaty of Versailles! Be Cautious of the Debt Question! Beware of the Middle East Question! Don't Speak about the Soviets!" *Le Rire,* April 15, 1922

David Lloyd George *(left)* and Louis Barthou *(right)* at Genoa

David Lloyd George *(center left)* and Carlo Schanzer *(center right)* at Genoa

Georgi V. Chicherin *(center)* and Members of the Russian Delegation at Genoa

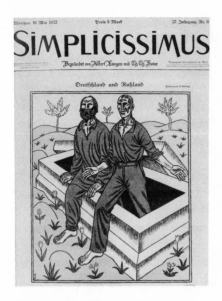

"Germany and Russia: A Beginning," *Simplicissimus,* May 10, 1922

"What Is Wrong with This Picture?" *Punch,* May 24, 1922

"Uncle Sam: 'Well, It's Good To Be Missed Anyhow,'" Cartoon by Clifford Kennedy Berryman

Die Deutsche Regierung , vertreten durch

[signature]

und

die Regierung der Russischen Sozialistischen Föderati
ven Sowjet-Republik, vertreten durch

[signature]

sind über nachstehende Bestimmungen übereingekommen.

Artikel 1.

Die beiden Regierungen sind darüber einig, dass
die Auseinandersetzung zwischen dem Deutschen Reiche
und der Russischen Sozialistischen Föderativen Sowjet
Republik über die Fragen aus der Zeit des Kriege -
zustandes zwischen Deutschland und Russland auf fol-
gender Grundlage geregelt sind:

a) Das Deutsche Reich und die R.S.F.S.R.
verzichten gegenseitig auf den Ersatz ihrer
Kriegskosten sowie auf den Ersatz der Kriegs-
schäden , d. h. derjenigen Schäden , die ihnen
und ihren Angehörigen in den Kriegsgebieten
durch militärische Massnahmen einschliesslic
aller in Feindesland vorgenommenen Requisitio
nen entstanden sind . Desgleichen verzichten
beide Teile auf den Ersatz der Zivilschäden ,
die den Angehörigen des einen Teiles durch di
sogenannten Kriegsausnahmegesetze oder durch
Gewaltmassnahmen staatlicher Organe des ander
Teiles verursacht worden sind .

b) Die durch den Kriegszustand betroffenen
öffentlichen

öffentlichen und privaten Rechtsbeziehungen, ein-
schliesslich der Frage der Behandlung der in die
Gewalt des anderen Teiles geratenen Handelsschiffe,
werden nach den Grundsatz der Gegenseitigkeit gere -
gelt werden .

c) Deutschland und Russland verzichten gegenseitig auf Erstattung der beiderseitigen Aufwendungen
für Kriegsgefangene . Ebenfalls verzichtet die Deutsche Regierung auf Erstattung der von ihr für die in
Deutschland internierten Angehörigen der Roten Armee
gemachten Aufwendungen . Die Russische Regierung verzichtet ihrerseits auf Erstattung des Erlöses aus von
Deutschland vorgenommenen Verkäufer des von diesen
Internierten nach Deutschland gebrachten Heeresgutes.

Artikel 2.

Deutschland verzichtet auf die Ansprüche,die
sich aus der bisherigen Anwendung der Gesetze und
Massnahmen der R.S.F.S.R. auf deutsche Reichsangehörige oder ihre Privatrechte sowie auf die Rechte des
Deutschen Reiches und der Länder gegen Russland sowie
aus den von der R.S.F.S.R. oder ihren Organen sonst
gegen Reichsangehörige oder ihre Privatrechte getrof-
fenen Massnahmen ergeben, vorausgesetzt, dass die
Regierung der R.S.F.S.R. auch ähnliche Ansprüche drit-
ter Staaten nicht befriedigt.

Artikel 3.

Die diplomatischen und konsularischen Beziehungen
zwischen den Deutschen Reiche und der R.S.F.S.R.
werden sogleich wieder aufgenommen . Die Zulassung
der

der beiderseitigen Konsuln sind durch ein besonderes
Abkommen geregelt werden .

Artikel 4.

Die beiden Regierungen sind sich ferner auch
darüber einig, dass für die allgemeine Rechtsstellung
der Angehörigen des einen Teiles im Gebiet des anderen
Teiles und für die allgemeine Regelung der beiderseitigen Handels-und Wirtschaftsbeziehungen der Grundsatz der Meistbegünstigung gelten soll. Der Grund -
satz der Meistbegünstigung erstreckt sich nicht auf
die Vorrechte und Erleichterungen, die die R.S.F.S.R.
einer Sowjet-Republik oder einen solchen Staate
gewährt, der früher Bestandteil des ehemaligen Russischen Reiches war.

Artikel 5.

Die beiden Regierungen werden den wirtschaftli-
chen Bedürfnissen der beiden Länder in wohlwollenden
Geiste wechselseitig entgegenkommen . Bei einer
grundsätzlichen Regelung dieser Frage auf interna -
tionaler Basis werden sie in vorherigen Gedankenaus-
tausch eintreten. Die Deutsche Regierung erklärt sich
bereit, die ihr neuerdings mitgeteilten ,von Privat-
firmen b-absichtigten Vereinbarungen nach Möglichkeit
zu unterstützen und ihre Durchführung zu erleichtern.

Artikel 6.

Die Artikel 1 b und 4 dieses Vertrages treten
mit der Ratifikation,die übrigen Bestimmungen dieses
Vertrages treten sofort in Kraft .

Ausgefertigt

Ausgefertigt in doppelter Urschrift in Rapallo
am 16. April 1922.

[signatures] Rathenau

Rapallo Treaty

Joseph Wirth *(left)* and Walther Rathenau *(right)* at Genoa

Edouard Beneš

Viscount Kikujirô Ishii, Head of the
Japanese Delegation at Genoa

7

French Plans for the Reconstruction of Russia: A History and Evaluation

ANNE HOGENHUIS-SELIVERSTOFF

France's policy toward Soviet Russia at the time of the Genoa Conference has been described both in the official government publications that appeared shortly afterward and in subsequent monographs.[1] However, the preparations for the conference, its various transformations, and the strategy and tactics of its participants have received little attention.

The private files of a number of French civil servants who took part in the preparations for the Genoa Conference provide revealing evidence about the above matters; they also permit a better understanding of this crucial period of French diplomacy with its mounting concern that France, just emerging from postwar reconstruction, was descending from the top of a wave and had to defend itself from both friend and foe. It was feared that considerable damage had already been incurred and there was only a very narrow margin for action to regain control.

At the end of 1921, diplomats and statesmen in Moscow, London, and Berlin called for an international conference to discuss the reentry of Russia into the European system, the settlement of the problem of German reparations, and the revival of traditional trade patterns that had been distorted by war and revolution. They hoped that this would restore peace, order, and prosperity to Europe. However, the various proponents of the conference were largely motivated by feelings of national interest, and some of their schemes would explode like bombs during the course of the Genoa Conference.

The situation was scarcely different in Paris. In the summer of 1921, Aristide Briand's government, with Louis Loucheur as its minister of

---

1 Ministère des Affaires Etrangères, *Documents diplomatiques. Conférence économique internationale de Gênes, 1922.* For a general bibliography and historical background, see Anne Hogenhuis-Seliverstoff, *Les relations franco-soviétiques, 1917–1924* (Paris, 1981).

reconstruction, had looked for practical ways of facilitating the recovery of French assets that had been lost in the war and revolution. On the one hand, the resumption of German trade with Eastern Europe might generate funds that could in part be used to pay the overdue installments of German reparations. On the other hand, the reintegration of Soviet Russia into the European trade system offered improved prospects for the repayment of Russia's debts to France. Moreover, the creation of an international consortium for economic cooperation with Russia might preclude independent German ventures into that country.[2]

By the end of 1921, Briand realized that the United States did not intend to provide aid for European reconstruction and also that France did not have the backing of David Lloyd George's government on the key issues of war debts, German reparations, and a treaty of guarantee. He thus had little choice but to accept the idea of an international conference on Russia and Eastern Europe with an agenda concentrating on the resumption of economic relations and excluding all other questions.

As is well known, Briand resigned during the meeting held in Cannes to prepare for this conference. Raymond Poincaré, who succeeded him on January 15, 1922, made it clear both in the governmental declaration of January 19 and in his message to Lloyd George dated February 6 that, although he did not plan to back out of the impending negotiations with the Soviets, he intended to take a hard line because he did not share Lloyd George's optimism about a possible re-Europeanization of Russia through trade.

Jean Monnet, at the time a financial expert for the League of Nations who was in London to discuss the Austrian loan, sent his comments on the February 6 note in the hope of reaching Poincaré. Monnet thought that the note, particularly the stipulation that Russia accept the conditions laid down in Cannes as a precondition for its participation in the conference, would make a favorable impression on most European governments. He therefore suggested that a good translation be distributed throughout Europe in order to counter the distorted reports appearing daily in the British press denouncing Poincaré as out to "sabotage" the conference. Monnet further suggested various ways to create publicity for the French position, for example, by engaging in a dialogue with

2 Note, Dec. 26, 1921, "Conférence de Londres et les relations intereuropéennes," Secret, Seydoux Papers, box 23.
3 Monnet to Bourgeois, Feb. 6, 1922, Bourgeois Papers, vol. 40 (SDN). See also comments in telegram from Fleuriau, London to Paris, Secret, Jan. 17, 1922, ibid.

European heads of state and thereby shifting the center of negotiations from London to Paris. He thought that this move had good prospects for success, since France still held the key to the European situation and Poincaré enjoyed considerable prestige abroad. A discussion under French leadership before the conference that dealt with a number of key points would "exclude fantasies or surprise blows" contemplated by some parties."[3]

In a subsequent letter on this subject, Monnet outlined the techniques of multilateral negotiation that were to become famous some thirty years later. However, at the time his advice was not followed; we do not even know if it ever reached Poincaré. In any case, it seems unlikely that there would have been sufficient time to accomplish such a strategy; moreover, French diplomacy lacked the energy required to rechannel the flow of negotiations. Poincaré, who made no secret of his dislike for holding negotiations "in public," was far more at ease in bilateral discussions.

I shall now proceed to analyze the French approach to the problem of Russian reconstruction, then examine the various plans put forward, and finally try to account for their failure.

From 1922 onward, historians have generally represented the French attitude at the Genoa Conference as backward-looking, resentful of British plans for Europe, irreconcilable toward the Germans, and uncompromisingly opposed to the Soviet government. Lloyd George's exaggerated view of Poincaré as a reactionary, chauvinist negotiating partner has imposed itself on the historical record.[4] It has been reinforced by the widespread acceptance of J. M. Keynes's interpretation of the European peace settlement, backed up in later decades by the success of his *General Theory*.[5] Indeed, there was no place for Poincaré in a Keynesian world.

Poincaré's policy toward Germany has recently been reappraised by French historians. In regard to his rejection of British monetary plans for Europe, a study published in 1986 has shown that in the light of the franc's weakness and the precarious state of France's economic recovery, any other attitude would have been suicidal.[6] Moreover, French

---

4 Wickham H. Steed, *Through Thirty Years,* 2 vols. (London, 1924). According to Steed, the press campaign against Poincaré was inspired by Lloyd George.
5 Robert Skidelski, *J. Maynard Keynes: Hopes Betrayed, 1883–1920* (New York, 1986).
6 Laurent de Saint-Aubin, *Les aspects monétaires de la conférence de Gênes* (Paris, 1986); rapport de la sous-commission préparatoire pour la conférence de Gênes, Mar. 16, 1922, box B322.82, FMF.

experts at the time considered currency reform to be unrealistic and even dangerous for the small central and east European countries and quite out of the question for Russia.

There is evidence that France tried seriously to establish a satisfactory de facto relationship with Russia that met France's specific needs, even if it did bypass the multilateral negotiations then under way. It may be wondered whether the statesmen who had been active before 1917 did not still tend to think of Russia as a possible counterweight to Germany; despite the erratic course of Soviet politics, the NEP suggested a Thermidorean turn to the Russian Revolution. Advisors such as former Russian ambassador Maklakoff suggested that France should avoid being too hard on the Soviets to prevent their teaming up with the British.[7] Moreover, the rumors of Soviet contacts with German industrial and banking circles revived French fears of a German–Soviet rapprochement.[8]

In France's preparations for the Genoa Conference, two sets of experts were consulted: private and semiprivate individuals in connection with the consortium, and officials from the ministries concerned with the conference agenda.[9] The different ministries were all convinced of the need for a return to normal bilateral economic relations with Russia, but for different reasons.[10] This sentiment was particularly marked in the Ministry of Trade but also in the Ministry of Finance, where the minister, Charles de Lasteyrie, kept a close watch on the balance of France's "suffering" assets abroad.

At the Quai d'Orsay, the task of coordinating the economic preparations for the Genoa Conference rested on the shoulders of the *sous-directeur des affairs commerciales,* Jacques Seydoux. Working at the same time on a solution for the reparations problem along the lines laid down by Loucheur, Seydoux placed the Russian problem in this framework. He acted under the direct supervision of Poincaré, who, in his position

7 Note on a conversation with Maklakoff, Dec. 30, 1921, FMAE 2619/20.
8 Anne Hogenhuis-Seliverstoff, "La perception du marché russe en France, 1922–1923," in *La Révolution d'octobre et les pays européens 1917–1924*, Proceedings of the Association Internationale d'Histoire Contemporaine de l'Europe, Moscow, September 7–13, 1987 (in preparation).
9 List of administrations and enterprises consulted are to be found in FMAE, Z628/6 sd, Classified, Nov. 22, 1921; "Préparation de la Conférence de Gênes, séance du 16 février 1922. Composition de la Commission chargée de préparer le programme des questions financières à soumettre à la conférence de Gênes," and "Liste des experts," Feb. 20, 1922, Millerand Papers, vol. 2.4.
10 There is no comprehensive French study on relations between bureaucrats and businessmen. See, e.g., Paul Gordon Lauren, *Diplomats and Bureaucrats: The First Institutional Response to Twentieth Century Diplomacy in France and Germany* (Stanford, 1976), and Stephen A. Schuker, *The End of French Predominance in Europe* (Chapel Hill and London, 1976).

as minister of foreign affairs and with no general secretary to act as counterweight to his authority, personally reviewed the files and made many of the overall decisions.[11]

Contrary to the sentiments of the other governments involved, the French experts shared an underlying assumption that the reconstruction of Russia was not a prerequisite for the reconstruction of Europe, or even of France. The building-up of Soviet Russia would clearly require a very long, complicated process. There were no immediate prospects for resumption of trade, whether internal or international, given Russia's dilapidated production facilities and apathetic, poverty-stricken population.[12]

Relief had been offered, but reconstruction was only possible on a sound basis. Of course, during the war most European states, including France, had turned their backs on liberalism, resorting to autarky, protectionism, and inflation. However, the emergence of this "age of immorality"[13] in economic relations was not welcomed. Since Russia had broken the links with the European system by such internal and external measures as nationalization of foreign property and the cancellation of foreign debts, it was the one that should take the first steps toward cooperation by making the effort to reenter the system.

Poincaré saw political recognition as a matter of principle, by definition not negotiable and reserved for consideration by the government. Such recognition implied reciprocal obligations, covering private debts, war debts, new credits, and then political recognition. To be sure, at the time, French business circles were not exerting much pressure for the recognition of Soviet Russia.

At the Quai d'Orsay, Seydoux translated these assumptions into an operational code of conduct. To him, the problem of resuming economic relations was a matter of trust, to which the question of political recognition contributed only in a formal respect. The solution was in the hands of the Soviet government. While the first of the conditions elaborated at Cannes stated that the Soviet government could impose on Russia whatever system it favored, the second and third conditions stated that in order to obtain credits the government would have to

11 Many minutes bear annotations in Poincaré's handwriting, cf. Seydoux Papers, boxes 23 and 24, and Millerand Papers, vols. 73 and 74.
12 Soviet statements about "selling the capitalists the rope to hang themselves with" and "seizing the outstretched hand in order to crush it" were taken at their face value at the time. The suggestion that they were only made to keep the left-wing opposition within the party happy did not appear until later.
13 Skidelsky, *J. Maynard Keynes,* 400–2.

change the laws that stood in the way of economic cooperation. If they wished not to do so, they would have to take the consequences.[14]

Within a context of multilateral discussions, a global approach like Poincaré's was difficult to maintain without the support of all the other parties. That is why France had insisted that the Soviet government accept the Cannes conditions as a prerequisite for the Genoa negotiations.

On February 16, the members of the first Comité interministériel des Affaires Russes set themselves the task of working out a plan that would be attractive to French and Russian interests and at the same time neutralize Lloyd George's attempts to promote the international recognition of Russia to help it reintegrate itself into the European system.[15] The plan would also protect Russia against "mercantile exploitation," such as the dumping of British surpluses that the prime minister had promised the trade unions as a means of solving Britain's unemployment problems.

France, in contrast, should act as befitted Russia's oldest ally, which knew best what Russia needed, and which was entitled to offer know-how and resume its former activities. The ten million odd gold francs that the French had already invested in Russia were a sad reminder of these claims. However, as de Chevilly, from the Ministry of Trade, stressed, France was not out simply to recoup its losses at the conference. Such an attitude not only would be unrealistic but would lay the French open to charges of money-grubbing. Accordingly, the discussions concentrated on two fields where, without requiring any major changes by the Soviets in industrial and commercial legislation, French and Russian interests might coincide: railways and oil.

In the summer of 1921, a German–Polish plan for the restoration of the Russian railways was submitted to the Quai d'Orsay, which, seeing no point in helping the Germans extend their influence in the East, treated it with suspicion. But because this scheme might conceivably be incorporated into the newly devised system of in-kind payment of German reparations, Loucheur was interested enough to have the Banque de France on December 15 ask the Ministry of Foreign Affairs whether the credits requested by the Polish government could be granted. In the

14 See Hogenhuis-Seliverstoff, "La perception du marché russe en France," and Questions à la Chambre et réponse, Mar. 16, 1922, FMAE Z619/20.
15 "Rapport de la Commission financière interministérielle," Classified, Mar. 7, 1922 (with 32 pages on Russia and 20 on the rest of Europe), Millerand Papers, vol. 75, and final version, "Rapport de la Commission financière préparatoire à la conférence de Gênes," Classified, Feb. 17, 1922 (60 pp.), FMF B 322/81.

meantime, the traditional rivalry for the Russian railway network between Mitropa and the Compagnie International des Wagons Lits had been resumed. Paris feared that the German steel magnate Hugo Stinnes might obtain a concession for the main railway lines.[16]

After the informal talks, which took place in December in London, British and German industrialists, soon joined by the French, began discussing the form of an international syndicate for trade with Russia.[17] Stinnes proposed that the reconstruction of Russia should start with the railways. On December 19, Seydoux drafted a plan intended to turn the reconstruction of Russia "from an apple of discord into a token of European reconciliation." Like Loucheur, he was concerned that Germany should pay its reparations but also sensed that the Reich was ready to venture eastward on its own. Germany was in many ways in the best position to work together with Russia, but it was short of capital.

Seydoux rejected the idea of lending to Poland and thus promoting a German–Polish rapprochement. He saw the solution in a geographical division, based on what had been drafted after the Russian armistice in December 1917: Britain would be responsible for the Baltic States and the North, and France for the Donets basin and the Ukraine. "Without going so far as partition," he went on, "we might foresee a consortium in which both Great Britain and the United States had a share. Germany would provide the equipment, and a percentage of Russia's payments would go to the reparations account."[18] A few days later, he added the suggestion that several other countries, in particular the Netherlands and Switzerland, should also take part in the consortium.[19]

On December 26, in summing up the conversations in London and also commenting on the difficulties arising from the isolationism of American Secretary of State Hughes, Seydoux concluded that what was needed was closer cooperation among the Allies: French, Belgian, and British industrialists should first agree on how to divide the Russian market before entering into negotiations with Germany.[20] According to this scheme, the reorganization of the Russian railways became the

16 Note dated Dec. 19, 1921, Seydoux Papers, box 23. The possibility of the Germans gaining a concession for the Russian main railway lines was emphasized by rumors of a takeover bid for the French interests with the aid of British and Canadian capital.
17 Dec. 16, 1921, FMAE B82/16. Unofficial meeting on the consortium in London: draft proposals, revised on Dec. 31.
18 Note dated Dec. 19, 1921, Seydoux Papers, box 23.
19 "Note sur la conférence de Londres," Secret, Dec. 26, 1921, Seydoux Papers, box 23.
20 Ibid., and "Note sur le paiement des réparations par l'Allemagne," Jan. 9, 1922.

operational part of the French official position and was accepted on February 16. The idea would be to approach Russia "in a friendly way, with a rational and progressive plan."

Adopting this concept of geographical division, Seydoux defined seven zones where France could offer particular assistance, which he saw as compatible with the Russian tradition of local autonomy. The first step would be to establish a minimum level of well-being in each zone through plans of limited scope to attain better living conditions for the impoverished, undernourished population. Once this had been achieved through a rise in the level of employment, this slight improvement in economic conditions could also benefit trade. With the revival of the internal market, normal industrial activities could gradually be resumed. Only then would foreign investment in local industry yield benefits. Without these initial steps, foreign funds would sink without a trace into the general disorganization and the bottomless needs of the country. One way to provide the necessary starting impulse was through local improvement of the run-down harbor installations, waterways, and railways. After the transportation network had been restored, the previous owners of industrial installations in the Donets basin could, wherever possible, start repairing their property.[21]

On February 17, de Chevilly contacted Dutch shareholders of Russian railways to sound them out on the idea of a Franco–Dutch coalition controlling a majority of shares. When de Chevilly asked if the Dutch were prepared to take up a common position against the Germans,[22] the answer was noncommittal.

There are no records of further initiatives in this field during the next months. In the numerous rumors of unofficial Soviet–French talks, railway reorganization was never mentioned.[23] Poincaré kept the matter in reserve, as evidenced by his instructions on March 19 not to relaunch the discussions about the consortium. In Genoa on April 30, the French negotiators themselves took the initiative when they broached this matter with their British counterparts, who reacted favorably and agreed to submit it to the Russians.[24] Seydoux wired Paris that the discussion concerned "the plan y[our] E[xcellency] knows and has

21 "Rapport de la commission interministérielle," Mar. 8, 1922, Millerand Papers, vol. 75. See also "Rapport Sergent," Feb. 26, 1922, vol. 74, on British plans for railways.
22 The Netherlands, Ministerie van Buitenlandse Zaken, Archief, A.81/Agenda, Box 1064.
23 Note, Mar. 14, 1922, FMAE, B82/16 sd IV.
24 Tel. from Genoa, n. 222-5, FMAE Z624/12.

accepted in its main lines." But L. B. Krassin's response, made during a subcommission meeting, was that his government did not intend to permit foreign interference in the railways. This surprising statement, in view of the numerous, contrary utterances of the past, clarified some of the nebulous limits of the NEP and also ended hopes of reviving earlier patterns of implementation.

The main concern of both groups of French experts was oil. Since the San Remo agreements in 1920, the French government had been looking for a dependable source of oil independent of the British and American companies. The Société Française des Pétroles, Essences et Naphtes was formed at this time. Under the chairmanship of Laurent-Eynac, the company started buying up shares of the nationalized oil wells, acquiring as much as 20 percent of the entire stock and with particularly high participation in the Grozny fields. At the same time de Martel, the High Commissioner of Georgia, arranged for contracts to be signed supplying fuel oil to the French navy. This continued until the Soviet government established its rule over the Caucasian republic and, although no clear proof is available, probably for some time afterward. In September 1921, Loucheur again took the initiative with his suggestion that the new Georgian authorities be contacted to negotiate a concession.[25]

As minority shareholders, the French were less vitally interested in the restoration of owners' rights than in contracts granting them the right to exploit wells and pipelines and export oil on a profit-sharing basis. Soviet profits from this scheme could be transferred to an account that would be used to repay some of their international debts. Hervé Alphand of the Office des Biens, which dealt with French property expropriated by the Soviets, agreed to this scheme, which placed the Caucasus at the head of the seven regions of projected French activity. Apparently the only point still open to discussion was whether the talks with the Soviets should be carried out in consultation with the British oil companies.[26]

At the first meeting of the above-mentioned interministerial committee, Lion, of the Banque de l'Union Parisienne, pleaded for the oil concession to be included within the framework of the international consortium; but there were objections that since this would require the agreement of former owners, it might be difficult to achieve. We may

25 Note, Laurent-Eynac, Oct. 18, 1920, note, Sept. 1, 1921, and *passim*, FMAE Z633/4; note, Sept. 7, 1920, on import duties, FMF B320.23.
26 "Commission interministérielle," Mar. 16, 1922, Millerand Papers, vol. 75.

infer that the inquiries about this possibility received no encouraging response, since at the next committee meeting on March 3, Pineau, the director of *Combustibles liquides* in the Ministry of Trade, proposed that "if circumstances do not allow us to take advantage of the common French and Soviet interest at this moment, the project should be postponed." Moreover, he stated, "By signing a contract at this moment, we [would] provoke the resentment of the owners in order to benefit the Anglo-Saxons."[27] It should be noted that both the Pineau and Lion proposals contained far-reaching implications, namely, that the Soviets did have sovereignty over the Caucasus,[28] that they owned the oil fields there, and that they had the right to dispose of them. They had virtually accepted the idea that the indemnification of the former well owners should be negotiated bilaterally and privately between the nationalized firms and the Soviet government.

During the months of March and April 1922, both groups of French experts did their best to display a positive attitude toward the international consortium in all their dealings with the British, while at the same time retaining the possibility of direct negotiations with the Soviets. They all agreed that even though the consortium did not favor French interests, it could not be ignored. They had to participate in order to be informed and to prevent the despoliation of French interests by foreign owners. This was the advice given to Poincaré by Sergent, the former under secretary of state for finance, when he returned from the discussions in London about the consortium.[29] Indeed, after Poincaré's meeting with Lloyd George in Boulogne on February 23, the Quai d'Orsay had decided unanimously to stop all further initiatives on the consortium scheme without, however, officially discarding it. Therefore Poincaré's reply to Sergent was that there was no need to inform his British counterparts about French plans for Russia.[30]

At the Quai d'Orsay, Seydoux, in his unobtrusive way, worked along similar lines. For example, when his British counterpart, Sidney Chapman, visited Paris on March 3, and when Francesco Giannini, who happened to be there at the time, was invited to join their talks, Seydoux only hinted at opposition to the consortium in French financial and industrial circles. Here he was on safe ground, since during a previous

27 Ibid. and rapport, Feb. 2, 1922, FMAE Z633/4, and Mar. 1 and 8, 1922, FMAE B 82/16 sd IV.
28 One of the reasons invoked for this might have been that since the Caucasian republics were not European but Asian territory, they fell outside the scope of a conference devoted to European reconstruction.
29 Note, Seydoux on conversation with Sergent, Feb. 26, 1922, Millerand Papers, vol. 74.
30 Note, Poincaré (handwritten), Mar. 9, 1922, FMAE B 82/16 sd IV.

visit Chapman had told him of similar feelings in Great Britain. Seydoux also confided to them his fears about the economic implications of the consortium for Eastern Europe.[31] After promptly reporting this conversation to the Belgian prime minister, Georges Theunis, he noted that the Belgians, who were as embarrassed as the French, would prefer a Franco–Belgian joint venture in the Donets basin but would be prepared to participate in the consortium, at least in its initial phase.[32]

In the meantime, tentative moves had been undertaken to remove the whole issue from a multilateral diplomatic meeting by placing the discussions under the aegis of the League of Nations. This idea was being actively promoted in Paris by Léon Bourgeois, one of the founding fathers of the League and the chairman of the Foreign Affairs Committee in the Senate, as well as by Jean Monnet. Bourgeois unleashed a campaign to obtain support for this proposal from the neutrals and other European members of the League of Nations. Monnet was in contact with Edouard Beneš, the unflagging go-between.[33] Monnet's letters to Bourgeois were passed on to French President Alexandre Millerand, who showed great interest and invited him for a long discussion. Monnet was also in touch with Poincaré, but it appears that their meeting was first postponed and then canceled.[34] Since Poincaré had agreed in Boulogne that the League would handle the follow-up to the Genoa Conference, this excluded the possibility that it would also be responsible for the initial conference.[35] Nevertheless, under various pretexts, he continued to promote the alternative construction.

It is difficult to resist the impression that Poincaré saw this whole process as a safe dead end. On March 16, he proposed to Rome and London that the League's procedures for meetings might be borrowed for the Genoa Conference. This suggestion had no impact, and it was too late to resist the pressure for definitive agreement on the meeting.[36] The oppressive uncertainty of the situation was accentuated by the Soviet approaches to Paris, which Poincaré mentioned in Boulogne.[37] The sig-

---

31 Note, Seydoux to Poincaré, Mar. 10, 1922, Millerand Papers, vol. 75.
32 Note, Apr. 1, 1922, ibid. Seydoux had received this information from Cattier and Witmeur on March 14, as they were passing through Paris before the joint meeting of experts in London.
33 Letters, Monnet, Jan. 21, 1922, on method, and Feb. 21, 1922, on conversation with Beneš, Bourgeois Papers, box 40, FMAE; memo., Beneš on conversation with Lloyd George, Feb. 23, 1922, Seydoux Papers, box 27.
34 Conversation Monnet–Millerand, Feb. 21, 1922, Bourgeois Papers, box 40.
35 Notes, Monnet on Boulogne conversations, Mar. 3 and 7, 1922, ibid.
36 Tel., Poincaré to Geneva, Mar. 15, 1922, and tels. to London and Rome, Mar. 16 and 21, 1922, note from Italian Embassy, Mar. 16, 1922, Millerand Papers, vol. 75.
37 De Peretti on the Boulogne minutes, p. 30, Millerand Papers, vol. 74.

nificance of this new development became clear when, on March 17, Seydoux asked Poincaré to state his views and put his instructions in writing, as the basis for Seydoux's impending meeting with his counterparts in London.

"This is an urgent matter," he wrote. "France cannot go on playing the scarecrow, as it did in Washington. We have good cards in our hands. Chicherin's telegram[38] proves this, and our relations are excellent. We cannot deliver a defenseless Russia into the hands of the British. We must study the possibilities offered by the consortium. If the consortium does not work, the conference makes no sense, and there is no point in the Russians – or ourselves – going to Genoa." In the meantime, he continued, they could not trust the British, who might have a secret plan. "Thus, we must take the initiative with a plan of reconstruction, with the understanding of the Belgians, Little Entente, and Balts. There is no reason why we should depart from the prudent expectations we have had of Russia during the past two years, if not to bring Russia positive assistance."[39]

The two years mentioned by Seydoux refer to the period of Laurent-Eynac's efforts to reinforce France's position in the Caucasian oil fields. In this respect, the Russians certainly appeared to be positively inclined. In the middle of April, the *Journée Industrielle* reported that the Soviets "are trying to put France, or some Frenchmen, under the spell of oil." We do not know very much about the talks that Soviet trade representatives may have had with French politicians and journalists in Berlin, Prague, or London. However, in a letter of March 3 to Poincaré from a Monsieur Maréchal, who together with Franklin-Bouillon had visited Krassin in London, there was an enclosure from Krassin describing Russia's misery and the urgent need for credits to restore the country's export capabilities, particularly of wheat but also of some other traditional commodities. In exchange for French official backing, he said that Russia would be prepared to recognize its financial obligations. A short covering note stated that the Soviet government intended to invite experts from all countries to make plans for the exploitation of Caucasian oil, even though Royal Dutch Shell was trying to obtain exclusive rights for the region. However, the note continued that the Soviet government would not like to grant privileges to the British, "because of Persia."[40]

---

38 This long telegram from Riga (eight pages), dated March 16, 1922, gave a general reassessment of Russia's overtures toward France; Millerand Papers, vol. 75.
39 Note, Seydoux to the President of the Council, Mar. 17, 1922, ibid.
40 Filed Mar. 5, 1922 (twelve pages), ibid.

We can therefore better understand the extremely restrictive instructions that Poincaré sent to Seydoux on March 17. They essentially said that if the British did not come forward with a plan for the reconstruction of Russia, there was no reason for the French to do so, "especially in the absence of the United States. The oil question is complicated. We shall certainly discuss it, but must respect American feelings in this matter. It would thus be better not to raise it at all at Genoa." As far as the consortium was concerned there was little to say. Finally, the matters that Seydoux should not discuss were listed: recognition of Russia, war debts, reparations, and so forth.[41]

These instructions must have seemed a poor reward to the teams in the various ministries who had worked throughout the winter to prepare the French position; but because of the constraints on French diplomacy and the menacing uncertainties that loomed, they accepted them. In fact, Seydoux learned in London that his British counterparts doubted whether the prime minister would endorse the plans they had prepared. They suspected that his only aim was to prepare de jure recognition of Russia, in order to save the Genoa Conference and provide a basis for granting trade-credit facilities. "He may do so if he wishes," Poincaré wrote on Seydoux's report, "but not until after the conference."[42]

It appears from the proceedings of the Genoa commissions and sub-commissions and from the formal and informal meetings[43] that both the French and British experts, with good mutual understanding, had done a great deal to prepare constructive proposals and open the way to multilateral discussions, while still anticipating the possibility of privately elaborated plans. On May 1, a French observer, André Siegfried, noted that delegates from the various countries were working on specific deals in the corridors while putting forward very general resolutions on very general matters during the sessions. He saw all this plenary activity as a cover under which the Russian question could ripen, which, he said, would soon happen.

Indeed, the French were ready to agree on the reply to be sent to the Russians in response to their successive proposals; under certain circumstances the Soviets were to be allowed to grant concessions of nationalized property to persons who were not the original foreign owners before expropriation. The Belgians alone opposed this formula. Siegfried wrote: "The [French] business world is stupefied at this betrayal

41 Note, Poincaré to Seydoux, Mar. 18, 1922, ibid.
42 Mar. 27 and 28, 1922, ibid.
43 Memo., June 1, 1922, Seydoux Papers, box 24, and *passim*, Millerand Papers, vol. 76.

of the Belgian position by our delegates."[44] As we know, the situation changed abruptly the next day, May 2, when Louis Barthou, the head of the French delegation, was recalled to Paris, and his stand-in was instructed to side with the Belgians. At the same time, Poincaré informed him that a concession agreement had been initialed by Krassin and Shell in December 1921; a friend (whose identity is unknown) had told him about this collusion against French interests.[45]

Explaining the situation to Laurent-Eynac a few days later, a very bitter Poincaré compared the affair to a second Rapallo: "Lloyd George came to Genoa with a treaty in his pocket, the rest was for show. He meant to discredit [the French] and prepare for the next elections. . . . There can be no doubt about the collusion between the Russians, English, Italians, and Germans." He immediately sought contact with Lloyd George and conferred with Laurent-Eynac concerning the points to be raised about the Grozny oil fields.[46]

The end of the Genoa Conference was in sight, although the negotiations continued while the Soviet delegates awaited new instructions from Moscow. All the participants concluded an undertaking not to sign a separate agreement with Russia at least until the end of the discussions between experts to be held in The Hague in a few weeks.[47] On the official level, the French seemed quite satisfied with the course of events, especially when the new proposals put forward on May 11 by the Soviet delegation went back on their previous offers and made further discussion pointless.

On the whole, the French press showed more relief at the pitfalls avoided than regret at opportunities lost.[48] A settlement for the losses incurred had receded into the realm of rhetoric. On the other hand, on the basis of the numerous talks held between various groups and individuals with Soviet representatives, hopes were high for private business projects between France and Russia, especially in the field of oil. It was expected that many of these plans would come to fruition in the second half of 1922. In Paris, contacts were established to organize

---

44 Letters, André Siegfried, Apr. 17, May 1 and 8, 1922, Millerand Papers.
45 Tel., Poincaré to Genoa and Brussels, 248–50, May 2, 1922, and to Washington, 279–84, May 3, 1922, FMAE Z633/4.
46 Poincaré to Laurent-Eynac, Genoa, Secret, asking for the points to be raised in a talk with the Soviets, ibid.
47 On the efforts to keep in line with the United States see tel., not numbered, May 14, 1922, Millerand Papers, vol. 79/80.
48 Renata Bournazel, *Rapallo: naissance d'un mythe. La politique de la peur dans la France du Bloc National* (Paris, 1974).

financial backing for a Franco–Belgian oil syndicate.[49] A French mission left for Russia on July 23 with Seydoux's approval and with the clear understanding that they went under their own responsibility and at their own risk. If concessions failed to materialize, it was hoped at least some contracts would be signed for the export of oil to France. In response to some protests about the purchase of "stolen oil," Seydoux noted that the oil question would not force France to reconsider its entire policy toward the Soviets, which was "a kind of expectant neutrality, with an economic policy under the motto of freedom of transactions. Three years of experience have proved its value."[50]

The French attitude at the time of the Genoa Conference, and the various changes it underwent, acquire more credibility when seen in the light of the search for oil concessions. This helps, for example, to explain both the rumors of a bilateral deal with the Soviets before the conference and the *volte face* by the French delegation in Genoa.

In his interpretation of the Genoa Conference, Louis Fischer viewed oil – and particularly the competition between Standard Oil and Shell – as the key to the entire negotiations.[51] But since his information came primarily from interviews with former Soviet officials, he followed their version of the story, which stressed France's responsibility for the failure of the Genoa Conference and overlooked the frustrations inflicted on the French.

Later publications, written against the background of peaceful coexistence and the Helsinki agreement,[52] discount the importance of oil and emphasize the possibility of a general, multinational agreement that was blocked by the debts/loans issue and the frustrations of the "gentleman in Paris."

One cannot escape the conclusion that the French attempts to combine multilateral negotiations with bilateral deals were poorly coordinated and hesitatingly implemented, while their attempts to prepare their strategy for the multilateral talks were ineffective: Railways were sacrificed for oil, and the hopes for an oil deal were discarded because

49 Note to the president of the Council on the oil question, June 23, 1922, Seydoux Papers, box 24.
50 Feb. 6, 1923, and July 10, 1923, FMAE Z633/4.
51 Louis Fischer, *The Soviets in World Affairs: A History of the Relations Between the Soviet Union and the Rest of the World, 1917–1929*, 2 vols. (Princeton, 1951).
52 See, e.g., Evgeni M. Chossudovsky, "Genoa Revisited: Russia and Coexistence," *Foreign Affairs* 50 (1972):554–77; Franklyn Griffiths, *Genoa Plus 51. Changing Soviet Perspectives in Europe* (Toronto, 1973).

of the commitment to lost assets. The consortium that had been proposed to check German advances in Russia made no sense after Rapallo.

The Shell negotiations were a severe blow to the credibility of French diplomacy. Although Seydoux's memoranda had contained warnings of possible secret deals, no alternative course had been devised. From the French standpoint, the situation was one of almost unrelieved gloom. The only silver lining lay in the possibility of a direct, pragmatic agreement with the Russians. However, it must not be forgotten that the French had less experience in dealing with the Soviets than the other Allies. Genoa was their first encounter with the new Russian diplomacy. Poincaré acted rather consistently in response to the Soviet signals beamed at France. However, no one seems to have been aware of what precisely was behind them.

We now know that Soviet diplomatic preparations for Genoa, guided by instructions from Lenin, rested on two main premises.[53] First, it was postulated that the inevitable antagonism between capitalists should be exploited and stimulated wherever possible. In view of the ever-present danger of a capitalist war against Russia, it might be advantageous to grant benefits to foreign capitalists whose property in Russia had been confiscated, because they then might exert a moderating influence on their governments' attitude toward Moscow. The second premise was that Europe's economic welfare required Russia as a market. The British government undoubtedly supported this view, and various British industrialists followed its lead. For example, after Rapallo, Vickers-Armstrong sent its representatives to Genoa in the hope of obtaining commercial advantages in the wake of the privileged Germans.[54]

Throughout 1922, a debate raged in Moscow over the trade monopoly and the need for a conciliatory gesture over foreign debts in order to attract new loans. Chicherin and Grigory Sokolnikov had pleaded for such measures. Lenin had led the resistance to any abandonment of the basic tenets of War Communism and finally imposed his views in November 1922.[55]

Krassin had had the courage to challenge the *Sovnarkom*, insisting that Russia at that moment was only a second-rate European power and

53 V. A. Shishkin, *Sovetskoe gosudarstvo i strany zapada, 1917–1923. Ocherki stanovlenija ekonomicheskih otnoshenii* (Leningrad, 1969) and *Polosa priznani i vneshne ekonomicheskaia politika SSSR 1924–1925* (Leningrad, 1983).
54 Jean de Pierrefeu, *La Saison diplomatique: Gênes (avril–mai 1922)* (Paris, 1928).
55 Jean-Pierre Saltiel, "Commerce extérieur et croissance économique en Russie et en URSS, 1861–1940" (thesis, Paris III, 1977).

not a vital factor in European recovery. He also proposed that the country be opened up to trade. But did the Soviet government expect that French capitalists, attracted by the offers of oil, would come to terms at Genoa? We know only that emissaries were sent out during the first months of 1922 to try to influence French and British opinion; Christian Rakovsky went on a similar mission to Berlin and Prague, where he made contact with Beneš.[56] Was Krassin acting under similar instructions? Or did he have hopes that he might manage to bring about an opening of Russia to foreign trade if some flexibility could be introduced in the negotiations? Did Krassin share the general strategy of two or three irons in the fire, or did he sincerely believe that the French needs for oil could be balanced against the necessity of finding an outlet for Caucasian oil over and against the claims of the big oil companies? Only Krassin's archives can reveal the answers to these questions.

What is certain is that during the discussions in Genoa in May 1922, the proponents of an autarkic line in Russia were supported in their views by the prospects of a good harvest. The exports of wheat might be resumed and, as advocated by E. A. Preobrazhensky and Ia. L. Piatakov, the profits reinvested in the Russian economy. There was no longer any urgency about granting concessions to foreigners, at least not in the key sectors of the economy. On the other hand, there was nothing against trading in the commodities that Russia could supply and that the other countries, including France, needed. This was precisely the line along which Franco–Soviet relations would steadily develop during the coming decade, despite the inevitable rhetoric about recognition and indemnification.

---

56 V. Ya. Grosup, "H. R. Rakovsky, revolucioner, diplomat i publicist," *Novaya i noveyshaya istoriya* 6 (1988):151–75.

8

The Oil Problem and Soviet–American Relations at the Genoa Conference of 1922

A. A. FURSENKO

Although the oil problem was not on the agenda at the Genoa Conference, it in fact had an impact on the course of the negotiations. The United States did not participate formally in the conference, but the American ambassador to Italy, Richard W. Child, was in Genoa as an observer. Behind the scenes, the ambassador and the representatives of the American oil industry were quite active, and their role in the conference was very important.[1]

Why speak about this in connection with the problem of European reconstruction? At least two reasons can be offered. First, the United States had acquired a new role in Europe as a result of World War I, and U.S. relations with Soviet Russia seriously influenced European diplomacy. Second, the oil problem had become an important issue in international relations. This could be seen in the sharp rivalry between the United States and the European powers over the oil fields of the Middle East: England and France had tried to establish their dominance by creating spheres of influence, while the United States insisted on the open-door policy.

Policy concerning the Russian oil fields was more or less similar in all the Western nations. After the October Revolution of 1917, the Russian oil industry had been nationalized, but no Western country wanted to accept this. During the Genoa Conference, the British businessman Leslie Urquart wrote in the *Financial Times* that in case the negotiations were successful and if foreign investments in Soviet Russia were accepted, Western corporations would receive "tempting"

---

1 Various aspects of this subject are described in several publications of the author: Alexander A. Fursenko, "S.Sh.A. i Genuezskaia Konferentsia 1922 g," in Victor I. Rutenburg, ed., *Problemy istorii mezhdunarodnyky otnoshenii* (Leningrad, 1972), 301–10; "Neftjanoe Dossier Gosudar- stvennogo Departamenta S.Sh.A. 1920-ch gg," in A. A. Fursenko, ed., *Problemy istochnikove- denia vneshnei politiki S.Sh.A.* (Leningrad, 1987), 150–63; *Neftianye voiny v konze 19–nachale 20 veka* (Leningrad, 1985).

advantages.[2] This viewpoint was basically accepted by the American representatives. The view of the Office of the Economic Advisor of the U.S. Department of State was that "the Russian oil fields are among the greatest in the world, with considerable undeveloped potentialities. . . . It would be ridiculous, therefore, to be indifferent to such a region, when we are taking a firm position with regard to Persia, Mesopotamia, and the Netherlands East Indies."[3] However, the United States' position on Soviet oil was in fact not one-dimensional. This was clearly revealed in the behind-the-scenes negotiations on the oil problem at Genoa.

Carole Fink's monograph on the history of the conference,[4] as well as the book by the American historians George Gibb and Evelyn Knowlton,[5] made it clear that the oil problem was an important issue at the Genoa Conference. I myself have worked on this problem using Soviet and American materials, and four years ago, when I had the opportunity to look through the files of the Public Record Office in London, I became convinced that this subject is most important for a better understanding of the very essence of European politics and Western relations with Soviet Russia.

Although they did not put the oil problem on the agenda, the Western powers intended to use the Genoa Conference to achieve the full or partial abolition of the Soviets' nationalization of the oil industry and to restore the former owners' rights to their property. From today's viewpoint, this intention seems absolutely unrealistic, but at that time it seemed possible. By considering the seriousness of the Soviet promises and the degree to which Western diplomacy transmitted an appropriate response, we can perhaps gain some insight into today's prospects for East–West economic cooperation.

In 1922, many people believed that the Soviet system could not continue for long. This belief was based on estimates of the situation made by special business interests involved in Russian affairs. The oil companies were among the most active lobbyists at the Genoa Conference, and their participation was clearly neither impartial nor unselfish. The governmental authorities certainly understood this, but they tried not to speak about it. In the debates over the oil problem during the Genoa

2 *Financial Times,* May 10, 1922.
3 Bureau of the Economic Advisor to the Secretary of State, June 3, 1922, USDS, RG. 59, file 8363, no. 83.
4 Carole Fink, *The Genoa Conference: European Diplomacy, 1921–1922* (Chapel Hill and London, 1984).
5 George Gibb and Evelyn Knowlton, *The Resurgent Years 1911–1927* (New York, 1956).

Conference, the starting point for all European delegates and American observers was their refusal to recognize the Soviets' nationalization decrees. Many documents in the archives of the Foreign Office and the Department of State show that the British and American governments were under strong pressure from special business interests, which took an implacable position: no recognition of the Soviet government.

What positive outcome could be expected from the Genoa Conference under these circumstances? It is doubtful that we can find a definitive answer to this question. Although the oil problem was discussed only on the periphery of the conference, there were some attempts to find solutions. The head of the powerful Royal Dutch Shell Company, Henry Deterding, in an attempt to defeat his American competitors, tried to conclude a separate arrangement with the Soviet representatives. These attempts took place even before the Genoa Conference, when representatives of Royal Dutch Shell met with Leonid Krassin, the Soviet trade agent in London. An experienced manager, Krassin had earlier worked for the German concern Siemens and Schuckert, where he had developed some skill in international business diplomacy. During his lengthy stay in England as a member of the Soviet delegation, Krassin had conducted negotiations with numerous Western businessmen. He had promised foreign companies that the Soviets would conclude contracts with them for profitable concessions. Despite the intransigent anti-Soviet policies of Western leaders, Krassin's statements aroused hopes in the business community.

On the eve of the Genoa Conference, the press reported that Deterding had reached a secret agreement with the Soviet representatives. The report provoked alarm among the Americans. Despite determined efforts, before 1917 the American Standard Oil Company of New Jersey had been unable to establish itself in the Russian oil business. But in 1920, the company had bought the stocks of the largest Nobel petroleum corporation, ignoring the fact that this company had already been nationalized by the Soviet government. As a result, the American corporation became directly involved in the struggle over nationalized Russian oil property.

The story of this affair is fully described in George Gibb and Evelyn Knowlton's book on the history of the Standard Oil Company of New Jersey. I shall only emphasize certain details that relate directly to the negotiations at Genoa and to the fate of the conference. My comments are based on relevant documents of both Soviet and American origin.

The relations between Standard Oil and the Russian Nobel corpo-

ration were in some respects enigmatic. Despite the fact that the czarist
government had introduced strict control measures to prevent American investments in the Russian oil industry, rumors constantly circulated of a secret agreement between these two companies. In 1911,
President William H. Taft asked some unknown person to investigate
American investments in Russia. According to confidential information
delivered to Taft, the Russian Nobel company was controlled by American Standard Oil. My research, based on the private Nobel papers,
indicates that this information was wrong, and several years ago I published an article devoted to this question, using all available material.[6]
There is no doubt, however, that some kind of understanding, in my
opinion beginning in the 1890s, existed between Nobel and Rockefel-
ler on the rules of the game in the world oil market. Hence, it is not
surprising that Standard Oil, and no other corporation, bought the
Nobel stocks in 1920. As a result, the American company became one
of the firms most closely concerned with the fate of nationalized property in Russia. The Standard–Nobel connection explains why the U.S.
government paid so much attention to the Genoa Conference,
although it refused to participate formally in its work.

Strictly speaking, Standard Oil was not considered a lawful claimant
to the property nationalized by the Bolsheviks, because the deal with
Nobel was made only in 1920. But its role in the attempts of Western
diplomacy to restore nationalized property in Russia to its former owners should not be underestimated. This is especially so because the purchase of Nobel stocks was sanctioned by the State Department, which
worked hand in hand with the Standard Oil Company representatives
during the Genoa Conference.

Soon after the purchase of the Nobel stocks, the Standard Oil Company board submitted to the State Department a complaint that the
British were playing a double game in trying to gain some advantages
by separate negotiations with Soviet Russia. The company criticized
the American government for its lack of initiative.[7] During a special
meeting at the State Department, the Standard Oil Company's representatives criticized American diplomacy as inefficient.[8] They wanted
more vigorous support for their efforts to establish themselves as the
lawful owners of the Nobel company.

---

6 Alexander A. Fursenko, "Mozhno li schitat' kompaniiu Nobelia russkim kontsernom?" In
   N. E. Nosov, ed., *Issledovaniia po sotsial'no-politicheskoi istorii Rossii* (Leningrad, 1971), 352–61.
7 Memo., Standard Oil Company of New Jersey to the State Department, Dec. 1920, USDS,
   RG. 59, file 8363, no. 31.
8 Minutes of meeting, Jan. 12, 1921, ibid., no. 238.

Several weeks before the Genoa Conference, the Standard Oil board sent its director, A. Bedford, to Europe, where he conducted negotiations in Paris and London with the assistance of the American diplomatic service.[9] On the eve of the Genoa Conference, the State Department received a memorandum from the company reminding the U.S. government of the need to form a united front with Britain and France against Soviet Russia.[10] In another memorandum several days later, when the Genoa Conference was already under way, the board of Standard Oil expressed its hope that no one at the conference table or behind the scenes would negotiate oil concessions with the Soviet delegates.[11]

The United States wanted to block any possible agreement with Soviet Russia if the latter refused to guarantee the return of property to the former owners. Soon after the opening of the Genoa Conference, Secretary of State Charles Evans Hughes, answering Standard Oil's request, assured the company that "the government will not countenance any arrangements to the prejudice of American interests in Russia."[12] One month before the conference, Bedford had written to Hughes that he was acting in full accordance not only with Nobel but also with Deterding. The company suggested that Washington collaborate with London because "the opinion of the United States carries more weight than that of any other government. We, therefore, earnestly request that the United States government should extend whatever assistance you may deem advisable in the protection of American interests in Russia."[13]

As already mentioned, the representatives of the oil concerns lobbied at the Genoa Conference. They set rumors afloat suggesting that the New Economic Policy would force the Soviet government to denationalize industry, and that some steps in this direction had already been taken. Representatives of the Nobel Company were especially active in spreading these rumors in the hope of persuading Western diplomats to reject any Soviet promises, except the unconditional return of all private property to the former owners. For obvious reasons, Standard Oil supported this actively.

No doubt Royal Dutch Shell followed the same course. It was even more interested in the Russian oil business, because its 1912 purchase of several enterprises in Baku, Grozny, and the Ural region had made

9 Bedford to Hughes, Mar. 10, 1922, ibid., no. 50.   10 Ibid.
11 Bedford to Hughes, May 5, 1922, ibid., no. 63.
12 Hughes to Child, May 4, 1922, ibid., no. 54.
13 Bedford to Hughes, May 5, 1922, ibid., no. 63.

Deterding the second largest owner of Russian oil after Nobel. Deterding was extremely hostile toward the Soviet government, but if the opportunity arose to negotiate an agreement, he was prepared to seize it. When rumors about his maneuvers reached Washington, they were received with indignation. Ambassador Child was instructed to verify them immediately and to report the results of his investigation.[14]

Any British attempt to contact the Soviet delegates outraged the Americans. Long before the Genoa Conference, the Standard Oil representative had visited Krassin, who was negotiating at the time in London. In his dispatch to Moscow, Krassin had written that he thought the Americans were attempting "to play a trick" on their British competitors.[15] One should note that Krassin took skillful advantage of Anglo–American contradictions, although according to the instructions from Lenin his main task was to obtain positive solutions in the negotiations on economic relations between Soviet Russia and the West. This was not an easy task, but the Soviet leadership relied on Krassin's previous business experience.

During the Genoa Conference the office of the Standard Oil Company's Italian affiliate, Italo-Americana, became Ambassador Child's residence, and all diplomatic correspondence went through this office. The head of Standard Oil's Italian affiliate, J. Mowinckel, attended the conference with Child and privately conducted negotiations with Western diplomats.[16] He also met with Krassin, invited him to his villa, and held informal talks on the question of possible Soviet–American negotiations and agreements. During his meeting with Krassin at Genoa, Mowinckel asked him not to conduct any kind of negotiations with the British until the possibility of a Soviet–American agreement had been discussed. Mowinckel expressed the wish that Krassin come to New York for an exchange of views.[17]

Standard Oil paid much attention to its contacts with Krassin, but it underestimated his extraordinary diplomatic ability. Walter Teagle, by then chief figure on the Standard Oil board, also met with Krassin, but the circumstances of their encounter have never been fully revealed. As far as I know, the Soviet archives contain no record of this event, but many files of the Soviet Foreign Office *(Narkomindel)* are still closed to scholars.

14 Hughes to Child, May 2, 1922, ibid., no. 52A.
15 Krassin to Chicherin, May 29 and June 11, 1920, *DVP SSR*, 2:552, 569.
16 Gibb and Knowlton, *Resurgent Years*, 338–9.
17 Bedford to Hughes, May 11, 1922, USDS, RG. 59, file 8363, no. 59.

All that is known about this comes from Gibb, who many years ago began working on a biography of Teagle. He spent a great deal of time with Teagle after the latter's resignation from Standard Oil and interviewed him extensively. As a result, Gibb wrote a book about his life and activities, but after Teagle's death his relatives vetoed the publication of the biography. Several years later, this book was revised and published by Bennett Wall, who became Gibb's coauthor.[18] In this book, the only reference to Krassin is in connection with his meeting with Deterding.[19] Krassin's talks with Teagle are not mentioned. But from my personal correspondence with Dr. Gibb, I have learned some details of the relations between Krassin and Teagle, which were described by the former head of Standard Oil in the interviews with his biographer.

After making an appointment with Krassin, Teagle was confident that his business experience would make it easy for him to get the better of the Soviet "commissar." In his account of the meeting to Gibb, Teagle claimed that he found the Soviet representative "a far cry from the polished European diplomats like Gulbenkian, Deterding, Riedemann, and the rest." The commissar was apparently "somewhat unpolished" and "dressed in a quite incongruous manner."[20]

Compared with the attire of oil magnates, the dress of the Soviet diplomat was no doubt more modest. But those who knew Krassin emphasize that he always comported himself with ease and grace and felt equally comfortable either in business negotiations or at formal receptions, where he was elegantly dressed. Here is the recollection of A. N. Ehrlich, who participated in the Genoa Conference as a Soviet delegate:

Before us stood a tall, well-proportioned man dressed in the European fashion, with a dark complexion and slightly grayish-white face. His energetic movements and speech somehow had an immediate impact on those around him. A small, trimmed, wedge-shaped beard and his graying hair gave him, if you will, the appearance of a businessman.[21]

In truth, Krassin was not only an experienced revolutionary and politician, but also a skillful businessman. However Teagle may have described him, those who met Krassin noted his brilliant knowledge and extraordinary capability. He found a way out of any complicated

---

18 Bennett Wall and George Gibb, *Teagle of Jersey Standard* (New Orleans, 1974).
19 Ibid., 221.   20 Gibb to Fursenko, Sept. 14 and Nov. 5, 1969.
21 S. V. Zarnitskii and L. I. Trofimova, *Sovetskoi strany diplomat* (Moscow, 1958), 150.

situation and possessed a rare sensitivity and quick reactions. Teagle was punished for his self-confidence and snobbishness. "The unpolished Russians," by Teagle's own admission, "held all the trump cards and played with consummate skill. Americans found the negotiations extremely difficult and frustrating." Neither Teagle nor the other representatives of Standard Oil succeeded in bettering the Soviet "commissar" as they wanted. "This was certainly one of the ironies of history," notes Gibb, "because Krassin pretty much made fools out of the Western diplomats who were trying to get a foothold in Russian oil-producing territories."[22]

In working on Teagle's biography, Gibb came to the conclusion that the refusal to recognize Soviet Russia was "an enormous blunder." "Teagle in his last years," writes Gibb, "admitted that this had been one of his greatest blunders." Teagle and his partners at Standard Oil were convinced that "Communism was a transient thing" and "the Bolshevik regime would fall to pieces." "He played a waiting game," writes Gibb, "always expecting that the communist movement in Russia would collapse and that a conservative government would restore to Standard Oil the vast investments in Russia." Shortly before his death, Teagle admitted that the purchase of Nobel's stock "was possibly one of the worst and most expensive mistakes for which he took responsibility."[23]

The obstruction that the oil magnates arranged at the Genoa Conference had a bad effect on the fate of European and international reconstruction. It also harmed the prospects for a Soviet–American dialogue. When the Soviet delegation departed for the Genoa Conference, Lenin had observed that they were going there like merchants, and that their aim was to make agreements on mutually beneficial forms of economic relations. He warned that Soviet Russia would not negotiate on any other terms. "If Messrs. capitalists think that they can procrastinate and that the longer they delay, the greater will be the concessions," said Lenin, "then I repeat, it is necessary to tell them: 'That's enough – tomorrow you will get nothing!'"[24]

In conclusion, let me raise the question of whether there was a real possibility at that time of achieving an agreement between Soviet Russia and the West. It is wholly justified to pose such a question, especially because it was in 1922 that the Rapallo Treaty between Germany and

---

22 Gibb to Fursenko, Sept. 14, 1969.   23 Gibb to Fursenko, Dec. 17 and 30, 1968.
24 V. I. Lenin, *Polnoe sobranie sochinenii,* 45:2, 13.

Russia was concluded. In principle, any other Western country, or all of them together, could have done the same. The opportunity for similar agreements with Soviet Russia did exist. Subsequent developments showed that the chance for rapprochement was lost, although the door had been opened. Only several decades later was an East–West accord, including agreement on European reconstruction, attempted, and, as we have seen, it was attainable.

At Genoa, the door was opened, but it was not used. There is no "if" in history, but had the negotiations ended in a positive solution to the oil problem and some kind of agreement on Soviet–American relations, I have no doubt that these would have favorably influenced the whole process of European reconstruction. I believe there was a real opportunity to solve at least some of the problems on the basis of a reasonable compromise. There were barriers of political animosity and prejudice, but later they were surmountable. This is one of the main lessons of those events for our time. Studying the Genoa Conference and its consequences cannot be considered a purely academic exercise. The lessons of the Genoa Conference are of vital importance to today's European policy. This is why the events connected with the Genoa Conference have not lost their meaning up to the present time.

9

Italy at the Genoa Conference: Italian–Soviet Commercial Relations

GIORGIO PETRACCHI

At nine o'clock on the morning of April 6, 1922, a special three-car-riage train entered the railway station in Genoa. On board was a Soviet delegation of about sixty people, invited to participate in the economic and financial conference that was to convene there. This was the first international meeting since the revolution in which the Russian Soviet Federated Socialist Republic, as it was then called, was to participate.

Sturdy carabinieri wearing three-cornered hats surrounded the sta-tion, and policemen in long black jackets and with whips in their hands patrolled the platform. Nearby, the prefect of Genoa and the general secretary of the conference, Romano Avezanna, were waiting to wel-come their guests according to diplomatic protocol. The conference staff wore the official badge on their arms, a blue silk band with white five-pointed stars.

When Chicherin, wearing a top hat and yellow gloves, descended from the train, one of the journalists made this hurried remark: "By these means the Bolsheviks want to keep up the pretence that bolshe-vism is not poles apart from the European legal order. This is why they make a show of the hats and gloves. Perhaps tomorrow they will show up in tails!"[1]

During the next days, the charming seaside resort of Santa Mar-gherita Ligure, where the Soviet delegation resided, became the scene of a veritable pilgrimage. Hundreds of curious people poured into the eastern Ligurian coast just to see with their own eyes the "new aliens." There was nothing surprising about this, considering the many years of Russian isolation as well as what had been said and written about the Bolsheviks. A massive security operation sealed off the area around the Soviet delegation. A division of carabinieri, public security officers, and

---

1 Quoted from M. Sonkin, *Kljuchi ot bronirovannych komnat* (Moscow, 1970), 298–9.

a group of communist workers who had volunteered to do surveillance service, all attempted to keep onlookers and journalists away.[2]

A few days later, on April 10, 1,254 delegates representing thirty-four countries inaugurated the conference, which is remembered today chiefly for the reentry of revolutionary Russia into the international arena through its conclusion of the Rapallo Treaty with Weimar Germany.

There is general agreement among scholars that the Genoa Conference originated from two sources: the Soviet plan aimed at establishing relations between Moscow and the rest of the capitalist world, and the British project to resume economic relations with Russia in order to recover wider Central European and Eastern markets.[3] France opposed Britain's aim of seeking collaboration with the Soviets. Mainly concerned that the Soviet government acknowledge the czarist debts and compensate or return the assets it had confiscated from former private owners, the French government wanted the Genoa Conference to conclude a debt settlement instead of recognizing the Soviet state.

Italy shared the English line. According to Italian experts, Russia's slender means should not be employed for a "settlement of the past," or to compensate the former owners of assets in Russia. Instead, those resources should be employed for a Russian economic program, in which Italian companies could also participate.[4] The Italian economic world looked forward to the Genoa Conference, confident that, with help from its government, profitable contracts could be drawn up with the Bolsheviks.

After the Cannes Conference, the Italian government appointed four committees charged with the tasks of examining the resumption of relations with Russia, as well as financial, economic, and transport matters. The experts' work was delayed by the fall of the Bonomi government and by the long political crisis of February 1922. Once the first

---

2 The workers came from the most important factories of Genoa (Ansaldo), Milan (Breda), and Turin (FIAT). Cf. N. N. Lyubimov and A. N. Erlikh, *Genuezkaia Konferenciia* (Moscow, 1963), 31. Precautionary measures were strengthened after the arrest on April 18 of the terrorist Boris Savinkov, who had come to Genoa from Constantinople under the cover of being a journalist named Elia Gvozdavo-Golenko. See Prefect of Genoa Poggi to General Director of Public Security Vigliani, Apr. 18, 1922, IACS, Ministero Interno, Direzione Generale di Pubblica Sicurezza, Divisione Affari Generali e Riservati, 1922 (DGPS, DAGR), Coll. A-5, busta 6, N. 169-2/1. It would be worthwhile to examine this episode more closely.

3 See Carole Fink, *The Genoa Conference: European Diplomacy, 1921–1922* (Chapel Hill and London, 1984).

4 Cf. Giorgio Petracchi, *La Russia revoluzionaria nella politica italiana. Le relazioni italo-sovietiche, 1917–1925* (Bari, 1982), 212 ff.

Facta ministry was set up, with Schanzer at the Foreign Office, the experts resumed their activity and presented their reports at the end of March.

The first committee's suggestions were of particular importance. Its members included the engineer Oscar Senigallia, vice-president of the influential Italian League for the Protection of National Interests;[5] Professor Felice Guarnieri, general secretary of the Association of Italian Joint-Stock Companies; the engineer Leopoldo Parodi Delfino; the honorable Gino Olivetti, general secretary of Confindustria; the honorable Ludovico D'Aragona; Dr. Alessandro Schiavi; and the lawyers Natale Rovina and Carmine Cajola, representing the General Confederation of Labor, the National League of Cooperatives, the Italian Confederation of Workers, and the Italian Cooperative Confederation. These experts advised the government to work for a single convention between the Western powers and the RSFSR that would settle these questions: 1) recognition of the Soviet republic; 2) acknowledgment of debts by the Bolsheviks; 3) guarantees for the resumption of trade with Russia; and 4) the basic conditions for the establishment of consulates or official agencies in the RSFSR and for the admission and protection of the contracting parties' citizens in each other's territories. Should this prove impossible to attain, the experts recommended that the Rome government work for a general agreement with the Allies on the essential conditions to be included in all bilateral agreements with Russia.

While avoiding the question of recognition, which it considered of a political nature and thus within the purview of the government, the committee expressed its opinions on several other issues. It recommended that the Soviets should: 1) acknowledge all liabilities contracted before and during the world conflict by the previous government as well as by provincial and municipal authorites; 2) return estates to their former proprietors; 3) allow trading with state organizations as well as with self-governing bodies; 4) afford full juridical validity to contracts and assume liability for the actions of government-controlled authorities who might contravene these contracts in either their letter

---

5 The Italian League was created in Rome on September 20, 1920, by a resolution of the *Associazione Nazionale Trento e Trieste*. Its president, Giovanni Giurati, had served in the D'Annunzio cabinet in Fiume, and later he became Secretary of the Fascist National Party. Mussolini dissolved the League in February 1923. See IMAE, Serie Affari Politici (AP), Italia 1923, busta 1273, fascicolo 5348.

or their spirit; and 5) freely permit imports and exports and undertake to stabilize their customs regime.

The committee also proposed that the Italian government, on its part, should recognize that the RSFSR was entitled to an indemnity for damages suffered at the hands of Western armies during the intervention and concede it most-favored-nation status. It outlined a navigation agreement based on reciprocal freedom of traffic in river and maritime ports as well as a plan for a convention on the exchange of consular agents and the establishment of norms for the status of foreigners in Russia.[6]

The most interesting part of the experts' work consisted of two reports. The first, edited by Confindustria and the Association of Joint-Stock Companies and approved by the entire committee, analyzed the Russian economy sector by sector in order to single out potentialities. In the conclusion, there was a list of Italian interests that existed before the Bolshevik regime. The largest outstanding claims against the Soviet government were from the banking consortia: At the top of the list was Italian Credit, claiming as of December 31, 1920, a total of 28,850,486.55 lire plus accumulated interest, followed by the Banca Italiana di Sconto, which was owed 14,320,243.95 lire plus interest. In addition, FIAT declared that its losses included both its Petrograd branch and some manufacturing patents handed over to a Muscovite financial group headed by Riaboucinski Brothers.[7]

The second report, signed by Olivetti, was confidential and was used exclusively by the delegates at the Genoa Conference. It examined the potential forms of Italian participation in Russian reconstruction. According to the report, the economic readjustment of Russia should

6 On the resumption of economic relations with Russia, see IMAE, Archivio Conferenze (AC), Posizione 52/37-9 (Conferenza di Genova), 12.
7 In 1917, an Italian bank consortium headed by the Credito Italiano had granted the Soviet government a credit of up to 110 million lire for purchasing aircraft and motor parts in Italy. The contract was guaranteed by Russian banks and by a deposit of 110 million lire in Russian Treasury Bonds in the Banca d'Italia. On the expiration date of December 31, 1920, the Italian banks were to be refunded by either the Russian banks or government. FIAT, LANCIA, Itala, Bianchi, Isotta Fraschini, Zust Fabbrica Automobili, Società Ceirano Automobili, and Società Italiana Motori Gnome-Rhone were interested in delivering the parts. When, at the end of 1918, the Russian banks did not fulfill their obligations under the contract, the Italian banks asked the Milan court to sequester the Russian goods still stored in Genoa, which were worth 69.7 million lire. The court consented to the request, and after difficult negotiations involving the banks, the Italian government, and the Soviet representatives in Rome, the creditors were able to recuperate 40.9 million lire. A contract with a volume of 75 million lire, concluded in 1917 to finance the Russian purchase of Italian war materials, had a similar fate. Ibid., 70–1.

begin in those areas and activities that required small investments and promised immediate production.[8]

The economic recovery of Russia depended upon its collaboration with the industrially more advanced countries. Moreover, the powers should pursue "an appropriate division of labor," based on the characteristics of their economy and the geographical position of each country in relation to Russia. For Italy, the Black Sea basin, linked by geography and longstanding economic activity, would be a "natural field of action." "The most profitable area" for Italian intervention was located in a circular area, whose circumference started from and included the Tauride governorship, cut through Ciscaucasia to incorporate the Kuban and the Grozny district, and arrived at the Black Sea around Poti.

This report tackled the problem of guarantees, which were indispensable to make investments if not attractive at least possible. On practical grounds, Olivetti rejected taking control over a part of Russian finances as a guarantee of loans to the Soviet government. He also conceded that economic concessions would be the "most general form of capital investment in Russia," but with the caveat that the "grantee" should be able to exploit concessions in an economically favorable way. Otherwise, these concessions would exist only on paper, and "foreign capital might as well beware of crossing the Soviets' borders."

In its program for Russian development, Olivetti's report mediated skillfully between the two Italian political and economic viewpoints. Some circles advised a slow, gradual penetration of Russia, characterized by a large number of "small businesses" and based on an exchange of manufactured articles for raw materials, in order to give the Soviets the means and opportunity to settle their obligations. On the other hand, Italy's industrial and especially its banking interests presented an opposing "big-business" strategy, looking to Russia in terms of large investments guaranteed by the Italian government, and a capitalist recapture of the Soviet market. The resolution of these two viewpoints involved a political decision; the supporters of small business were favorable to the recognition of the Soviet government, whereas those of big business were hostile, because this would subject them to bonds, guarantees, and conditions. The big-business strategy did not, however,

8 Report, Apr. 17, 1922, Torre Papers, busta 3, fascicolo 10, Segretariato Generale della Conferenza di Genova.

underestimate the possibility of modifying the structure of the Soviet economy.

Italy's political parties split over the Soviet question. The conservative right was unwilling to recognize the government in Moscow; as a prerequisite to resuming normal economic relations, it demanded that precise conditions be placed on the Soviets, requiring them to fulfill their obligations and guarantee investments. On the other hand, the Socialists, Communists, and Popular Party of Don Sturzo, which sent representatives to Genoa, set no preliminary conditions and advocated a general reestablishment of relations between victors and vanquished. The Fascists were "possibilists," with unprejudiced realism claiming for Italy the right to negotiate over all its policies.

Foreign Minister Carlo Schanzer followed "a line of close connections with the right" but was also influenced by his reluctance to fall out of step with Britain. Because Schanzer's behavior throughout the conference reflected his efforts to reconcile these opposing principles, Italian participation appeared feeble and uncertain.[9]

The small-business policy had been anticipated by the reformist Socialists. Before the Genoa Conference, the reformists and some industrialists had set up a committee for Italo–Russian initiatives, consisting of Giovanni Agnelli, Alberto Pirelli, Franco Marinotti, Raimondo Targhetti, Oscar Consulic, Angiolo Cabrini, Emilio Colombino, Ludovico d'Aragona, and Oddino Orgari. On April 26 the reformist Socialist leader Turati held a conversation with Chicherin intended to facilitate commercial arrangements.

During the conference, Italian groups negotiated three preliminary agreements with the Soviet delegates at Genoa. The first reflected the thesis of the small-business faction; the other two tried to implement a system of directing excess Italian labor, which might otherwise be forced to emigrate at random to America, into an agricultural colonization system in Russia. It may be recalled that before World War I, in Kerk in the Crimea, a small agricultural colony called San Nicola had been established, consisting of families from Puglia. Moreover, there were colonies of farmers from Venetia and Lombardy in the northern Caucasus, at Vlodicavkas (today's Ovxiornikize) and at Verbludogorskoj.

The first deal was made on May 23, when the Italian corporation Ernesto Breda signed an option for 200,000 tons of coal in exchange

---

9 Cf. Petracchi, *La Russia rivoluzionaria*, 215–8.

for supplying the Soviets with railway material and agricultural machinery.[10] Although it was evident that Breda was simply bartering some Italian-made machinery for a raw material in which Russia was particularly rich, Lenin himself attached particular importance to the agreement and intervened decisively to bring the talks to a successful result. On May 13, he personally telegraphed the Soviet delegation, instructing them to offer coal to the Italians at a lower price than they were paying elsewhere.[11]

On May 24, a preliminary agreement was concluded that assigned an agricultural concession of 100,000 hectares in the Don governorship, a day's trip from Rostov by train or by horse, to a group headed by Angelo Parodi Delfino. On June 5, the Italian Iron Working Consortia and the Red Cooperatives of Forli were also granted a concession of arable land in the Don governorship.

The agricultural concessions were to last for twenty-four years, with the Soviet government reserving the right to renew them for the same period or revoke them. The concessionaire was allowed to export 50 percent of all production but was to give the Soviet government a percentage estimated at the rate of 15 percent for cereals and 15 to 20 percent for cattle. Also, the Soviet government retained the option of purchasing any remaining product, to be paid for at world market prices in gold rubles, foreign currency, or oil. The concessionaire was granted free import allowances and exempted from customs duties for items considered necessary to get the concession going. He was also granted full freedom in credit transactions with foreign banks. In addition, the concessionaire was permitted to import the necessary manpower, up to 50 percent of the total personnel; and he was allowed to enforce contracts according to Italian practices so long as these were not inferior to local standards in regard to the "interests of workers."

These basic terms of agreement for both agricultural concessions are worth remembering. Although the projects were unsuccessful, they represented ambitious, historically important projects of Italian colonization of Russia and were closely linked with Italy's emigration problem in the post-World War I era. Both the political parties and the government believed that they had found in Russia the solution to an agelong problem. As soon as the Italian press released news of the concession agreement between the Consorzio Cooperativo and represen-

10 IMAE, AP, Russia 1922, busta 1532. The option was signed by Krassin and Guido Sagramoso, Breda's managing director.
11 M. I. Trush, *Vneshnepoliticskaja dejatel'nost V. I. Lenina, 1921–1923.* (Moscow, 1967), 336.

tatives of the Soviet government, many agricultural workers appealed
to the Communist Party to be sent to Russia to work. These workers
were not only attracted by the Soviet mystique but were also hoping to
escape the pressure of the Fascists, who were forcing them to join in
order to keep their jobs.[12] Indeed, when the Soviet government was
finally recognized by Fascist Italy, Mussolini adopted the idea of finding
an outlet in Russia for the waves of Italian migration. By then, the
United States, through the Emergency Quota Act of 1921 and the
Immigration Act of 1924, had virtually closed its borders to Italians.[13]

At the end of April 1922, when everyone realized that the Genoa
Conference was doomed to fail, even the Italian government reclaimed
its freedom of action. On May 24, Ettore Conti, Gino Olivetti, Guido
Jung, and Salvatore Contarini signed a commercial convention with
Chicherin and Krassin, which had been envisaged in the preliminary
Italo–Soviet agreement of December 26, 1921.[14] The Italian negotiators obtained some significant concessions from the Soviets: preferential treatment for citrus-fruit exports, permission to store goods in free
ports on the Black Sea, and most-favored-nation status for goods in
transit, except those to be sent to Persia. They were also granted an oil
concession, which will be discussed later.

This commercial convention was not ratified by the Soviet government because Schanzer, despite the repeated entreaties of the Soviet
delegation, had refused to insert a clause granting de jure recognition.
The Italian foreign minister later explained that after the shock of the
Rapallo Treaty, he did not want to turn his back on the remainder of
Europe by granting political concessions to the Soviets. Indeed, it was
only on condition of this reservation that the Allies had agreed to a separate commercial agreement between Italy and Soviet Russia.[15]

The Soviets, on the other hand, had counted on using Italy to obtain
a second significant political breakthrough and to split the Entente
front. At Genoa, Chicherin and Krassin offered Italy substantial concessions and economic advantages; although they were dropped at that
time, two years later they would become the basis for the commercial
and naval agreements drawn up between the Fascist and Soviet states.

During the years preceding political recognition, contacts between

12 Schanzer Papers, busta 13. In 1923, an influential member of the Italian Communist party,
   Anselmo Marabini, wrote a report on a visit to the Italian settlements. IACS, Ministero
   Interno, DGPS, DAGR, Atti Speciali 1898–1940, busta 10, fascicolo 85.
13 Petracchi, *La Russia rivoluzionaria*, 185.
14 "Convenzione commerciale Italo–Russe," Schanzer Papers, busta 13.
15 Ibid. Schanzer's notes are handwritten.

Italy and the Soviet world were maintained by Franco Marinotti, the future president of Snia Viscosa. With the intuition typical of a businessman, Marinotti revived the idea of "commercial companies" (more precisely, bodies of commercial intermediaries), which would overcome the difficulties of Italian producers in developing adequate promotional activity within the Soviet market. In May 1921, he founded CICE (the Industrial Company for Foreign Trade), which came to represent as many as thirty-four industries in the Soviet market, including FIAT, Pirelli, and Targhetti as well as some two hundred factories and 130,000 workers. This commercial body, which united Italian industry into a virtual monopoly, enabled it to compete with the official Soviet state monopoly for foreign trade.[16]

In 1923, Italy's participation at the Pan-Russian Industrial Exhibition was remarkable. The pavilion erected by CICE was the most impressive of all the foreign ones. On this occasion, FIAT increased its prestige by the victory of Allesandro Cagno, who drove the "510" in the Leningrad–Moscow–Leningrad motor race; FIAT repeated this victory two years later in the Leningrad–Moscow–Tiflis–Moscow motor race, with the "519" models driven by Cagno and Piccin. By 1925, one year after the restoration of diplomatic relations, Italian–Soviet economic exchanges started to take off. As in the prewar period, Russia now became one of Italy's principal suppliers of raw materials, and especially of oil.

The Italian government was highly interested in exploiting the oil fields of the Caucasus. The Anglo–French San Remo convention of April 1920 had practically excluded Italian companies from controlling oil production sources, not only in the Mediterranean but also in the Caucasus. Italy had therefore directed its diplomacy toward eliminating the Anglo–French monopoly, both through efforts in London to revise the San Remo convention and by seeking a direct agreement with the Soviets.

On March 16, 1921, Italian Ambassador Gaetano De Martino had attempted to win Lord Curzon's approval to include Italian enterprises in the Anglo–French oil agreement. The Foreign Office's response was not encouraging. On July 22, 1921, Curzon stated that although the San Remo convention did not exclude cooperation between British and Italian enterprises, any British firm that threatened the interests of soci-

16 See Marinotti's memorandum on his meeting with Mussolini on July 19, 1933, IACS, Segreteria particolare del Duce, busta 98 X R, sottofascicolo 7.

eties already receiving official support would not be eligible for governmental assistance.[17] This ruling, for all practical purposes, excluded the possibility of a British–Italian oil combination; the Anglo–Persian and Royal Dutch Shell companies, already backed by the British government, would continue to control all the Middle Eastern sources of production.

As to demarches with the Soviets, in January 1921 the Italian commercial attaché in London, Francesco Giannini, discussed with Krassin the purchase of a few lots of crude oil. The negotiations proceeded quickly, and on March 14, Krassin announced in a letter to Giannini that a general agreement had been reached. The Rome government undertook to sell to Russia 350 tanker trucks that would be paid for with oil supplies. As a guarantee for the payment, Moscow was to deposit in a Swedish bank a quantity of gold equivalent in lire to the value of the Italian goods; the gold would be returned to the Soviet government in proportion to the value of its fuel deliveries. The Soviet government also declared its willingness to discuss the construction by an Italian group of a refinery at Grozny and an oil pipeline from Grozny to Novorossisk. Nevertheless, the March 14 agreement, despite its secure guarantee of trading tankers for crude oil, became a dead letter. Because of the difficulty in finding the 350 trucks, Italy missed an opportunity to benefit from its concrete initiative.[18]

On the eve of the Genoa Conference, the Italian government had made no progress on the question of oil. It decided to revive the Giannini–Krassin accord and also to tackle the oil matter directly with Lloyd George. Between May 2 and 7, 1922, oil dominated the Genoa Conference and made the atmosphere rather "greasy." The news of an agreement between Deterding, the head of Royal Dutch Shell, and the Soviets exploded like a bomb in Italy. Until then, the press had scarcely dealt with oil nor understood the conflict among London, Paris, and Brussels over article seven in the memorandum presented to the Soviets on May 2, the clause that dealt with compensation of former proprietors of confiscated properties. Suddenly, Italian newspapers probed the subject for an entire week. Industrial associations, political circles, and

17 The Italians attempted to support the British against the Americans in the competition for Russian oil concessions. In exchange they hoped to obtain the advantages the Anglo–French companies enjoyed under the San Remo convention. IMAE, AC, Posizione 52/32 (Conferenza di Genova).
18 Krassin to Giannini, ibid.

the Italian League for the Protection of National Interests all put pressure on the government to free Italy from foreign dominance.

"We cannot bear to repeat at Genoa what happened at San Remo two years ago," wrote the League on May 3 to Schanzer. Prime Minister Facta was urged to make Schanzer act forcefully. The League suggested that the government recognize the Royal Dutch concession in the Caucasus on the condition that Schanzer wrench from Lloyd George the promise of Italian participation or collaboration in the proposed concession. If he could not, then Italy must protest the British oil monopoly in Russia and proceed to secure and exploit its own concessions.[19] The nationalists favored independent exploitation of the Caucasus oil wells. On the other hand, the free traders represented by the *Corriere della Sera* advocated assigning the Caucasus fields to the International Consortium, in which Italy would participate.

The League represented that part of Italian opinion that desired a radical solution to the energy-supply problem. It pressed for an official state body to act as the principal instrument of Italian oil policy. Only such a body could reduce Italy's "dangerous servitude" toward the major oil companies and their Italian branches, which maintained price ceilings and market control. Although the idea of creating a national petroleum body was not original, the new component was the League's pressure on the government.

Exposed to these various strong pressures, Schanzer moved in three directions. First, he attempted to obtain guarantees from Lloyd George on the entry of Italian firms into the Middle East and the Caucasus. During a conversation with the British prime minister on May 4, he referred to oil collaboration by asking for "a little assistance in these

---

19 In 1920–1, three syndicates that were particularly interested in exploiting Soviet oil resources were established: the Consorzio Utenti Nafta Società Anonima (CUNSA), the Sindicato Imprese Provviste Minerali (SIPOM), and the Società Mineraria Italo-Belga di Georgia. CUNSA was founded in Turin in August 1920 with a capital of 34 million lire and with the support of the Italian Admiralty. Among its shareholders were FIAT and Pirelli. Its purpose was to import naphtha for a group of Italian companies, but until 1922 it made very few transactions. The first published balance sheet showed a deficit of 2 million lire, but according to a report of the Direzione Generale di Pubblica Sicurezza, the "real losses" were "several millions more." CUNSA's Amministratore Delegato Gadda, a relative of Senator Ettore Conti, was the principal negotiator of the Italo–Russian agreement of May 24, 1922. SIPOM was created in Rome in December 1920 with a task similar to that of CUNSA but with less capital. Its president was Di Scalea and its chairman Gian Battista Antonelli. The early history of the Società Mineraria Italo-Belga di Georgia, founded in Turin in 1921, is poorly documented. For the activities of CUNSA and SIPOM, see the report of May 9, 1922, IACS, Ministero Interno, DGPS, DAGR, 1922, Coll. A-5, busta 6.

questions concerning Italy,"[20] and took one step further by asking for a revision of the San Remo convention. Replying with a personal letter, Lloyd George expressed the British point of view stated a year earlier by Lord Curzon, which was neither hostile nor very encouraging toward Italy's requests.[21]

Schanzer's second initiative was directed toward Krassin. During the negotiations for the failed commercial agreement, he asked for some oil concessions, whereupon Italy was granted a "fair interest" in the oil field of Bibi-Eibat, near Baku.[22] Finally, he also attempted to obtain control over the few oil fields available in Galicia and reinforced this action with negotiations aimed at obtaining crude oil supplies directly from the governments in Moscow and Warsaw.

The Fascist government would at least temporarily solve Italy's oil-supply problem, which had been raised at the Genoa Conference. When AGIP, an entity created with state participation in 1926, found in Soviet Russia a source of supply independent of international trusts, the price of petrol in Italy decreased remarkably for the next two years. A joint Italian–Soviet company, PETROLEX, which used distribution plants in Italy, was created in 1927. Until the early 1930s, the Italian Navy secured almost all of its oil supplies from the Soviet Union.[23]

---

20 *DBFP* 19:728.
21 Lloyd George to Schanzer, May 17, 1922, IAME, AC, Posizione 52/105-4 (Conferenza di Genova).
22 For the negotiations on the Italo–Russian commercial agreement, see IMAE, AC, Posizione 52/37-37 (Conferenza di Genova).
23 Petracchi, *La Russia rivoluzionaria,* 248–52.

10

The European Policy of Czechoslovakia on the Eve of the Genoa Conference of 1922

FRANK HADLER

"The historian of European politics will have to dwell seriously on the Genoa Conference," said Edouard Beneš in a speech to the Czechoslovak National Assembly four days after the end of the conference.[1] Thereby the head of government and foreign minister of the First Republic referred not simply to the immediate results of the Genoa Conference but also to the fact that this meeting of the major political leaders of thirty-four governments, including Soviet Russia and Germany, which had lasted six weeks, had been the "first international expression of the political and economic community of Europe" after World War I.[2] This evaluation has survived for almost seven decades, as witnessed by Carole Fink's work published in 1984.[3] There is little to add to this monograph, which draws on the materials of all the important archives of Western Europe and the United States. Nevertheless, this contribution will describe the events preceding the Genoa Conference from the viewpoint of Czechoslovakia on the basis of sources little used up to now.[4]

At the end of 1921, Europe was in crisis. The conflicts of interest between the European Great Powers, France and Great Britain, which had burst open during the peace negotiations at Paris, began to endan-

1 Speech to the Plenary Session on May 23, 1922, quoted in Edouard Beneš, *Problémy nové Evropy a zahraniční politika Československa. Projevy a úvahy z r. 1919–1924* (Prague, 1924), 192.
2 Ibid., 191.
3 Carole Fink, *The Genoa Conference: European Diplomacy, 1921–1922* (Chapel Hill and London, 1984).
4 In the archives of the Foreign Ministry of the ČSSR in Prague (CAMZV) there are twelve volumes on the Genoa Conference, entitled "Janov 1922." Scarcely any materials contained in them have appeared in the literature up to now. Other documentary materials from CAMZV, in particular legation reports, have been referred to in: Věra Olivová, "Postoj československé buržoasie k Sovětskemu svazu v době jednání o prazatímní smlouvu z roku 1922," *Československý Casopis Historický* 3 (1953):294–323; Alena Gajanová, "La politique extérieure tchécoslovaque et la 'question russe' à la Conférence de Gênes," *Historica* 8 (1964):135–76; Vladimír Soják, ed., *O československé zahraniční politice, 1918–1939*, Sbornik statí (Prague, 1956).

171

ger the guarantee mechanisms of the Versailles system even before they were firmly established. The clarification of such important questions as the affiliation and inclusion of Soviet Russia and Germany in the postwar economic order was still pending when the leaders of the major European powers traveled for the first time to the United States in November 1921. At the Naval Disarmament Conference in Washington decisions were made about the postwar regulation of the Pacific and the Far East.[5] In response to the economic crisis that had affected the victors as much as the defeated states – unemployment and inflation were the order of the day – British Prime Minister David Lloyd George made an effort to expand the program of the Washington Conference to deal with the economic consolidation of Europe. Such a proposal was brought forward by the Belgians in the middle of December, but it encountered such a "cool" reception in Washington "that it was dropped at once, and the project of a European economic conference began."[6] One important result of the active European policy of Woodrow Wilson was that the United States had become a major creditor of France and Britain;[7] under his successor, Warren G. Harding, the "Pacific-first" orientation became increasingly dominant in American foreign policy. Washington's obvious indifference toward the reconstruction of Europe marked the beginning of a type of isolationism: Postwar Europe was again left to its own resources.

In Prague, this development was observed with great concern. As a successor state dependent on the preservation of the status quo created by the Paris Peace Treaties, the first Czechoslovak Republic was extremely interested in maintaining concerted action by the Great Powers toward Europe. Increasing differences, especially between France and Great Britain, had induced Beneš, who was both prime minister and foreign minister, to journey to Paris, London, and Rome for several weeks in the spring of 1921. Without adhering to the position taken north or south of the Channel, he declared to the Senate after his return on March 8: "Intimate cooperation with France and Britain is the *conditio sine qua non* of our entire policy."[8] This evaluation was unchanged in Prague at the end of 1921. Beneš's response to the events

---

5 The Washington conference began on November 12, 1921; European questions are dealt with in Fink, *Genoa Conference*, 24–30.

6 Henry W. Steed, *Třicet let novinářem, 1892–1922. Vzpomínky*, vol. 2 (Prague, 1929), 364.

7 In 1922, England's debt amounted to $4.221 billion and France's to $3.404 billion (American billion). Fritz Klein, *Die diplomatischen Beziehungen Deutschlands zur Sowjetunion, 1917–1932* (Berlin, 1953), 121.

8 Státní Ústřední Archiv Prague (SÚA), MZV-VA, 1485, kart. 2826, projevy E. Beneše.

in Washington was reflected in his article in the *Prager Presse* on December 25.[9] In view of the "international economic crisis" and the strongly diverging economic interests of the European countries, the Czechoslovak leader expressed doubt about the success of an international conference. However, at the same time he underlined the necessity of working for the reconstruction of Europe. He foresaw problems in the growing refusal to grant most-favored-nation status, in the rejection of long-term commercial treaties, and in the widespread tendency toward economic nationalism. Beneš's reservations about holding an international economic conference for the reconstruction of Europe were not based exclusively on these symptoms of disintegration. He also regarded the "circumstances in two major states, Germany and Russia," as considerable obstacles to international economic negotiations. He understood that Germany's efforts to obtain reparations relief would be construed as catastrophic by the French. As to Soviet Russia, the foreign minister insisted that the country would for some time need "help without offering any prospect of return or repayment." The proposed economic conference would merely confirm these facts. Beneš doubted the possibility of organizing the necessary international relief.

Following the termination of the Entente's blockade of Soviet Russia in January 1920, Czechoslovak foreign policy had increasingly viewed Moscow, despite its Bolshevik government, as a great power, although Beneš declared in May 1920 that "for the foreseeable future European politics will proceed without it."[10] After several months of discussion in the Foreign Affairs Committee of the Chamber of Deputies, it was decided no longer to avoid negotiations with Moscow.[11] With the mutual establishment of trade missions, this new course of Czechoslovak foreign policy was put into practice.[12]

The Prague government increasingly recognized the importance of the Russian factor for the economic consolidation of Europe. Following London, not Paris, Beneš in his article in the *Prager Presse* at the end of 1921 affirmed the necessity of integrating Russia into the efforts for international reconstruction. He also referred to the fact that with the NEP, the Bolsheviks had acknowledged that their country would not be able to escape its desperate situation without a "new, constructive

9 *Prager Presse*, Dec. 25, 1921; also published in Beneš, *Problémy nové Evropy*, 157–64.
10 Report on the political situation, May 24, 1920, CAMZV, PZ, Paris, 1920, č. 158a.
11 Věra Olivová, "Die russische Linie der tschechoslowakischen Aussenpolitik, 1918–1938," in *Die Entstehung der Tschechoslowakischen Republik und ihre international-politische Stellung. Zum 50. Gründungsjubiläum der ČSR* (Prague, 1968), 169.
12 The trade missions were opened in Prague (June 14, 1921) and in Moscow (Oct. 10, 1921).

economic policy." But in order to create an "atmosphere of international rapprochement, from which there would be only one step to a real, common international relief action,"[13] Beneš outlined an alternative to the economic conference that had been decided upon by an Anglo–French agreement that month in London, and which would be convened the next month in Cannes. He proposed concrete diplomatic steps to be taken by individual states to resume former contacts, remove conflicts, enter into trade treaties, intensify international communication, and reduce isolation. The Czechoslovak foreign minister set conditions for relief efforts for Soviet Russia, which shortly afterward would be echoed in the French preparations for the Genoa Conference: recognition of international law, czarist obligations, individual property rights, and the rights of foreign nationals, as well as a willingness to conclude "normal," and particularly commercial, treaties.[14] Although Beneš equated the fulfillment of these conditions with the "capitulation" of the Soviet regime to the rest of Europe, he also indicated that "reasonable elements (i.e., Lenin) in the Soviet government know this, do not conceal it, and shift the world revolution twenty years forward."[15] In Beneš's opinion, Europe was now faced with the important question of "whether it was time to commence an active policy toward Russia or to delay still further."[16] Since Britain, the United States, and even Germany were already embarking on economic activities on the basis of the opportunities offered by the NEP, the Czechoslovak leader warned that his country must do everything possible to avoid being "too late." Beneš, whose longstanding policy of military nonintervention had ultimately been adopted by the Allies, now proposed that "generous economic intervention" would be the only means of achieving the main goal of European reconstruction: "to open Russia for Europe."

Contrary to the interpretations of Czechoslovak historians in the 1950s, this "economic intervention" was not simply a new version of an aggressive anti-Soviet policy.[17] It was based on the following assessment:

Nowadays, the serious observer of conditions in Russia is less concerned with whether the Soviet regime will fall or not, whether Lenin and Trotsky will remain at the helm or not, or whether things will move faster or slower to the right. Today we have moved much further. Today, in the interests of millions

13 Beneš, *Problémy nové Evropy*, 160.   14 Ibid.   15 Ibid., 161.   16 Ibid.
17 Overemphasis of anti-Sovietism especially in Soják, *O československé zahraniční politice*, 98–111.

of starving people, we have risen above these matters and want to place all of Russia in the realm of world politics and in world economic cooperation. From the moment that we embark on a common effort, all these controversial issues of regime and personalities will be quietly settled by themselves.[18]

Nevertheless, according to Beneš, only an international economic conference, with a nonideological framework, had a real chance of success.

Prague was not informed of the plan worked out in London by Lloyd George and Briand to hold a conference in January 1922 in Cannes on European economic questions.[19] The six resolutions passed at Cannes,[20] and the prospect of an international economic conference that included Germany and Soviet Russia, raised serious questions for Beneš; the impending conference moved abruptly to the center of Czechoslovak foreign policy. On January 6, 1922, Jan Masaryk telegraphed from London: "People are saying that the Prime Minister [Beneš] will invite the international conference for European reconstruction to Prague."[21] A day later he communicated the information that France supported Prague as the conference site, but Italy favored Genoa.[22] Beneš, who had obviously not expected such an interpretation of his *Prager Presse* comments, cabled his emissaries in London and Paris on January 9 that because "it is not in our interest that the conference take place in Prague," they "not promote this course."[23]

Nevertheless, Czechoslovakia's participation in the preparatory work of the Genoa Conference was considered extremely significant. President Thomas Masaryk, who was ill at the moment, was not involved. Beneš, though lacking "great hopes for the results of the conference," was firmly resolved to take an active part in its preparation and implementation. Any other course would have isolated Czechoslovakia diplomatically. He stated the direction of his foreign policy in a circular letter to the missions abroad on January 13, 1922. He started with the "Russian question": "I regard it as a great mistake to press for the de jure recognition of the Soviets, particularly through the convocation of an international conference at Cannes." The "correct tactics" should instead involve "slow action," taking account of the anti-Bolshevik standpoint and making gradual political, diplomatic, legal, and

18 Beneš, *Problémy nové Evropy,* 162.   19 Soják, *O československé zahraniční politice,* 102.
  20 *Material über die Konferenz von Genua* (Berlin, 1922), 7.
  21 J. Masaryk to Beneš, London, Jan. 6, 1922, CAMZV, PZ, London 1922, č. 3.
  22 J. Masaryk to Beneš, London, Jan. 7, 1922, ibid., č. 4.
  23 Beneš to Osusky (Paris) and Mastny (London), Prague, Jan. 9, 1922, ibid., č. 6.

economic concessions to the present Russian regime. His third point was that a European conference, "as proposed in Cannes, will produce not clarification but confusion. . . . A quick and immediate recognition of the Soviets will only complicate conditions in Europe, because we are not prepared for this, especially in view of the internal politics of individual states." Against the background of postwar Europe's disastrous economic situation, the Czech leader feared the political radicalization that would result from the strengthening of leftist forces by the international recognition of the Soviet government.[24] Beneš was no doubt concerned specifically about Czechoslovakia, which had had a Communist party since May 1921.[25]

According to Beneš, there was a practical way to deal with the Russian question: "a) first, an agreement between the Great Powers, Czechoslovakia, Poland, Yugoslavia, and Romania over common policy and tactics toward Russia; b) after political principles were agreed upon, an agreement over the division of common tasks; c) an orientation of everything on an economic basis, which would encourage Russia to move politically toward the right." Finally, Beneš informed the foreign missions that if a European conference took place, the Prague government would participate, but he considered the venture "a mistake, especially . . . when presented to the public as it was in Cannes."

On January 16, Bararo, the Italian *chargé d'affaires* in Prague, handed Beneš the invitation from Foreign Minister Marquis della Torretta to participate in the economic and financial conference.[26] Afterward, the question of the international economic conference moved temporarily to the background of Czechoslovak foreign policy. The foremost issue was Czechoslovakia's relations with Austria. In December 1921 a Czechoslovak–Austrian agreement had been signed at the country residence of President Masaryk in Lany near Prague.[27] This event signified the Prague government's affirmation that, contrary to widespread opinion and to the conviction in Vienna, the Austrian state was completely viable politically and economically, even if it was urgently in need of international assistance. Because of the *Anschluss* movement stimulated

24 Beneš circular, Prague, Jan. 13, 1922, CAMZV, PZ, Vienna 1922, č. 5.
25 On the founding of the Communist party of Czechoslovakia, see Jan Galandauer, *Od Hainfeldu ke vzniku KSČ. České dělnické hnutí v letech, 1889–1921* (Prague, 1986).
26 Invitation, with the six Cannes Resolutions, CAMZV, Cabinet Ministry (KBM), věcné, kart. 15, konference, obal Janov.
27 The treaty was signed during the meeting of Presidents Masaryk and Hainisch on December 15 and 16, 1921. For background, see Věra Olivová, "K historii československo-rakouské smlouvy z roku 1921," *Československý Časopis Historický* 9, no. 2 (1961):198–219.

by Austria's mounting economic crisis,[28] Prague had undertaken an active policy aimed at the economic rehabilitation of its southern neighbor.

This consideration had a significant impact on Czechoslovakia's attitude toward the Genoa Conference. As a follow-up to the Lany treaty, negotiations between the Austrian and Czechoslovak finance ministers, Gürtler and Novák, began in Prague on January 22, 1922.[29] As envisioned in his *Prager Presse* article, Beneš was creating an alternative to a European economic conference, with concrete steps toward establishing an "atmosphere for European rapprochement." Though aware of Lloyd George's doubts concerning Austria's ability to survive,[30] on February 2 Beneš notified his minister in London: "You may announce that it is possible to save Austria, that we believe in it, and shall lend money to it. This week we shall formally offer Austria a loan of more than 500 millions, which we shall translate into action after we secure our own credits abroad. Please pass on the information confidentially that France is ready to act with us in helping Austria in the manner we have proposed."[31] Two weeks later, Jan Masaryk reported that a credit of 5 million pounds could be raised in London.[32] Later, during his trip to Paris and London, Beneš negotiated about the credit for Austria.[33]

These developments were followed attentively by the German Foreign Office. According to the charming description of the Czechoslovak–Austrian rapprochement by the German representative in Vienna, "the well-behaved Austrian child has received a *Zuckertüte* from its godfather . . . because it has obediently shaken hands with its sister, Czechoslovakia, instead of reaching for mother Germania's apron."[34]

---

28 Cf. Lájos Kerekes, *Von St. Germain bis Genf. Oesterreich und seine Nachbarn, 1918–1922* (Vienna, Cologne, Graz, 1979).

29 Cf. final protocol of negotiations from January 22 to February 8, 1922, in Prague in the enclosure to the report of the minister of finance to the Foreign Ministry, Prague, Feb. 8, 1922, Archiv Ústavu marxismu-leninismu (AÚML), Benešův Archiv (BA), Rakousko 1922, sl. 1.

30 Jan Masaryk had telegraphed that "Lloyd George took a negative view toward an Austrian loan. He doubted that Austria could be saved." J. Masaryk to Beneš, London, Feb. 1, 1922, CAMZV, PZ London 1922, č. 33.

31 Telegram, Beneš, Prague, Feb. 2, 1922, ibid., č. 34. A few days later, Beneš informed the Czechoslovak Embassy in Vienna that the loan could possibly be increased even to one billion. He regarded this "as indispensable for Austria and for the restoration of the economic situation in Central Europe." Without coordinated action by Britain and France, which he hoped would be organized by the League of Nations, this action would not be sufficient. Telegram, Beneš, Prague, Feb. 6, 1922, CAMZV, PZ Vienna 1922, č. 15.

32 Telegram, J. Masaryk, London, Feb. 18, 1922, CAMZV, PZ, London 1922, č. 60.

33 Cf. Telegram Beneš, Paris, Feb. 15, 1922, CAMZV, KBM, věcné, kart. 56, správa veřejná.

34 Report by Pfeiffer, Vienna, Feb. 14, 1922, Zentrales Staatsarchiv, Potsdam, Auswärtiges Amt, 43139, Bl. 33.

The fact that the Cannes Conference had taken place without the Entente's small allies, just after Italy in September 1921 had thwarted Czechoslovakia's mediation efforts between Austria and Hungary over the Burgenland,[35] provided Beneš with additional proof of the necessity to emphasize his state's importance in European affairs through steps like the loan attempts for Vienna. Two days after he received the invitation to the Genoa Conference, Beneš announced to the Foreign Affairs Committee of the Parliament that his foreign policy was "neither a French, nor a British, nor a German, nor a Russian of either today's Soviet or any other one, but only our Czechoslovak policy."[36] The thesis that Beneš at this time had embarked on a form of solo venture is supported not only by the credit action on behalf of Austria but also by the fact that the Little Entente had not been included in this phase of the planning of Czechoslovakia's foreign policy. Beneš was conscious of the fact that it would be difficult to win over Belgrade and Bucharest for his constructive "Russian policy."[37]

After being informed by Ambassador Osusky in Paris of the contents of a note from Poincaré to Lord Curzon, which among other things indicated that the Quai d'Orsay was considering the possibility of not attending the Genoa meeting,[38] Beneš began to alter his attitude toward the conference. He recognized an opportunity to profit from the dissension that had erupted between the two Great Powers after Cannes and to promote Czechoslovakia's interests by functioning as mediator, particularly in regard to the Russian question. Czechoslovak opinions on conditions in Soviet Russia were highly regarded, as witnessed in January 1922 by the request for information sent by U.S. Secretary of Commerce Herbert Hoover to President Masaryk.[39] In the League of Nations, a Czech member of the secretariat, Vladimir Slavik, functioned as an expert advisor on Russian affairs.

Beneš's revived interest in the Genoa Conference was not only a result of Paris's adoption of a similar policy toward Russia. There was also point 8 of Poincaré's note to London, which called for participa-

---

35 Cf. Stefan Malfèr, "Das Venediger Protokoll vom 13. Oktober 1921 und die politischen Parteien in Oesterreich," *Oesterreichische Osthefte* 23 (1981):184–6.

36 SÚA, MZV-VA, 2823, Projevy E. Beneše, zahraniční výbor, Jan. 18, 1922.

37 Cf. A. Gajanová, *ČSR a středoevropska politika velmocí (1918–1938)* (Prague, 1967), 103. As Gajanová emphasizes, Yugoslavia pursued a generally anti-Soviet policy, while the tensions between Bucharest and Moscow were due primarily to the Bessarabian question.

38 Osuský to Beneš, Paris, Feb. 9, 1922, CAMZV, II. sekce, konference, kart. 165.

39 Cf. Soják, *O československé zahraniční politice,* 103.

tion of the Little Entente as well as the activation of Polish diplomacy on the eve of the conference. On February 10, Maxa, the Czech envoy in Warsaw, wrote: "In local political and economic circles there are indications of strong interest in cooperating with us at Genoa."[40] Maxa also reported that Karachan, the Soviet representative in the Polish capital, had proposed a preliminary agreement between Czechoslovakia, Poland, Yugoslavia, and Soviet Russia before the Genoa Conference. European diplomacy was moving swiftly. Czechoslovakia had either to take part or lose its claim to be an active participant in European questions.

Beneš traveled to Paris, where on February 13 he met with Poincaré. Joined by Finance Minister Charles de Lasteyrie, they discussed the Russian question in the context of the preparations for Genoa. At the Quai d'Orsay, Beneš's long talk with Jacques Seydoux, the head of the Commercial Department, encompassed "all the financial and economic questions which were to be discussed at the Genoa Conference; mutual agreement on all issues was obtained."[41] In addition to his official accounts, Beneš sent reports directly to President Masaryk.[42] These indicate that the Czechoslovak prime minister found the situation in Paris "essentially unstable, but not disastrous. . . . In Russian affairs Poincaré agreed with me, and France will undoubtedly alter its policy. On German questions it was more difficult."

As to Franco–British relations, Beneš drew the impression from Paris that there would be an agreement. Moreover, he accentuated France's positive attitude toward Czechoslovakia, as witnessed by the Quai d'Orsay's agreement that the Prague government participate in the work of the Allied preparatory commission for the Genoa Conference. Beneš ascribed particular importance to the fact that Seydoux, the "organizer of the preparatory work for Genoa," "fully accepted" his proposals for resuming economic relations with Soviet Russia as well as for a more moderate policy toward Germany.

On the other hand, his talks the next day with the French president dampened the optimism of the Czechoslovak government leader: "The negotiations with Millerand [were] more difficult. He agrees with moderation toward Germany but refuses to hear anything about an

---

40 Telegram, Maxa, Warsaw, Feb. 10, 1922, CAMZV, II. sekce, konference, kart. 165.
41 Report of the Czechoslovak Embassy, Paris, Feb. 13, 1922, CAMZV, KBM, věcné, kart. 56, správa veřejná.
42 Beneš to Masaryk, Paris, Feb. 13, 1922, ibid.

agreement with Russia."[43] Beneš again defended the basic German and Russian elements of Czechoslovak foreign policy, which he had formulated in December 1921, but he was forced to admit that in Paris "there were not many people who see things clearly." There was little prospect of an agreement between the Allied powers before Genoa.

In view of this situation, Beneš, shortly before his trip to London, made an arrangement with the Italian ambassador, Bonin-Longere, to visit Rome. It is especially noteworthy that up to this moment Beneš had attached far less importance to the Little Entente than he would at Genoa. Only at the end of his Paris conversations did the Czechoslovak foreign minister in his multilateral reflections bring the triple alliance into a concrete relationship with the Genoa Conference.[44]

In his report, Beneš commenced with assessments of the state of Franco–British and Franco–German relations, the question of Bolshevik participation in Genoa, the recognition of the Soviet regime, and the attitude of the United States toward Europe, and then listed eight points that required "clarification and explanation" by the Allies before the Genoa Conference. At the top of the list was that Czechoslovakia, "which had organized the Little Entente, was to play a significant role in establishing order in Central Europe." Further, Prague was aligning itself with Poland and helping Austria. Czechoslovakia had also conducted a positive policy on the Russian question, consisting of "strict nonintervention and restraint toward official Moscow" as well as private relief efforts. He gave special emphasis to the internal consolidation of Czechoslovakia, stating: "As a result of our policies, our communism has been largely tamed and is now virtually harmless." Finally, he wanted to call the Great Powers' attention to the fact that "out of the new states at least one should, as soon as possible, be completely consolidated." As the "cultural and geographical center of a large zone of small nations and states," Czechoslovakia was the likely candidate for this role in the interest of all of Europe.[45]

In London, Beneš was able to complete his picture of the attitude of the Great Powers toward the economic consolidation of Europe.

---

43 Beneš to T. G. Masaryk, Paris, undated (Feb. 14, 1922), ibid. On February 15, 1922, he informed Ambassador Tusar in Berlin about his talk with Millerand: "Toward Germany he is already more moderate. . . . In Russian affairs, Millerand refuses to get involved, and he is against opening negotiations with the Soviets," CAMZV, KBM, věcné, kart. 56, správa veřejná.

44 Beneš to Czechoslovak embassy in Rome, Paris, Feb. 15, 1922, ibid., in which Beneš also asked for a meeting with Yugoslav Foreign Minister Ninčić, which took place in Bratislava on March 2, 1922.

45 K janovské konference, Feb. 15, 1922, CAMZV, KBM, věcné, kart. 15, konference.

Between February 17 and 19 he held discussions with Lord Curzon and with Arthur James Balfour and met twice with Lloyd George. He learned that the indispensable agreement between Paris and London, which he termed the "international authority" for postwar Europe,[46] would be extremely difficult to obtain. As the leading statesman of a country whose existence was largely dependent on the system established by the Great Powers in the Paris Peace Treaties, Beneš was exceptionally interested in functioning as a mediator. There is evidence of the results of his efforts in London in two extremely optimistic press reports[47] as well as in his private telegrams. On February 21, he wrote: "Negotiated with Lloyd George: 1) The Genoa Conference will be postponed until the end of March. 2) The peace treaties will not be discussed. 3) Reparations will not be discussed. 4) The Little Entente will take a semi-official role in the preparations in London. 5) The League of Nations will be consulted. 6) Although participating in the conference, the Bolsheviks will not be granted de jure recognition; the question of recognition will depend on the results of the work. 7) There will be an attempt to formulate a European nonaggression pact. Lloyd George has asked me to present these points to Poincaré as a basis for a compromise between England and France."[48] The last sentence is obviously an amplification of a message he had sent earlier to Paris on February 19: "I have information [*vzkaz*] from Lloyd George for Poincaré." Beneš stressed the urgency of his being able to speak with the French premier on the very day of his return (February 20) to Paris.[49]

There is no indication in the Czech documents about the Quai d'Orsay's reaction to Beneš's reports from London. What is certain is that the British prime minister crossed the Channel on February 25 and met Poincaré at Boulogne-sur-Mer to discuss their existing differences over Genoa.[50] Boulogne was undoubtedly the result of Beneš's mediation. However, whether or not the Franco–British summit meeting was due solely to the Czechoslovak prime minister's initiative, as Soviet Foreign Minister Chicherin asserted on March 21,[51] cannot be answered defin-

---

46 Ibid.
47 Cf. press reports Feb. 19, 1922, from London and Feb. 22, 1922, from Paris, CAMZV, KBM, věcné, kart. 56, správa veřejná, which include the statement that a "complete agreement was achieved. . . . All questions are settled and the standpoint was exactly formulated."
48 Beneš to the Czechoslovak Embassy in London, Paris, Feb. 21, 1922, CAMZV, PZ, London, č. 70.
49 Beneš to the Czechoslovak Embassy in Paris, London, Feb. 19, 1922, CAMZV, KBM, věcné, kart. 56, správa veřejná.
50 Fink, *Genoa Conference,* 79.
51 Cf. report J. Girsa, Moscow, Mar. 21, 1922, CAMZV, Janov 1922, spis 128.

itively on the basis of the sources available for this study. Beneš never commented on this subject again.

Nevertheless, he was not dissatisfied with the results of his Paris and London negotiations. To be sure, he no longer felt it necessary to travel to Rome.[52] Also, he was in no hurry to commence the discussions with the Little Entente that had been scheduled to take place in Belgrade.[53] Both of these facts indicate that on Beneš's return from Paris and London the Prague government considered that Czechoslovak interests had been fully taken into account in the preparations for the Genoa Conference.

During the final weeks before the conference there were increased contacts between Czechoslovak diplomats and foreign figures, who for the first time since World War I were to be represented in an international forum. As early as February 18 there were talks in Berlin between Ambassador Tusar and Karl Radek. The Comintern delegate stated: "The Soviet government would welcome a Czechoslovak–Russian agreement even before the opening of the Genoa Conference which would delineate the role [*uloha*] which the Republic . . . wishes to reserve for itself in the future reconstruction of Russia."[54] In the middle of March, in response to attacks by the Soviet press against his active role in the preliminaries to the Genoa Conference,[55] Beneš instructed Jaroslav Girsa, the head of the Czechoslovak Trade Mission, to inform Chicherin personally that the Prague government had in fact urged Paris and London to expedite the resumption of "economic and trade relations between Europe and Russia." He denied Moscow's accusations that it was he who had proposed a six-month waiting period for

52 There were at least three reasons not to go to Rome: 1) the rapprochement had been achieved; 2) Belgrade was opposed to close relations between Prague and Rome (see Ninčić to Beneš, Belgrade, Feb. 21, 1922, CAMZV, KBM, věcné, kart. 56, správa veřejná, drawing attention to Italian aggressiveness); and 3) in view of the tense domestic situation caused by a general strike of miners (February 3–10, 1922), Beneš as prime minister had a compelling obligation to return to Prague.

53 Beneš even considered delaying the meeting of the Little Entente until a few days before the conference. Beneš to the Czechoslovak embassy in Bucharest, London, Feb. 18, 1922, CAMZV, KBM, věcné, kart. 56, správa veřejná. One reason for his hesitation was no doubt his disagreement with Bucharest and Belgrade over Poland's participation: Gajanová, *ČSR a velmoci,* 104, n. 126.

54 Report, Tusar, Berlin, Feb. 18, 1922, CAMZV, PZ, Berlin, č. 24. The seriousness of this offer was minimized by Soviet Foreign Minister Chicherin in the beginning of April, when in a talk with Tusar he said that Radek "is a private man; neither he [Chicherin] nor the government assumes responsibility for his statements." Chicherin added that Radek's statements were not always appropriate. Tusar to Beneš, Berlin, Apr. 4, 1922, CAMZV, Tusar Papers, úřední korespondence.

55 Report J. Girsa, Moscow, Feb. 27, 1922, CAMZV, II. sekce, konference, kart. 165.

the recognition of the Soviet regime.[56] When Chicherin received Girsa on March 21, he blamed Beneš for Britain's retreat from the conciliation policy that had begun with the trade treaty of March 16, 1921, and for London's adherence to the French line. The People's Commissar nevertheless admired Beneš as a politician who "through his influence and stature was capable of achieving the political and economic rapprochement of Russia and Europe."[57]

During the month of March in Prague, there were deliberations on a statute to establish consular missions in Soviet Russia based on a report from the trade mission in Moscow and also on information from the state police.[58] The draft of March 3 indicates that the underlying hindrance to instituting economic relations lay in the two disparate legal systems.[59] Without concessions by the Soviet government on the question of legal guarantees, the Prague government considered it very difficult to restore "normal" contacts between a "communist" system and a system "based on the principle of private property." But one effort had worked: the Anglo–Soviet trade agreement of March 1921. Beneš, who in December 1921 had warned against being "too late" in the impending integration of Soviet Russia into the European economic system, was therefore prepared to consider the transformation of the "ad hoc mission" to full consular status. To avoid any suspicion that this step amounted to a "de facto recognition of the Soviet government," Prague hoped to extract "concessions" from Moscow in the form of enlarging the authority of the Czechoslovak consulate, particularly in legal questions. These deliberations on the question of recognition were expanded during the course of the Genoa Conference and led, in the beginning of June 1922, to the conclusion of the first Czechoslovak–Soviet trade agreement.

Czechoslovak foreign policy was also concerned with the German role at the Genoa Conference. On March 16, Tusar met with Foreign Minister Walther Rathenau, who declared that Germany would go to Genoa despite the exclusion of the reparations question.[60] In response to Beneš's mediation offer, Rathenau stated that he would prefer to

---

56 Telegram, V. Girsa to J. Girsa, Prague, Mar. 16, 1922, ibid.
57 Report, J. Girsa, Moscow, Mar. 21, 1922, CAMZV, Janov 1922, spis 128.
58 Report of Police President Bienart, based on information obtained by a delegation of the Communist party of Czechoslovakia that had gone to Soviet Russia in connection with Genoa, CAMZV, Janov, 1922, spis 363.
59 Draft of a consular statute, Prague, Mar. 3, 1922, CAMZV, II. sekce, konference, kart. 165.
60 Tusar to Beneš, Berlin, undated (before Mar. 21, 1922), CAMZV, Tusar papers, úřední korespondence.

negotiate directly with France, though he feared being reproached as a francophile. He would also have to take account of Great Britain. Tusar replied that Czechoslovakia's foreign policy was based on supporting all its neighbors in the direction of "peace and economic revival." Beneš, according to the ambassador, advocated an improvement in German–French relations in the interest of Europe. Rathenau responded that he would like to meet with his Czech colleague to discuss steps to alleviate Germany's isolation. Berlin, which was searching for friends, valued Prague for its eminent reputation in Central Europe. But the head of the *Wilhelmstrasse* doubted whether Czechoslovakia could move appreciably in Germany's direction, because of the extent of Beneš's other commitments. Tusar, while expressing his personal support for closer relations with Berlin, acknowledged that this was dependent on improved ties between Berlin and Paris. Beneš's reaction to this report is not documented, but a month later he did negotiate with Rathenau at Genoa.

Within the framework of all these events, the preparatory conference of the Little Entente took place in Belgrade from March 9 to 12. A representative of the Polish government participated. On the basis of his trip to Paris and London, Beneš had concluded that Czechoslovakia would be unable to play a solo part in an international conference to promote economic consolidation. His public foray as a small-power statesman attempting to set the tone for the European concert of powers had proved abortive. As a substitute for the broad goal of the Genoa Conference, the revival of the "European community of interests,"[61] Czechoslovak foreign policy now endorsed the Polish proposal, supported by Romania and Yugoslavia, for concerted action by the Little Entente on questions relating to the Genoa Conference. Beneš nevertheless refused to participate in a subsequent conference in Warsaw.[62]

Despite the longstanding tension between Warsaw and Prague over the Teschen conflict and apparently minimal support in Paris for a permanent connection between Poland and the Little Entente, Beneš during his March 2 consultation with Yugoslav Foreign Minister Ninčić in Bratislava had agreed to a coordinated action at Genoa by the four Central European states. In return, his partners had accepted the moderate Russian policy of the Czech foreign ministry. But whether the idea of a "fourth great power" was actually born in Belgrade, as Von-

---

61 Beneš before the Foreign Affairs Committee, Prague, Apr. 4, 1922, Beneš, *Problémy nové Evropy,* 167.
62 Gajanová, *ČSR a velmoci,* 104.

dracek asserts,[63] cannot be established by the available documents. The Belgrade resolution[64] simply emphasized that the participating states, which "due to their geographic situation formed a unified area between Western Europe and Russia as well as the Near East," were of special importance for the economic reconstruction of Europe.

It would be incorrect to view the discussions at Bratislava and Belgrade of a unified Little Entente under Beneš's direction as the realization of his foreign policy statements of late 1921 and early 1922. From the start, Prague had not considered the Genoa Conference a "prime opportunity" for the essentially anti-Hungarian alliance to "exert its influence outside the Danubian basin."[65] Until now, scholars have paid scant attention to the efforts by Czechoslovakia to establish an independent course in matters pertaining to the economic consolidation of Europe. There is indeed evidence that Czechoslovak foreign policy, as manifested during the last stages of the Genoa Conference, did not necessarily serve the interests of the Little Entente.

---

63 Felix J. Vondráček, *The Foreign Policy of Czechoslovakia, 1918–1935* (New York, 1937), 144.
64 Resolution of the Belgrade Conference, Mar. 9–12, 1922, CAMZV, Janov 1922, první sekce, Noty a dokumenty, spis 582. The text was published on April 29, 1922, in Genoa.
65 Pierre Crabites, *Beneš, státnik střední Evropy* (Prague, 1935), 166.

11

The Genoa Conference and the Little Entente

MAGDA ÁDÁM

The role of the Little Entente at the Genoa Conference has not yet been explored. The books that have been written about the conference merely hint at it.[1] We know relatively more about the role of Czechoslovakia because there is a work devoted exclusively to this.[2] However, its author was not able to consult either the published British records[3] or the documentation on the Bucharest and Belgrade meetings, which, although not yet available, is indispensable for an objective analysis. The problems treated at these two preliminary meetings, the viewpoints represented there, and the debates among the participants are still scarcely known. The sources found in the archives of Prague, Budapest, and Paris only partially fill this gap, and the official published statements of the time are not completely reliable.

This study is based on sources in the archives of Czechoslovakia, Hungary, and France, on the published British documents, and on other publications dealing with the Genoa Conference.[4] I shall try to offer a broad, nuanced picture of the role of the Little Entente and its individual members at the Genoa Conference.

It becomes clear from the documents that there was a strong duality in the policy of the Little Entente toward the Genoa Conference and its antecedents. In general, its views were closer to those of France than to those of Great Britain, but the members of the Little Entente were

---

1 Carole Fink, *The Genoa Conference: European Diplomacy, 1921–1922* (Chapel Hill and London, 1984), an outstanding monograph, deals several times with the role of the Little Entente.
2 Alena Gajanová, "La politique extérieure tchécoslovaque et la 'question russe' à la Conférence de Gênes," *Historica* 8 (1964):135–76.
3 *DBFP*, First Series, vol. 19, documents the conferences of Cannes, Genoa, and The Hague.
4 In addition to Gajanová's study, see Alla A. Jazkova, *Malaja Antanta v Evropejskej politike* (Moscow, 1974), and V. Soják, ed., *O československé zahraniční politice 1918–1939* (Prague, 1956). Both works are based on the idea that the Bolshevik regime was surrounded by enemies both at home and abroad. The authors view the international discussions aiming at Soviet Russia's political recognition and reintegration into European economic life from this perspective.

also acutely sensitive about their relationship with London. They took great care not to provoke a confrontation with Great Britain and did their best – especially Beneš – to contribute to the reconciliation of Paris and London. This was highly important for the stability of Europe after the Paris Peace Conference. Moreover, there were sharp differences of opinion among the member states concerning the agenda of the Genoa Conference. It was mainly due to Beneš's efforts that they finally presented a unified front at the conference.

All three members of the Little Entente followed the diplomatic events preceding the Genoa Conference with considerable attention. If the background and aims of these diplomatic maneuvers were not entirely clear, some things were apparent: The goal of the Genoa Conference was to alleviate the severe economic and political consequences of the war and the peace treaties; to reintegrate the two Great Powers that had been excluded from European political and economic life, Germany and Soviet Russia; and to promote the reconstruction of central and southeastern Europe regardless of a particular state's position as one of the victors or the vanquished. Indeed, Britain was rumored to be ready to recognize Soviet Russia and enter into discussions over reducing Germany's reparations, which would have entailed political concessions. Although all the members of the Little Entente considered these concessions inadmissible, the intensity of their resistance was not uniform. Czechoslovakia was the least opposed to concessions; Romania was most strongly against them.

All, however, agreed to the economic reconstruction of Europe, since they all wished to obtain loans from the West to overcome their serious economic problems. They were nevertheless opposed to any concession regarding the recognition of Soviet Russia, to discussing the reparations problem, or to allowing the reconstruction of Hungary.[5] Although there were certain differences regarding the first two points, all three states were in full agreement on the third.

On the Soviet question, there was from the very beginning no harmony within the Little Entente. Their relationship toward Moscow was determined partly by their fear of bolshevism and partly by other political, economic, and geographical factors that were far from iden-

5 Considering the economic reconstruction of Hungary dangerous, they found it unacceptable to obtain loans through Budapest or Vienna banks. Cf. *DBFP*, 19:222–4. According to the Romanian government, Hungary and Austria should not be supported "at our expense." The two countries were to receive relief only after the victorious small states had been rehabilitated, and only under the condition that they pay the reparations imposed by the peace treaties. See H MOL Küm K.69-1922-109-5-7947.

tical in all three states. Czechoslovakia and Yugoslavia were not neighbors of Soviet Russia and therefore had no territorial disagreements with it. Also, the "Bolshevik threat" was not next door as it was with Romania, whose annexation of Bessarabia had not yet been recognized by the Allies. Moreover, industrial Czechoslovakia was far more interested in establishing commercial relations with Soviet Russia than were agrarian Romania or Yugoslavia.

These perspectives determined the three states' attitudes toward Soviet Russia. Romanian Foreign Minister Brătianu was opposed to any kind of connection. Yugoslavia, although neutral toward commercial contacts, was opposed to political recognition because of the influence of the large number of Russian emigres inside its borders. Czechoslovakia, on the other hand, thought that economic cooperation with Soviet Russia was not only possible but also necessary, and even indicated an inclination toward political recognition.

The three states were in full agreement that the peace treaties should remain intact and that no concessions should be made in regard to reparations. Nevertheless, Beneš was not opposed to economic aid to Germany, which he considered indispensable to the preservation and further development of economic relations between Prague and Berlin.[6]

In spite of their differences, and in order to prevent their exclusion from the talks on the reconstruction of Europe, the members of the Little Entente thought it important to take a united stand and create a common front toward the outside world. They had especially resented their exclusion from the discussions that had taken place in December 1921 in London.[7]

In January 1922, the Allied Supreme Council met in Cannes to convene the Genoa Conference and passed six resolutions. The first resolution, which produced anxiety in Bucharest, Belgrade, and Prague, stressed the right of every nation to choose the system under which it wanted to live and barred any interference with this choice.[8] The mem-

6 During their talks in London in February 1922, Beneš told Lloyd George that Czechoslovakia had industrial and economic problems similar to those of Great Britain. It too was to a significant extent dependent on trade with Germany. Czechoslovakia could not support Poincaré's hard line on the German question and was interested in reviving Germany's economic life and stabilizing its currency. Because a solution to the reparations problem was of primary importance to European reconstruction, Beneš thought it was possible to modify Germany's payments, but not, as he repeatedly insisted, Hungary's. Cf. *DBFP,* 19:151; also H MOL Küm, K.69-1922-109-57947-286.

7 CAMZV, PZ, London, Jan. 2, 1922.

8 On the Cannes meeting, see Fink, *Genoa Conference,* 37–43. The resolutions were delivered by the Italian minister in Budapest to the minister of foreign affairs, Count Miklós Bánffy. H MOL Küm K.69-1922-109-5-7947.

bers of the Little Entente feared that the recognition of Soviet Russia, which none of them desired, was imminent.

The first Cannes resolution worried the members of the Little Entente for another reason. They suspected that the memorandum of the Council of Ambassadors of February 1920[9] concerning the Habsburg question would become invalid. They considered a Habsburg restoration a menace to their sovereignty as independent nations, and its prevention was one of their primary collective tasks.[10]

There was thus considerable basis for concern among the Little Entente powers. Beneš expressed his view on January 15, 1922, in a communication to Czechoslovak diplomats abroad: "I think that it [i.e., the first Cannes Resolution] is a serious mistake and will encourage the recognition of the Soviets." Although he added that Czechoslovakia would participate in the Genoa Conference, he also predicted from the outset that the enterprise would fail.[11]

The Little Entente's anxiety was increased by the fact that after Cannes, the relationship between France and Britain became extremely tense. This strain was caused by the resignation of French Premier Briand, who had agreed to the Cannes Resolutions, to holding the Genoa Conference the next month, and to including those governments that had previously been excluded from the Paris peace negotiations and the series of international conferences that had followed: Germany, Soviet Russia, Austria, Hungary, and Bulgaria. Briand's foreign policy had provoked opposition from French conservative circles, which had forced his resignation. His successor, the diehard Poincaré, did not agree with Britain's appeasement policy and strove for French hegemony in Europe.[12]

When the Anglo–French discussions produced a deadlock, a total break in the Entente appeared imminent, which would have meant the collapse of the Versailles system. It was therefore natural that the Little Entente, and above all its leading member Czechoslovakia, was aroused

9 Because the Treaty of Trianon had not settled the Habsburg question, the successor states, Yugoslavia and Czechoslovakia, had urged the Allied powers in February 1920 to issue a memorandum to the Hungarian government expressing their opposition to a Habsburg restoration in Hungary. FMAE, Jugoslavie, vol. 62.

10 The treaties establishing the Little Entente were concluded in 1920 and 1921. They compelled the three governments to hinder Hungarian revisionism and a Habsburg restoration at all costs.

11 CAMZV, PZ, Paris, Jan. 15, 1922. See also Gajanová, "Politique extérieure," 140.

12 In the course of their conversations in London (see footnote 6), Lloyd George told Beneš that both the United States and Great Britain believed that France aspired to military hegemony in Europe. The Czechoslovak foreign minister pointed out that President Thomas Masaryk thought the same.

to action. Despite reservations concerning the Cannes Resolutions, especially the first one, the Little Entente did not wish for a rupture in the Entente. The reestablishment of friendly relations between Paris and London was essential for the stability of the postwar order. Moreover, there was the danger that Britain might join forces with Germany and start separate talks with Soviet Russia.

Beneš therefore decided to visit Paris and London. As Czechoslovakia's minister for foreign affairs, he wished to mediate between the two countries to reach a possible compromise, to make Poincaré reconsider his attitude toward Soviet Russia and Germany, and to convince Lloyd George that it would suffice to maintain economic relations with Russia, that political recognition was untimely, and that the attendance of the Little Entente at the preliminary London Conference was justified and important.

Beneš's mission was not an easy one, and he was fully aware of this. He claimed to be representing the eighty million people of Central Europe,[13] the population of the Little Entente members and also Poland – whose membership, however, he had steadfastly blocked.[14] Indeed, there were strong differences between the Warsaw government and the Little Entente in regard to the Genoa Conference. The Little Entente itself was not in agreement on all points, although efforts had been made to smooth difficulties and elaborate a joint stand. Beneš's activity in Paris and London provoked renewed tension and jealousy in Bucharest and Belgrade.

In spite of all this, Beneš proceeded to negotiate in the name of the victorious successor states, and his mediating efforts were widely reported in the world press.[15] Arriving in Paris on February 11, he conducted difficult talks with Poincaré and Millerand. In his report to Masaryk, he described the former as more intransigent toward Germany and the latter as more rigid toward Russia, but he felt that his arguments had been noted.[16] When he met Lloyd George on February 17, he

13 Jazkova, *Malaja Antanta*, 215.
14 From the very beginning Beneš had opposed the efforts of Take Ionescu to include Poland. The Romanian minister of foreign affairs kept this issue on the agenda until his death in June 1922.
15 Beneš's conciliatory diplomacy was resented in Moscow, which preferred a divided Europe.
16 "Premier Poincaré agrees with us in the Russian question and is going to revise French policy concerning Russia. As regards the German question, it will be much more difficult to carry our point here. . . . My talks with Millerand proved much more difficult. His attitude toward Germany is not as intransigent, but he simply does not want to discuss coming to terms with Russia. I again suggested a moderate policy toward Germany without any obligations to maintain economic and commercial relations with Russia. My arguments seemed to impress him greatly." CAMZV, PZ, Paris, Feb. 12, 1922.

informed him of his talks with Poincaré and explained that the French premier opposed the Genoa Conference because of his lack of sympathy with Britain's economic problems and also because of the political statements he had made while in opposition. Beneš suggested that Britain meet France halfway. A bridge had to be constructed for an agreement, which was the precondition of a conference whose success was crucial for Central Europe, and therefore for Czechoslovakia.

Lloyd George insisted that unless Poincaré came to England for informal talks the breach in the Entente might become irreparable. The French premier's policy was driving Britain more and more toward Germany: "Trade was life to us, and if we were attacked in our trade and France stood in its way, we shall drift toward other friends. . . . Italy stands with us in this." Beneš agreed with Lloyd George because Czechoslovakia's commercial relations with Germany were similarly burdened by severe problems.[17] In his view, Germany was intent on weakening itself financially to a point where it would be unable to pay reparations; it should pay reparations to France but be given a moratorium in order to improve its financial position. France and Germany must come to an agreement or else Europe would fall to pieces. "Not only the question of Russia but also that of reparations was of the first importance in the reconstruction of Europe."[18] Beneš insisted that he was not anti-German and claimed he had told Poincaré that it was essential that he move to the left in regard to both Germany and Russia and come to an agreement with Britain on these two problems. He concluded that it would be very difficult for Central Europe if Anglo–French differences were not alleviated.

Lloyd George told the Czechoslovak foreign minister that Take Ionescu had said the very same thing, but that Romania was unable to adhere to either France or Britain's side.[19] The British prime minister was well aware of the fact that the Little Entente stood much nearer to the French viewpoint; although its members wished to avoid deciding between the two, if a choice had to be made they would undoubtedly pick Paris over London. The British leader therefore wanted to diminish their role both before and during the Genoa Conference. That was why he refused to consider Beneš's request, which had been supported by Poincaré, to include experts of the Little Entente in the preliminary work of the Genoa Conference.[20] He also refused the idea of postpon-

---

17 *DBFP*, 19:146–56. 18 Ibid.
19 But in fact the Romanian government identified with Poincaré's hard line and its relations with Britain were relatively cool, primarily as a result of Lloyd George's plans for Russia.
20 *DBFP* 19:146–56.

ing the Genoa Conference, rejecting Beneš's argument that the Little Entente needed time to formulate a common stand and suspecting that the Czech leader ultimately intended to support Poincaré's policies. Citing the fact of more than two million unemployed in Britain, he insisted that "he could not postpone anything which might help to restore trade because of M. Poincaré's objections."[21]

Lloyd George asked Beneš to inform Poincaré of the essentials of their talks, namely, that Britain was determined to go ahead even without France's support. It would still be better to come to terms, and he would be happy to meet Poincaré in London to discuss their mutual problems. He asked Beneš to return with Poincaré and participate in these talks, which would give the Czechoslovak foreign minister an opportunity to express his views on Central Europe. Gladly accepting the assignment, Beneš said that "his services were entirely at Lloyd George's disposal for this purpose."[22]

But Beneš did not return, and he was not present at the meeting between Poincaré and Lloyd George that finally took place not in London but at Boulogne-sur-Mer in France. On the morning of February 20, before departing for France, Beneš sent Lloyd George the *aide-mémoire* that he intended to present to Poincaré and asked for his comments.[23] The memorandum centered on the following points: 1) the conference should be postponed until the end of March; 2) the peace treaties and reparations should not be discussed there; 3) Soviet Russia's participation could not mean its political recognition; and 4) the Little Entente was to participate at the London preparatory conference in an indirect way.[24]

The British prime minister sent word to Beneš that the *aide-mémoire,* and especially the point relating to Russia, was unacceptable. When they met in person, he told Beneš that it was senseless to convene a conference just for the sake of concluding a general trade agreement with Russia. Britain already had such an agreement, and Czechoslovakia could have one when it wished. A commercial treaty was not enough to solve the problem of the economic restoration of Russia. Loans were needed for that, but loans would go to Russia only if the Soviet government was recognized. This was a priority.[25]

Beneš argued that expanded commercial contacts with Soviet Russia

---

21 Ibid.   22 Ibid.   23 *DBFP* 19:166–7.
24 Two additional, significant points included the participation of the League of Nations at the Genoa Conference and the nonaggression clause, ibid. The Little Entente would play a significant role in formulating the latter; Beneš and Ninčić both discussed this problem with Lloyd George in Genoa, *DBFP* 19:565–71, 747.
25 *DBFP* 19:159–67.

were more urgent than political recognition, which could follow later and only under certain conditions. In the end he promised Lloyd George that he would amend the point concerning Russia.[26] He then left for Paris, where he met Poincaré again and informed him of his talks with Lloyd George. In his report to Prague, he indicated that Lloyd George had accepted his memorandum, with slight stylistic modifications.[27]

Undoubtedly it was due to Beneš's mediation that Poincaré agreed to meet Lloyd George at Boulogne on February 25, 1922.[28] The records of the discussions reveal that Beneš's proposals were highly influential.[29] But the talks also represented a compromise, which strengthened Poincaré's rigid course. "This is our mutual success," he said, that of France and of the Little Entente.[30] Indeed, Beneš's negotiations did contribute to strengthening the role of the Little Entente in international affairs and firmly established the position of Czechoslovakia within the alliance.

On his return from Western Europe, Beneš had to tackle his most important task, the formulation of a common policy for the Little Entente. He opposed the decisions that had been taken at the meeting in Bucharest, which had been held during his stay in the West.[31]

At Bucharest, Yugoslavia had been represented by Foreign Minister Momcilo Ninčić, Romania by Prime Minister Ionel Brătianu, and

26 The amended sentence referred to the possibility that should certain conditions be fulfilled (i.e., Moscow accept the Western demands), Soviet Russia could receive political recognition. Ibid., 167.

27 According to this communication, it was agreed: 1) to postpone the Genoa Conference until late March; 2) not to discuss existing treaties and reparations; 3) to make the recognition of Soviet Russia dependent upon the results of the talks; 4) to solve the problem of Little Entente participation in the work of the London Committee in an indirect way; and 5) to present the draft of a European nonaggression pact.

28 In the event he did not return to London, Beneš had promised Lloyd George to communicate Poincaré's views via Jan Masaryk, the Czechoslovak minister in London. *DBFP* 19:146–56.

29 Lloyd George made certain concessions on the Russian question, agreeing to major conditions regarding political recognition. Furthermore, he agreed to a quasi-official participation of the Little Entente in the London meeting. This concession did not satisfy Yugoslavia and Romania, and the latter country protested energetically. Both considered the British offer a denigration of the three-power bloc, which cherished the ambition of being on equal terms with the Great Powers. CAMZV, PZ, Bucharest, Feb. 23, 1922.

30 Quoted in L. Marceilin, *Politique et politiciens d'après-guerre,* vol. 3 (Paris, 1924), 333.

31 Gajanová, "Politique extérieure," 142. CAMZV, PZ, Bucharest, Feb. 22, 1922. Indirect sources indicate that at the Bucharest meeting Prime Minister Ionel Brătianu announced that Romania would demand compensation for its losses during the war and the costs of its occupation of Hungary. According to the report of the Hungarian minister in Bucharest, from information he had received from the Italian minister, one of the Little Entente's decisions at Bucharest was to attempt to curb the right of minorities to appeal directly to the League of Nations.

Czechoslovakia by its ambassador. Skrzynski, the Polish minister for foreign affairs, who had attended as an observer, had suggested the formation of a *"bloc de quatre,"* with Poland joining the Little Entente. Brătianu and Ninčić agreed at once, but Beneš was adamantly opposed, because this would have endangered Czechoslovakia's leading role in the alliance. Moreover, he did not want to burden the Little Entente with Poland's tangled eastern problems, and in this he agreed with Lloyd George. The Polish question thus caused further strain in Czechoslovakia's relations with its allies. Beneš declined the invitation by the Polish government for a meeting of Little Entente foreign ministers in Warsaw.[32] He did so in the name of the Little Entente, even though Romania and Yugoslavia would gladly have accepted the invitation. Both of them, but especially the former, resented that Beneš had negotiated and decided questions in their name without first consulting them. As an indication of the chill in relations between Czechoslovakia and Romania, the Bucharest government did not send a representative to the foreign ministers' meeting in Bratislava on February 28.[33]

At Bratislava, Beneš and Ninčić discussed problems relating to the Genoa Conference. They deliberated over how to surmount differences within the Little Entente and formulate a common standpoint. According to the minutes of their talks, the Yugoslav foreign minister accepted all the points in the text drafted by Beneš and Lloyd George except for point four. Beneš managed to sway his colleague on the Soviet question, namely, on the restriction of Russian émigrés in Yugoslavia. He also won his support on the Polish question; according to the minutes, they concurred that "the diverse interests do not make it possible to create a common stand for the Little Entente and Poland."[34] Thus, the Yugoslav–Romanian decisions that were made at the Bucharest meeting were revised at Bratislava in several important respects, notably on the issue of Poland.

The leading role of Czechoslovak foreign policy was demonstrated by the convocation of another conference on March 9 in Belgrade. Poland once more sent experts to deliberate with the Little Entente. But Romania sent its representative two days late, probably to indicate its reservations concerning the Bratislava meeting and the Genoa Conference.

32 Marceilin, *Politique et politiciens,* 333.
33 It is also possible that Beneš himself wished to consult Ninčić first and did not even invite the more hard-line Foreign Minister Gheorge Ion Duca.
34 CAMZV, PZ, Mar. 2, 1922.

The six-page instructions of the Romanian delegates sum up the Bucharest government's views on several important issues. Romania was convinced that the purpose of the Genoa Conference was to undermine the clauses of the Treaty of Versailles, place disarmament on the agenda, establish commercial contacts with Russia, and install the defeated countries at the conference table. But because of Anglo–French differences and France's open unwillingness to negotiate over the peace treaties, reparations, or the recognition of Soviet Russia, Romania anticipated the failure of the Genoa Conference.[35]

It also becomes clear from these instructions that Romania was willing to agree to negotiations with Soviet Russia only on condition that the Romanian–Soviet border would be recognized. On the other hand, the Bucharest government wished to seize the opportunity to obtain financial support at the Genoa Conference. It based its monetary claims on the fact that it had to mobilize an army even after hostilities had officially ceased and fight an additional year on the Dniester and Tisza rivers against Lenin and Béla Kun.[36]

At the Belgrade Conference, Romania asked its Little Entente allies to support its claims at Genoa. Without access to the documents of the meeting, it is impossible to ascertain their response. Through indirect sources, we can reconstruct the Yugoslav standpoint. Belgrade, which also wanted loans, asked its allies for support in the event of a conflict with Italy and for solidarity over the minorities question, especially on the issue of international control.[37]

The Belgrade Conference produced few gains. Poland, which had exerted considerable efforts after Boulogne, was unable to establish a common platform with the Little Entente over guaranteeing its eastern borders.[38] Ninčić admitted afterward to the British ambassador that he had not anticipated any major accomplishments. The parties had simply concurred that they must have a common platform in Genoa to guard against any proposals that might endanger their independence.[39]

---

35 H MOL Küm. K.69-1922-109-57947-10-16.   36 Ibid.
37 The official communiqué on the Belgrade conference, issued in Belgrade, Prague, Bucharest, and Warsaw, stressed that the program of the Genoa Conference had been established by the Cannes Resolutions and nothing further could be discussed there. Ninčić said the same thing in his reply to an interpellation in parliament, adding that such political problems as reparations and disarmament would not be dealt with and that Yugoslavia was not interested in the Russian question. H MOL Küm K-1922.109-57947-34. A. Young, British ambassador in Belgrade, informed Foreign Secretary Lord Curzon of the failure of the Belgrade Conference. *DBFP* 19:222–4.
38 The Yugoslav and Romanian representatives refused to consider this question after the Beneš–Ninčić meeting at Bratislava.
39 *DBFP* 19:222–4.

It was also agreed to meet again before the conference, but that meeting did not take place. The Little Entente powers found it unnecessary, or, to be more precise, impossible, to come to a mutual agreement. For example, when, just prior to the conference, Chicherin, the Soviet commissar for foreign affairs, invited the three governments to discuss outstanding problems, first Beneš and then Ninčić declined.

Once Poland learned it could not rely on the Little Entente's support, it ceased pursuing membership in the alliance and worked for an accord with its eastern neighbors. On March 17, the foreign ministers of Finland, Estonia, Latvia, and Poland signed an agreement in Warsaw on a common platform for the Genoa Conference. But in response, deeming it indispensable for Soviet Russia to secure its western borders, Chicherin proposed a follow-up conference. After a short hesitation, the four Baltic states convened at Riga where they signed an agreement with the Soviets on March 29.[40]

Despite three months of preparations, the Little Entente did not manage to formulate a common platform for the Genoa Conference. At Genoa, Beneš convened a meeting of the foreign ministers of Czechoslovakia, Romania, Yugoslavia, and Poland which decided on 1) participation in every commission, 2) refusal to recognize Soviet Russia, and 3) full cooperation with France.[41]

It was also important for the Little Entente to pay attention to the Hungarian delegation at Genoa. On the very first day of the meeting, Beneš clashed with Count Istvan Bethlen when the Hungarian prime minister called attention to the plight of the Hungarian minorities in the neighboring states and the neglect of international enforcement procedures. Bethlen proposed an international commission to deal with the problem, but Beneš firmly rebuffed this request, stating that the minorities question fell within the province of the League of Nations.[42] At the same session a serious quarrel also erupted between Brătianu and Chicherin.

It is not the purpose of this paper to detail the events of the Genoa Conference. The representatives of the Little Entente did work assiduously on the various commissions and subcommissions to protect their

---

40 *DBFP*, 19:231–4.   41 A long debate preceded these decisions.

42 The representatives of the Little Entente opposed the proposition that separate subcommissions be set up to discuss the problem of the successor states. Beneš found it inadmissible to discuss "political" problems at the conference, despite the fact that the Little Entente had decided at its Bucharest meeting to work for the revision of unfavorable points in the Minority Treaties. Cf. H Küm 1922 Genoa 3 136–45; *DBFP* 19:359–65; H MOL Küm 69.1922-109.37 947.

interests.[43] I shall, however, comment on the reactions to the most spectacular result of the Genoa Conference, the Rapallo Treaty.

Neither the Little Entente members nor Poland anticipated the Russo–German treaty, and they reacted with fear and indignation. All four signed the protest note to Germany,[44] but they did not share the intransigent position of France. When the French delegation inquired unofficially if the Little Entente would be willing to follow France and leave the conference, Beneš answered in the negative, explaining that they could not take this step against Britain's interests.[45] At Genoa, the Little Entente continued to maneuver between France and Britain; Czechoslovakia and Yugoslavia moved closer to the British view on Russia.

These maneuvers are reflected in a secret telegram that Beneš sent to Prague: "I think I shall join Lloyd George if his negotiations on the Russian question are successful. But I shall not do anything openly against France."[46] The Czechoslovak foreign minister mentioned that he and the Poles were afraid of siding openly with France; Romania, because of its anti-Russian sentiments, stood resolutely on Paris's side; and Yugoslavia was still hesitating.[47] During the conference, Beneš contacted Chicherin, and their talks led to a provisional treaty that virtually meant the recognition of Soviet Russia.[48]

Ninčić too met with Chicherin and assured him that Yugoslavia would not agree to any anti-Soviet measures.[49] However, the Yugoslav government did not consider normalizing relations with Moscow.

43 Beneš, Ninčić, and Brătianu made sure that members of their delegations were represented on every subcommission; they took part personally in the most important commissions. They were most active in the First (Political) Sub-Commission, where they guarded against any infringements on their sovereignty or the peace treaties. They were generally opposed to the suggestions of the London preparatory committee. They were also against the Hungarian proposals to develop a liberal economic policy and economic cooperation with its neighboring states. They stood firmly against Hungarian suggestions that the participating governments conclude mutual trade agreements with most-favored-nation clauses and replace prohibitions with simple protective tariffs. For the Hungarian proposals, see H MOL Küm 69-1922-109 54947-328-470. For the activity of the representatives of the Little Entente in the various subcommissions, see *DBFP*, 19:630–6, 508–12, 559–60, 630–6; and H MOL Küm K. 69.1922. Genoa 3-153-169.

44 Lloyd George recommended a collective protest note to the German delegation by the Little Entente and Poland condemning the separate agreement between Soviet Russia and Germany. Cf. Gajanová, "Politique extérieure," 161; *DBFP*, 19:431.

45 Jazkova, *Malaja Antanta*, 223.   46 Ibid.   47 Ibid.

48 This act of Beneš's aroused dissatisfaction at the conference in general and, especially, within the Little Entente. There had been agreement not to conclude a treaty with Soviet Russia before the follow-up conference at The Hague.

49 V. Vinaver, "O jugoslavsko-sovietskoj trgovini izmedu dva rata," *Prehled* 12 (1957):96.

Romania stuck to its original stand concerning Russia and continued to support Poincaré's views.

The Little Entente thus failed to display a uniform attitude toward the most important question of the Genoa Conference, namely, the Russian question. Nevertheless, Beneš in his official statements stressed the harmony among the three powers, asserting that "the Little Entente [had been] an active factor of European politics at the Genoa Conference, [had] fully represented its interests, and fulfilled its task."[50] But he neglected to mention the controversies among the three states during the preliminary phase and the course of the conference.

The attempt at the reconstruction of Europe failed at Genoa. The Anglo-French conflict, the wavering of the Little Entente between Britain and France, and the passivity of the neutral states all led to the failure of Lloyd George's reasonable idea. The Rapallo Treaty also contributed to the failure. This diplomatic coup left its mark not only on the conference but also on the whole future development of Europe. "The Russo–German treaty cast its shadow on the whole Genoa Conference and is sure to have serious political consequences," wrote Beneš in his report.[51]

50 Edouard Beneš, *Problémy nové Evropy a zahraniční politika Československa. Projevy a úvahy z R 1919–1924* (Prague, 1924), 187–91.
51 CAMZV, PZ, Paris, Apr. 20, 1922.

12

The Role of Switzerland and the Neutral States at the Genoa Conference

ANTOINE FLEURY

Prior to World War I, very few European states possessed a statute of neutrality. Europe was dominated by the great empires and by the new and expanding nation states. The few small states were, for the most part, located in disputed areas between the Great Powers and were frequently assigned the role of buffer states.

Switzerland, which over the centuries had asserted its right to a statute of neutrality, had been the subject of guarantees by the Great Powers. In the Acts of the Congress of Vienna in 1815, the signatories had recognized that "the neutrality and inviolability of Switzerland and its independence from all foreign influences are in the best interests of the political structure of all of Europe." After its independence in 1831, Belgium too had benefited from international guarantees, which were reinforced by a statute of perpetual neutrality in the 1839 treaty. This statute was respected by the Great Powers until the German invasion in 1914.

During the nineteenth century, a period characterized by the growth of nationalism and the formation of nation states, the small state[1] appeared to be an outdated concept that contraindicated the general tendency toward the creation of large political/economic entities such as Germany and Italy. In Scandinavia, on the other hand, the Swedish–Norwegian union was dissolved in 1905. At the beginning of the twentieth century, a new volatile spirit emerged in some of the small states in the Balkans, but neither Switzerland nor the Scandinavian states attempted to increase their power through an alignment with one or another of the Great Powers.

In 1914, the Scandinavian countries, Sweden, Norway, and Den-

---

1 D. Kosary, "The Development Types of the Minor States in Europe 1715–1919," in H. U. Jost, ed., *Les Petits Etats face aux changements culturels, politiques et économiques de 1750 à 1914* (Lausanne, 1985), 3 ff.

mark, chose, like Switzerland (which was the only country, with the unhappy exception of Belgium, to have an international statute of neutrality), to distance themselves from the European conflict; by opting for nonbelligerency, Spain also became a member of the group of neutral states. The wartime neutrals were therefore a rather diverse group, consisting of traditionally neutral states such as Switzerland, states that had chosen a policy of nonbelligerency, states in the center of Europe and states at the edges of the continent, states that were content to remain small, and states that dreamed of the restoration of their former glories.

Certain minor states, notably Switzerland, Belgium, and the Netherlands, had maintained an active role in prewar European diplomacy. To be sure, the foreign policy of a minor power had to be developed with care; it was necessary to guard against establishing any policy whose implementation depended on the will of the Great Powers. If a small state wished to maintain its integrity, it was not in its interest to declare its allegiance to any of the Great Powers.

The foreign policy of a small state could be directed fruitfully toward areas other than large-scale strategic diplomacy. Since the middle of the nineteenth century, international conferences concerned with technical questions (communications, transport, public health, social legislation, and the protection of patents) had offered a new type of diplomatic activity to states regardless of their size.[2] A state's level of involvement and competence in these areas was frequently a measure of its industrial, economic, and social development, to the point that some small states played a more active role in this form of diplomatic activity than did some of the Great Powers.

Switzerland, for example, played an active and central part in several international technical conferences. It became the site of such agencies as the International Postal Union and the International Office for the Protection of Intellectual Property (established in Berne), and it hosted international conferences on labor legislation, which took place in Berne, and Red Cross conventions.[3] Another small country, the Netherlands, hosted the two great peace conferences of 1889 and 1907, and The Hague was the site of the International Court of Justice.

Thus, within the framework of multilateral diplomacy before 1914, the small state discovered a new role that reinforced its international

2 On the impact of communications see Verdiana Grossi, "Technologie et diplomatie suisse au XIXe siècle: Le case de télégraphes," *Relations Internationales* 39 (1984):287 ff.
3 Swiss diplomatic activity prior to 1914 is documented in *DDS*, vols. 1–5.

position without forcing it to subordinate itself to the Great Powers. In the case of Switzerland, this also gave additional justification to its neutrality policy and to the consolidation of the statute of 1815 in the interests of European peace. By understanding the diplomatic experience of Switzerland and other small states before, and especially during, the First World War, we can better understand the position they took at the Genoa Conference in 1922.[4]

The First World War considerably increased the international profile of certain minor states, notably Switzerland. The latter was entrusted with twenty-two mandates of representation of the interests of the warring states. Its diplomatic service was called on, from 1915 onward, to arbitrate in numerous sets of negotiations for the exchange of prisoners of war. Swiss territory served as a haven for thousands of military and civilian internees of the warring powers, their numbers rising from 18,000 in 1916 to 27,000 in 1918; during the course of the hostilities, 472,000 individuals evacuated from enemy-occupied territory were repatriated to their homelands by way of Switzerland.[5] Finally, the population of Switzerland supported the humanitarian projects of the Red Cross, which aided civilians affected by the war. More than any other neutral country, Switzerland, with its industrial advantages and central location, was in a strong position to contribute to the economic plans of all the warring countries. This however necessitated a skillful balancing act on the part of the Swiss federal authorities to implement a strict policy of economic neutrality, which was extremely difficult to maintain.[6] The result was a much greater dependency of the Swiss economy on the economics of its larger neighboring states, which caused a considerable number of problems at the end of the war.

In response to the extremely complex situation facing the neutral states, the Swedish government in 1916 proposed the convocation in

4 Most sources used in this essay are in the Swiss Federal Archives in Berne (SAF). The dossiers relating to the Genoa Conference, notably the reports of the Swiss delegation, are in boxes E 2001 (B) 3/67, 70, and E 7800 4/4. The main texts have been reproduced in *Documents Diplomatiques Suisses (DDS)*, vol. 8 (Berne, 1988), section 3: "La Conférence economique internationale de Gênes." Swiss historians have shown some interest in the Genoa Conference; see, e.g., Julia Gauss, "Motta an der Konferenz von Genua," *Revue Suisse d'Histoire* 4 (1978):453–81; and Peter Stettler, *Das aussenpolitische Bewusstsein in der Schweiz, 1920–1930* (Zurich, 1969), 234–7.

5 *DDS* 6:876.

6 Pierre Luciri, *Le Prix de la neutralité: La diplomatie secrète de la Suisse en 1914–1915* (Geneva, 1976); Heinz Ochsenbein, *Die verlorene Wirtschaftsfreiheit, 1914–1918* (Berne, 1971); Marjorie Farrar, "Le système de blocus suisse (1914–1918): Les interactions de la diplomatie, de la stratégie et des priorités intérieures," *Revue d'Histoire Moderne et Contemporaine* 21 (1974):591–622.

Stockholm of a conference of neutral states for the purpose of discussing issues of common interest, particularly commercial questions and the application of regulations concerning their rights and obligations as established in the Hague Convention of 1907.[7] The Swiss government was in favor of this, stating "that it would be of great benefit for us, as for all the neutral states, to be able to discuss together the new questions which the war has raised."[8]

This was the first attempt at cooperation among the neutral states. However, this hopeful prospect of joint action, which might have led to offers to mediate among the warring states and the opportunity to participate in the peace negotiations, came to nought because of fears of displeasing one or the other belligerent side. Moreover, when America entered the war in 1917, the neutral states realized that any attempt at mediation that lacked the approval of the president of the United States would be perceived by the Entente powers as a maneuver orchestrated by the Central powers.

Thus the neutral states lost the opportunity to take responsibility for the construction of the postwar world, especially after Wilson presented his peace program in his famous speeches of January and February 1918. The neutrals contented themselves with setting up study commissions to deal with the problems that would face the new League of Nations, which Wilson had indicated would maintain equality between small and large states.

By 1918, the political leaders of Switzerland shared the internationalist views of President Wilson.[9] They were conscious of the necessity of a "radical transformation of the economic order, a transformation based upon the existence of a state of peace in internal as well as external politics."[10] Without harboring any illusions about the establishment of a liberal commercial system, they supported the idea of a "most-favored nation system with also an open-door policy for less-developed countries such as China and Africa." They supported free access to raw materials, the "cornerstone of any reorganization of international relations," in the form of an "equitable distribution guaranteed by international agencies." From their deliberations in 1918 on the reorganization of international relations, the Swiss experts concluded that "one of the principal tasks of the League of Nations will be to assure an equitable

7 *DDS* 6:426.   8 Ibid., 427.
9 Antoine Fleury, "La Suisse et la réorganisation de l'économie mondiale: l'expérience du premier après-guerre," *Relations Internationales* 30 (1982):141–57.
10 Ibid., 147.

international economic situation, since economic peace is one of the essential prerequisites for political peace."[11]

At the end of the war, Switzerland recognized almost immediately that the new political and economic order was primarily the creation of the Great Powers; it was aware that as a neutral state it would have little impact on the Great Powers and their allies. Nevertheless, the Swiss government expressed its willingness to work within the new system of international relations based on the principles enunciated by the victorious coalition. For the first time, it therefore attempted to establish a collective position among the neutral states toward the issues discussed at the Paris Peace Conference in 1919.[12] Since the neutrals did not take part in the conference, it was important that their views be made known on certain key points of the treaties that would have a significant effect on them.[13]

This attempt by Switzerland to coordinate the diplomacy of the neutral states toward the peace treaties and the League of Nations did not meet with the expected success. Indeed, on March 19, 1919, a conference of the five neutral states, chaired by Switzerland, was held in Paris, to prepare for an appearance before the League of Nations commission of the peace conference. This meeting took place on March 20 and 21, and thirteen neutral countries were represented. They were able to formulate their observations concerning the draft of the League of Nations Covenant and to obtain detailed commentaries on the articles therein.[14] However, it was not long before the fear of creating a "neutrals' bloc" that might conflict with the aims of one or another major power outweighed any inclination to serve as a catalyst for the tensions and rivalries of the Great Powers.[15]

The Swiss government nevertheless appreciated the importance of its full participation in the multilateral diplomacy that developed after 1919. It derived satisfaction when the League of Nations Council appointed a Swiss citizen, Gustave Ador, the former president of the International Committee of the Red Cross and president of the Confederation in 1919, to preside over the International Financial Confer-

---

11 Ibid., 149; see also *Message du Conseil fédéral à l'Assemblée fédérale concernant la question de l'accession de la Suisse à la Société des Nations du 4 août 1919* (Berne, 1919), 32 ff.

12 *DDS* 7-1, section 1: "La conférence de la paix."   13 Ibid., 586 ff.   14 Ibid., 532 ff.

15 *DDS* 7-2, in particular those parts concerning the cautious stance of the Netherlands, made clear in April and August 1920 (632–3, 778–9), and the refusal of the Norwegian government to respond positively to a Swiss memorandum of April 8, 1920, addressed to the governments of Sweden, Denmark, Norway, and the Netherlands "in the knowledge that they were disposed to establish long-term discussions concerning the activities of the League of Nations where the post-war political structure of Europe was being established" (615, 708–9).

ence that was held in Brussels in the autumn of 1920.[16] The purpose of this conference was to deliberate over the reestablishment of credit mechanisms within Europe.[17] It also sought a remedy for the exchange crisis, which had paralyzed attempts to improve commercial relations. In view of the fact that the economic life of Switzerland was tightly connected with global economic patterns, the Swiss government was particularly interested in being involved in all discussions or agreements that affected international exchanges and loans.[18]

When the Brussels meeting failed to produce positive results, it was decided to entrust the follow-up work to the secretariat of the League of Nations, which had an economic and financial service; this, according to Jean Monnet, who as deputy secretary-general had worked hard to prepare the Brussels meeting, was the "only concrete result of the first great global economic conference."[19] According to the partisans of an active role for the League in economic questions, it was necessary to establish a quasi-permanent structure for consultation and negotiation on major international financial and economic issues. It was hoped that a resolution of these questions would lead to an improvement in international relations.

The fact that the most critical economic and financial problem of the postwar period, the reparations question, had been withheld from the League of Nations deprived the latter of an effective role, much to the great regret of countries such as Switzerland, which preferred a truly international and purely financial solution to the reparations question. Thus in the spring of 1921, the Swiss Federal Council endorsed a plan for financial reconstruction conceived by a Swiss banker, Léopold Dubois, which he presented to German and French officials.[20]

The doubts surrounding Germany's future – and particularly the state of its economy, which was hamstrung by reparations – were of primary concern to the small states and especially to the neutrals, which had traditionally enjoyed close economic ties with the Reich. It is against this background that one can understand the neutrals' interest in the idea of a global economic conference that would be open to all states, whether or not they were members of the League of Nations.

---

16 *DDS* 7-2:665.

17 Marie-Renée Mouton, "Société des Nations et reconstruction financière de l'Europe: La conférence de Bruxelles (24 septembre–8 octobre 1920)," *Relations Internationales* 39 (1984):309–31.

18 *DDS* 7-2: 654–61, 812–16.

19 Jean Monnet, *Mémoires* (Paris, 1976), 131.   20 *DDS* 8: 189–93, 203–4, 211–17.

After the Supreme Allied Council, on the initiative of the British prime minister, Lloyd George, issued (on January 6, 1922) an invitation to all the European states and to the United States to participate in the Genoa Conference, the Swiss government closely followed its preparation. The Swiss were alarmed by the widening gap between the policy of France, which was closely tied to the clauses of the Treaty of Versailles, and that of Great Britian, represented by Lloyd George,[21] which was guided by the urgency of creating new conditions, the reconstruction of Europe, and conceivably a new association of nations.

The Berne government carefully studied the six Cannes Resolutions.[22] On the basis of these, the Swiss government again took the initiative on March 1, 1922, inviting the remaining neutral states – Sweden, Norway, Denmark, the Netherlands, and Spain – for an exchange of views over certain important aspects of the agenda of the Genoa Conference.[23] A preliminary conference of the neutral states was held in Stockholm on March 18, 1922, at the invitation of the Swedish prime minister, H. Branting. Some refinements were suggested concerning the interpretation of certain obscure statements in the Cannes Resolutions,[24] and the parties presented their positions on the establishment of free trade, the gold standard, and the proposal for an international consortium for the reconstruction of Russia.

Finally, on the eve of the Genoa Conference, a meeting of experts and delegates from the neutral states convened in Berne from April 5 to 8, 1922.[25] The representatives of Denmark, Spain, Norway, the Netherlands, Sweden, and Switzerland expressed their views on a number of major points pertaining to the conference. Although it was hoped they would establish a common position, it proved impossible to obtain unanimity on all points, notably on those concerning relations with Soviet Russia and on the economic measures proposed by the Swedish economist Gustav Cassel.

Despite the equivocal results of the neutrals' meeting, it is significant that the first point of the instructions of the Swiss Federal Council to its delegates specified "that the Swiss delegation remain in close contact with the delegates of the other states which are in a similar situation to that of Switzerland. They were to avoid wherever possible becoming isolated on important questions with broad implications."[26] These instructions also reflected a concern for maintaining the stature of the

---

21 Ibid., 427 ff.   22 Ibid., 434 ff.   23 Ibid., 450 ff.   24 Ibid., 435–6.
25 Ibid., 479–80. On the work of this conference, see SAF, E 2001 (B) 3/67.   26 *DDS* 8:480.

League of Nations; rumors were circulating to the effect that the British prime minister sought to create a new international organization, more universal than the League of Nations, which would from the outset include Germany and the Soviet Union.[27] The policy of the Swiss government at Genoa was that "all the recognized European states should be invited to join the League of Nations," if possible by the next Assembly in September 1922.[28]

As the initiator of the Genoa Conference, Lloyd George was undoubtedly interested in Switzerland's viewpoint. As early as January 1922, he had expressed the desire to meet the federal councillor E. Schulthess, the head of the Department of Public Economy, to discuss the attitude of the small neutral powers toward the conference.[29] Despite the fact that these preliminary conversations might have provided Switzerland, particularly in its role in international economic relations, with an extremely favorable position at the conference, the federal councillor refused to respond to this personal invitation, invoking the traditional Swiss reluctance to allow members of their government to become involved in international politics. This extreme reticence on the part of Swiss officials was largely aimed at avoiding the risk that their actions might be misinterpreted or disapproved of by any of the protagonists in the international political arena.

The weeks preceding the Genoa Conference were notable for the maneuvers of the Entente, Germany, and Soviet Russia; the last, making its entry into the great diplomatic game, took advantage not only of the opportunities offered by the meeting itself, but also of the new conditions that had been created as a result of its convocation. Thus, the Swiss were strongly encouraged to sign an agreement with the Soviets before the conference took place.[30] Berne, on the contrary, wished to avoid strengthening the Soviet position prior to Genoa; it preferred to await the results of the conference before negotiating any agreements or becoming involved in any collective actions directed

27 Ibid., 446 ff. On the apparent threats facing the League of Nations, see also the alarming report, dated April 1, 1922, from Professor William Rappard, director of the Mandates section of the Secretariat, to G. Motta, head of the Swiss Diplomatic Service, entitled "La Conférence de Gênes et la Société des Nations," *DDS* 8:476–8.
28 Ibid., 481.
29 According to a letter from Rappard to Schulthess, Feb. 6, 1922, ibid., 440–3.
30 On Swiss–Soviet relations during this period see ibid., section 2.22 "Russie," in particular 443–6, 448–50. Cf. Antoine Fleury, "Les autorités fédérales suisses et le gouvernement soviétique: contacts et rupture 1917–1924," in *La Révolution d'octobre et les pays européens 1917–1924*, Proceedings of the Association Internationale d'Histoire Contemporaine de l'Europe, Moscow, September 7–13, 1987 (in preparation).

toward the economic reconstruction of Russia. The Swiss government did not favor a unilateral action toward Soviet Russia because the interests it wished to safeguard were similar to those of most of the Great Powers. It was through collaboration with the latter that Berne could best safeguard its own interests in Russia.

To be sure, the other neutral states were just as cautious as Switzerland, if not more so. Thus, when the Swiss government in the beginning of March proposed that the neutral states conduct an exchange of views over the problems that were to be tackled at Genoa, the foreign minister of the Netherlands, van Karnebeeck, was skeptical about the prospect of bringing together all the European states that had remained neutral during the war.[31] In his opinion, since the neutral states did not share identical interests, it would be preferable to invite only those that were involved in the same problems. He pointed out, for example, that a discussion of the gold standard would be of interest only to Switzerland, the Netherlands, and Sweden; moreover, it would be necessary to make contact with the Bank of England, without whose cooperation nothing could be accomplished in this area. As a general approach, it was "dangerous and disadvantageous to maintain in times of peace the distinctions that had been established between states in wartime."[32] He advised against using the term "longstanding [*anciens*] neutrals" and against inviting Spain to become a member of the group: "everything that is disclosed to them is promptly reported to Paris," because Madrid "endeavors by all possible means to place itself in good graces with the Entente."[33] This standpoint had no other adherents, and during the Genoa Conference the Dutch minister himself became a zealous promoter of concerted action by the former neutral states. It is nevertheless obvious that on the important issues of reparations, relations with the Soviet Union, the international consortium, and the restoration of the monetary system, the neutral states did have very different interests to promote and, consequently, a wide range of opinions.[34]

This explains why during the first phase of the Genoa Conference, up until the famous German–Soviet treaty signed at Rapallo on April 16, the group of neutral states did not play a particularly active role. Some of their delegates shared the resentment of the representatives of the other small states at being excluded from the important discussions in progress, especially those with the Soviet delegation. Following the

31 *DDS* 8:452. 32 Ibid. 33 Ibid., 453.
34 See also Carole Fink, *The Genoa Conference: European Diplomacy, 1921–1922* (Chapel Hill and London, 1984), 113 ff.

announcement of the Rapallo Treaty, the neutrals reacted similarly to the other states, that "the agreement concluded by the Germans and Soviets represented an unwise and incorrect action, contrary to the spirit of international cooperation."[35] It was also at this juncture that the Swiss delegation, under the direction of the foreign minister, G. Motta, and E. Schulthess, seized the initiative on Tuesday, March 18, to convene a neutrals' meeting at the Miramare Hotel, where they were staying, in order to examine the new situation. This invitation was successful, for all the delegations of the neutral states responded to the call. They agreed unanimously that "the discussions by separate groups (Inviting Powers and Russians; Inviting Powers and the Little Entente; Germans and Russians) were contrary to the principles and aims of the conference," which had been called primarily to reestablish confidence between governments. The individual discussions that had taken place outside the legitimate bodies set up by the conference had "undermined the very foundations by which such confidence could be built."[36] The delegations reached agreement on the necessity to "approach the President of the Conference and the President of the Political Sub-Commission in order to request a meeting of the Political Sub-Commission as soon as possible." That same evening, Motta and Branting proceeded to the Villa Raggio, the residence of the Italian prime minister, Facta, and the Italian foreign minister, Schanzer, to express the sentiments of the neutral delegations and their concern over the risk that the Genoa Conference might collapse.

The risk of a rupture sprang from the threatened departure from Genoa of the German delegation, which had been frustrated by the favoritism the Inviting Powers had shown to the Soviet delegation. In order to appease the Germans, Schanzer, on the same evening that he received the neutrals' delegation, unofficially asked the Swiss delegates, who were on very good terms with the Germans, to use their influence to prevent a break.[37] Without refusing to cooperate, Motta and Schulthess chose to act with caution. They sent an invitation to one of the members of the German delegation, Ernst von Simson, a senior official in the *Wilhelmstrasse,* who met promptly with them. The Swiss delegates advised Simson "of the disquiet which the German–Soviet Treaty had produced, even among the neutrals"; the latter wished to see this diplomatic incident resolved quietly. After explaining the German position and the delegation's desire not to disrupt the negotiations,

35 *DDS* 8:483.   36 Ibid.   37 Ibid., 484.

Simson emphasized his government's rejection of the accusation that in concluding a treaty with the Soviet delegation it had acted treacherously and in bad faith.

Three days after this conversation, Schanzer again requested that Motta make an informal approach to the German delegation so that the incident could finally be resolved.[38] However, on this occasion the Swiss foreign minister preferred not to take part because he found it dangerous to interfere. In his opinion confidence had been lost; he no longer had any illusions about the outcome of a conference that, as he wrote to the president of the Swiss Confederation on April 20, 1922, "had been inadequately prepared and continued to function on an unsound basis."[39] Motta wondered how in this strange climate to handle the thorny question of reparations, "one . . . in which we have a particular interest." But according to the report of the Swiss foreign minister on April 24, all that remained on the agenda was the Soviet question, whose solution would determine "the failure or success of the conference."[40]

It was necessary that the neutrals take part in the discussion of this central question. At the suggestion of van Karnebeeck, who was intent on protecting the considerable Dutch investments of some 5 billion (American billion) gold francs in Russia, Branting and Motta agreed to be represented by the Netherlands, in the person of the legal expert Struycken.[41] With this gesture, the Swiss and Swedish delegates not only established an effective cooperation between the neutrals but they also assured their rather cautious Dutch colleague of the advantages of solidarity. The neutrals began working together on the Russian question, despite their divergent, and even opposing views before the conference. It was really at Genoa that the delegates, including van Karnebeeck, recognized the importance of cooperation between the small states, which had begun in Stockholm and in Berne. But without these preliminaries, even though there had been no agreements beforehand, the neutrals, according to Motta, would merely have been "political nonentities" at the Genoa Conference.[42]

Motta reported with evident satisfaction that it was van Karnebeeck himself who on April 25 issued an invitation to the delegates of the neutral states – Branting for Sweden, Unden for Norway, Bernhöft for Denmark, Motta for Switzerland, and Urrutria for Spain – for the next day to discuss the state of negotiations between the Great Powers and

---

38 Ibid., 487.   39 Ibid., 485.   40 Ibid., 488.   41 Ibid.   42 Ibid., 490.

Russia. They were duly alarmed by the news of an ultimatum addressed by the Allies to the Soviets. During their meeting all the neutrals agreed that forceful methods would not produce a satisfactory result; instead, it was necessary that "the conference at least establish the general basis of an accord with the Russians, and that it was the duty of all true supporters of the conference to prevent a rupture of the negotiations."[43]

This position of the neutral delegations was immediately communicated to the Great Powers and apparently impressed the British prime minister, who was concerned over the possible failure of his initiative. The next day, April 27, he asked to see Motta, to whom he expressed satisfaction with the Swiss and the neutrals' views.[44] Lloyd George, according to Motta, considered that "a break with Russia would truly be a disaster for Europe." He also believed that the "present French policy, which was designed to exasperate the Germans, was extremely dangerous" and would only reinforce the Soviet–German bloc; this could be prevented only by Europe-wide cooperation for the reconstruction of the continent and of Russia. Lloyd George added that the neutrals' view of this issue would be extremely valuable, if in only a small way, to counteract the stance of France and Belgium, both of which were held hostage by a public opinion opposed to any concessions toward the Soviets.[45] Motta, who was reassured by his meeting with the British prime minister, felt that Switzerland should not hesitate to make its voice heard, "if its opinions, or mediation could have any influence, however minor, on international politics."[46]

Filled with a new determination to play a mediating role, Motta on the day after his meeting with Lloyd George invited the other neutral delegates to his hotel to discuss the Russian question.[47] Having learned of the British prime minister's intention to meet the representatives of the neutrals, he immediately relayed this information to his colleagues, who felt, however, that a visitation by all the neutrals would provoke an adverse reaction. Thus, the meeting did not take place. But that day, April 28, Motta encountered Lloyd George in the elevator and told him that the neutrals had decided to examine the British and French proposals for an arrangement with the Russians before meeting with him. Scarcely concealing his irritation, Lloyd George warned Motta: "If we cannot arrange something [concerning the Russian question], then each state will follow a road dictated by its own interests."[48]

---

43 Ibid., 491.   44 Ibid., 493.   45 Ibid., 494.   46 Ibid., 493.
47 Ibid., 508.   48 Ibid., 509.

That afternoon, the neutrals reconvened to exchange views on the two projects. According to their experts, the differences between the British and French texts did not appear insurmountable. Nevertheless, the neutral delegates were divided. While Branting was in favor of the British proposal, van Karnebeeck opted for a more cautious approach. Motta, on his part, was of the opinion "that the neutrals should make every effort not to become divided; it would be unfortunate if the harmony among the neutrals, whose value had so recently been confirmed, were to be damaged by the disagreements over the Russian problem. Although prudence was a virtue, it did not preclude the possibility of playing the role of peacemaker."[49] Because his colleagues did not disagree, Motta intervened in the reconvened Political Sub-Commission, which met late in the afternoon on April 28.[50]

The Swiss delegate took the floor after a particularly harsh exchange between the French delegate Barthou and Lloyd George. Motta commented on their two proposals, with which he was somewhat familiar and which in practical terms did little to create the harmony and confidence that were necessary for the achievement of their goals. Motta also did his best to lighten the tense atmosphere by explaining his difficulty, as a neutral representative, in judging which of the statesmen that had preceded him had made the better case. Having diverted the delegates, he then raised a procedural question, that the delegations had too often been asked to give their opinion on key documents without sufficient time to study them. "It would be desirable," he said, "if every important proposal first be transmitted to the Secretariat, who would communicate them to all the delegations or, at least, to the members of the Sub-Commission." As to the proposal before them, he announced, the position of his delegation was that "the two views appear easily reconcilable; an attempt at mutual understanding was essential,"[51] and he suggested that experts draft a single text.

This idea was immediately endorsed by Schanzer, the president of the Political Sub-Commission, who suggested that his delegation prepare the single text. However, the British prime minister preferred Motta's idea of assigning the task to a group of experts. He proposed the appointment of a drafting committee and invited Motta to take part. The committee was thus composed of a neutral representative, along with Barrère of France, Delacroix of Belgium, Avezzana of Italy, and Lloyd-Greame of Great Britian. A single text was rapidly drafted. This

49 Ibid.   50 Ibid.   51 Ibid., 510.

memorandum was presented to the Soviet delegation, which, however, refused to accept certain conditions proposed by the European states for the economic restoration of Russia. In order to relieve itself of the burden for the failure of the Genoa Conference, the Soviet delegation suggested the convocation of a special meeting to deal specifically with the Russian question; this was the Hague Conference of July 1922, which also failed to find a solution.[52]

At the Genoa Conference Motta believed that it was necessary to avoid a final split with the Soviet delegation. To be sure, the Swiss foreign minister was well aware of the problems of providing the huge amounts of capital required for the reconstruction of Soviet Russia. Earlier, when the neutrals had met in Berne to discuss the terms and conditions for aiding the economic revival of Soviet Russia, there were serious objections to the British plan for an international consortium with a capital of 200 million pounds sterling.[53] The difficulties envisaged beforehand were not resolved during the course of the Genoa Conference, even though the Soviet delegation did indicate in several instances that it understood the concern of the European governments to protect the freedom and property of their citizens. In addition, despite the clearly-stated willingness of the European states to come to the aid of Russia, Motta recognized that these governments lacked sufficient finances to satisfy all the Soviet demands and were not in a position to offer guarantees to those private firms that were prepared to deal directly with the Soviets along the lines proposed by Lloyd George.[54] Moreover, those businesses that could provide financial backing had little confidence in the Soviet regime, and the results of the Genoa Conference did little to encourage them. Motta was nevertheless sympathetic to Lloyd George's efforts and determination to have the British government stimulate private initiatives in Russia by ensuring them against the risks of their enterprises.[55]

In the end, it was a meeting with the papal representative that reinforced Motta's view on the necessity of preventing a rupture with the Soviets at Genoa. Motta had two opportunities to speak with the Vatican's representative at Genoa, Msgr. Pizzardo, who stated that Pius XI "*ardently* desired that the conference result in a general agreement with the Russian government" and "would consider a break in the negotiations a very great calamity."[56] The pope's objective was to insert in a resolution agreed upon by the conference the principle of freedom of

---

52 On the participation of the Swiss in the Hague Conference, see ibid., 547–8, 564–8, and Fink, *Genoa Conference,* 266 ff.
53 *DDS* 8:479.   54 Ibid., 530.   55 Ibid.   56 Ibid., 530 ff.

conscience and religion; he had already received an encouraging response from the chief Soviet delegate, Chicherin, on this crucial point. Pizzardo explained that the Vatican had also prepared a memorandum on the restitution of the property and sacred objects that the Soviet government had expropriated, not only on behalf of the Catholic church but of all religious denominations. However, the latter point concerning ecclesiastical property had been deleted from the memorandum in order not to complicate the pope's efforts to obtain the essential: freedom of conscience and religion. Motta also learned from Pizzardo that the pope had *personally* given his opinion that there was "no hope of an end to the Soviet regime" and that it was "pointless to count on a restoration of the old regime."[57] In reporting this conversation with the papal representative to his colleagues in Berne, the Swiss foreign minister stressed "that our obligation is not to hinder, but in an appropriate and prudent manner to support all efforts to bring about an accord with Russia."[58]

According to the Swiss delegation, the other neutrals also favored searching for an arrangement that would permit the reintegration of Soviet Russia into global politics. Thus, when they met at Pegli on May 10, 1922, the neutral states gave their support to the projected non-aggression pact, by which the signatories would abstain from all hostilities during the impending negotiations with Russia and for a period of four months afterward.[59] In the opinion of the delegates this pact could facilitate the entry of Russia and Germany into the League of Nations. The participation of these two powers in the organization of international collective security and cooperation would be the best indication of a new stability in Europe and the best guarantee of the economic reconstruction desired by the protagonists at the Genoa Conference.

The delegates of the neutral states also played a full and active role in the conference's technical commissions: economic, financial, and transport. They each expressed the interests of their governments and played a noteworthy part in the discussions of financial questions, particularly on increased collaboration among the central banks to regularize exchange markets and facilitate credit operations as well as on the economic and financial reconstruction of Austria.[60]

57 Ibid., 531–2. Cf. Antoine Wenger, *Rome et Moscou, 1900–1950* (Paris, 1987), 137 ff. Wenger omits to mention the mission of Msgr. Pizzardo to Genoa and the compromise offered by the Vatican in case certain essential demands were met.
58 *DDS* 8:532.   59 Ibid., 541–2.
60 Ibid., 520–2, 537–9. Cf. Nicole Pietri, *La reconstruction financière de l'Autriche, 1921–1926* (Geneva, 1970).

But above all it was in the very center of the Genoa Conference, the Political Sub-Commission, where the neutral states were proportionally well-represented. Motta had been pleasantly surprised to be elected, by twenty-one votes out of a possible twenty-four. This gave him a certain moral authority, not only among the other neutral states, which he had convened on two occasions and represented as their spokesman during the crisis moments of the conference, but also among the delegates of the Great Powers like Lloyd George, who had sought his opinion and appreciated his role as an arbitrator between the French and the Germans. However, even though Motta (unlike his colleague Schulthess, who returned to Berne on May 8) was involved in the Genoa Conference from beginning to end, he held very few illusions about the outcome; on many occasions he had the "impression of a void, incoherence, and confusion."[61] In his eyes what was important at Genoa was to make sure that the thread of the discussions was not snapped and that the dossiers that had been opened at Genoa would be turned over to the League of Nations.

Motta was well aware of the challenge that this major gathering had created for the delegates, who represented thirty-four governments, were responsible for defending their vital interests, and were charting a new direction of international diplomacy without precise rules and contrary to the orderly agendas and procedures of the League of Nations. Motta's testimony clearly indicates that the statesmen at Genoa were unfamiliar with the methods and aims of a new kind of multilateral diplomacy inaugurated in the wake of World War I.[62]

Although the diplomats from the small states could have been the main beneficiaries of a multilateral diplomacy conducted on the basis of equality among the powers, they failed to accomplish any more than the representatives of the Great Powers. Nevertheless, in spite of his many criticisms of the meeting, the Swiss delegate was convinced that "the Genoa Conference was, after all, an historic event." It remained up to the statesmen, and notably the representatives of the small states, to maintain responsibility for establishing an atmosphere of international solidarity, which represented the best guarantee against the resurgence of deadly conflicts in Europe.[63]

61 *DDS* 8:490.
62 The special problems encountered by the Swiss government are described in Antoine Fleury, "La politique étrangère de la Suisse et la 'Nouvelle Diplomatie,'" *Itinera* 7 (1987):54–75.
63 Cf. Motta's report of May 18, 1922, SAF, E 2001 (B) 3/70.

13

The Genoa Conference and Japan: A Lesson in Great-Power Diplomacy

TAKAKO UETA

Following the Paris Peace Conference of 1919–20 and the Washington Naval Conference of 1921–2, the Genoa Conference was the third significant international meeting after the First World War in which Japan participated. According to the two monographs on Genoa,[1] Japan played but a minor role at the conference and exerted little influence over its outcome. Indeed, no Japanese scholar has written an article on the Genoa Conference and Japan. On the other hand, there are a considerable number of works devoted to the Washington Naval Conference, because of the great interest in the origins of the Pacific War and in the history of U.S.–Japanese relations.[2]

Although the Genoa Conference has been virtually ignored by Japan's diplomatic historians, Japan's role there did signify an initial encounter with European diplomacy dealing with the reconstruction of Europe. A close analysis is in order, particularly in view of the developments that seventy years later have again led to a restoration of Europe, one in which Japan is once more taking part. This essay, based mainly on the Japanese diplomatic archives,[3] will clarify the Japanese attitude toward the Genoa Conference.

On April 5, 1922, Foreign Minister Uchida dispatched a telegram to Ambassador Ishii in Paris, whom he had appointed Japan's delegate to

---

1 Carole Fink, *The Genoa Conference: European Diplomacy, 1921–1922* (Chapel Hill and London, 1984), 205–6; Stephen White, *The Origins of Detente: The Genoa Conference and Soviet–Western Relations, 1921–1922* (Cambridge, 1985), ix, 15.

2 Chihiro Hosoya and Makoto Saito, eds., *Washington taisei to Nichi-Bei Kankei* [The Washington System and Japanese–American Relations] (Tokyo, 1970). Akira Iriye, *After Imperialism: The Search for a New Order in the Far East, 1921–1931* (Cambridge, 1965). For detailed information, see Sadao Asada, ed., *Japan and the World 1853–1952: A Bibliographic Guide to Japanese Scholarship in Foreign Relations* (New York, 1989).

3 JFMA, 2.3.1.109.1–15. *Nihon Gaikô Bunsho* [Documents on Japanese Foreign Policy]. Taishô 11-nen (1922), vol. 3 (Tokyo, 1977).

the Genoa Conference.[4] This telegram contained his principal instructions. The Japanese government regarded the Genoa Conference as an important meeting, whose outcome might significantly influence not only Europe but also the world's economy. Uchida ordered Ishii to follow the course of the conference carefully. He instructed the delegation to give full cooperation to every state and to work for agreements to stabilize their economies, restore international trade, and secure freedom of commerce. But they were also to convince the other delegations that because of its own economic difficulties Japan had only meager material resources to provide for European reconstruction.[5]

Japan nevertheless had special interests to protect. The foreign minister asked the delegation to secure the privileged status that Japan had obtained as a result of the peace treaties. The Tokyo government, which was extremely concerned with the Russian problem, also expected its delegation to pay careful attention to the situation in the Far East; it was necessary to establish friendly relations with Russian nationals and also to obtain support from other interested parties.[6]

Japan's overriding concern was over the recognition of the Bolshevik government. Ishii's telegram dealt with this difficult problem as follows: "We have no choice but finally to adapt ourselves to the course set by the Great Powers."[7] Nonetheless, Japan, because of the special situation in the Far East and the temper of its public opinion, wished to add two items to the decisions made at Cannes and London concerning the prerequisites for recognition. The first was that the Bolshevik government should take responsibility for the Nikolaievsk incident. From March to May 1920, in Nikolaievsk in Siberia, hostilities had erupted between the Japanese expeditionary troops and the Russian partisan army, which, before its withdrawal, had massacred Japanese prisoners of war and about four thousand Japanese citizens and had burned the town. Although the government of the Far Eastern Republic had proposed to settle the incident with Japan, it was not certain whether the two parties would reach a satisfactory solution. And if in the meantime the Bolshevik government were to annex the Far Eastern Republic, Japan would have no choice but to negotiate directly with Moscow; it wished for a satisfactory settlement as a condition of recognition.[8]

Tokyo's second concern involved the generally unstable political

4 On April 4, 1922, the government appointed three plenipotentiaries and twenty-six attendants. The plenipotentiaries were Baron Gonsuke Hayashi, ambassador in London; Viscount Kikujirô Ishii, ambassador in Paris; Kengo Mori, overseas financial commissioner. Foreign Minister Uchida to Hayashi, no. 136, Apr. 5, 1922, *Nikon Gaikô Bunsho*, 3:103–4.

5 Uchida to Ishii, no. 179, Apr. 5, 1922, *Nikon Gaikô Bunsho*, 3:104–5.　6 Ibid.

7 Uchida to Ishii, no. 180, Apr. 5, 1922, ibid., 105–6.　8 Ibid.

conditions in the Far East. As long as the Far Eastern Republic existed and was recognized by the Bolshevik government, Japan believed that the geographic scope of Soviet Russia did not include the Far Eastern Republic. But if the Moscow government were to annex the republic, then it would have to agree to honor the agreements that had been concluded between Japan and the Far Eastern Republic. Referring to these two key conditions, Foreign Minister Uchida advised that if at the Genoa Conference the other Great Powers moved toward recognition of the Bolshevik government, Japan's delegation should express its reservations and solicit new instructions from Tokyo.[9] This in sum was the Japanese government's initial position.

Japan regarded itself as an honored guest during the Genoa Conference, since it had no vital interest in the meeting's main goal: the reconstruction of Europe. Japan's principal political and economic pursuits were in Asia and the Pacific. Except for the Russian problem, Japan functioned primarily as an "observer." A telegram from Genoa on April 12, 1922, aptly characterized the power relationships of the European states. The Japanese delegation described the British plan for the economic reconstruction of Europe, which was backed by Italy and provided for the return of Germany and Russia as great powers. Japan would also be accepted as a great power, but Belgium might be demoted to the second rank because of its subservience to France. The French, who strongly opposed the British plan, had found support only from Belgium and Poland and had encountered fierce opposition from Italy. Isolated in its opposition to recognizing Russia and to placing Germany on an equal footing with the other great powers, France could neither withdraw from the Genoa Conference nor present its views effectively.

Despite the fact that Japanese sympathies coincided with the antibolshevism of France and Belgium, the delegates decided to adapt themselves to the tide of the conference. There was no reason to support France and Belgium openly. The Japanese delegates were afraid of taking an unpopular stance in a conference devoted to European problems and of being blamed for Genoa's probable failure. They tried to cooperate with the other great powers, but also declined the presidency of one of the commissions because the object of the conference was the reconstruction of Europe. The telegram of April 12 stressed that everybody appreciated the conciliatory attitude of the Japanese.[10]

On April 17, the Japanese delegation reported the negative reaction to the unexpected conclusion of the Rapallo Treaty between Germany

9 Ibid.   10 Delegate to Uchida, no. 20, Apr. 12, 1922, JFMA, 2.3.1.101.5, vol. 1.

and the Soviet Union. In their view, Germany's conduct represented not only a lack of sincerity but also an act of dishonesty that violated the Cannes Resolutions. It was regrettable that Germany had concluded the agreement without consulting other powers in view of the importance of the Russian problem and the difficult efforts under way to solve it.[11]

Ambassador Hayashi met with Lloyd George on the afternoon of April 26 to exchange views on the Soviet question. In his telegram to Uchida, he reported Lloyd George's warning that Germany, as a result of its treaty with Soviet Russia, had established its status as a great power and that it would make use of Russia and even provide armaments to the Bolshevik government. Hoping to prevent this development, the British prime minister had held discussions with Barthou and had inquired about France's response if Germany were now to act in a recalcitrant manner toward the reparation problem. At Bar-le-Duc on April 24, Poincaré had indicated a hard-line response. Lloyd George, who was greatly concerned about the repercussions of German–Russian collaboration, invited Hayashi to take part in the deliberations the next day among the ten governments which were preparing an ultimatum to Russia.[12]

Throughout the Genoa Conference, the Japanese delegates remained very sensitive to the Russian problem. Neither Japan nor any of the great powers except Germany had recognized the Bolshevik government. Japanese expeditionary troops were still stationed in Siberia, and the Tokyo government sought an adequate face-saving pretext for their withdrawal.[13] The other great powers had already withdrawn their troops by 1921, and the continuation of Japanese military intervention had been criticized during the Washington Conference. The Nikolaievsk incident, which was exploited by Japanese military leaders who favored prolonging the intervention, made matters more delicate. The negotiations on withdrawal between Japan and the Far Eastern Republic, held between August 1921 and April 16, 1922, proved to be a failure.[14]

At Genoa, the Japanese delegates carefully followed the statements of the Bolshevik delegates and refuted them when necessary. At the opening session of the First (Political) Commission, on April 11,

11 Foreign Ministry Report, Apr. 1922, JFMA, 2.3.1.109.14.
12 Hayashi to Uchida, no. 110, Apr. 26, 1922, JFMA, 2.3.1.109.5, vol. 1.
13 See Chihiro Hosoya, *Siberia Shuppei no Shiteki Kenkyu* [A Study of the Siberian Intervention] (Tokyo, 1955).
14 Uchida to delegate, no. 3, Apr. 18, 1922, no. 14, Apr. 18, 1922, JFMA, 2.3.1.109.5, vol. 1.

Chicherin protested against the Japanese occupation of a part of the Far Eastern Republic, which was allied to the Bolshevik government. He challenged Japan's participation in the commission, whose purpose was to establish solid relations between Soviet Russia and other countries. Countering this statement, Ambassador Ishii asserted Japan's right to participate and refuted the need for Russian authorization.[15]

To be sure, Japan was excluded from the secret four-power talks that took place with the Soviet representatives at the initial stage of the conference. Ishii communicated his concern to Barthou that Japan's non-participation would cause misunderstandings. Barthou justified the exclusion on two grounds: first, that Japan had no direct interest in the private talks; and second, that because its troops occupied a part of Soviet territory, the Allies worried that the Russian delegate would not speak frankly in front of a Japanese diplomat. Ishii, however, insisted that Japan had a considerable interest in the Russian debt.[16] And when the Russian problem proved too difficult for the four powers to solve, Japan was included in the consultations from April 17 on.[17]

The problem of Russian debts was extremely complex (see table). The Imperial government had given it careful study, and the Ministry of Finance had forwarded specific proposals to the Foreign Ministry.[18]

Russian debts (in thousands of yen)

	Before WWI	War debts	Total
Japan	—	29,000	29,000
United Kingdom	387,500	5,680,000 (Oct. 19, 1918)	6,067,500
France	4,400,000	3,600,000 (Mar. 1, 1918)	8,000,000
Germany	2,000,000	—	2,000,000
Belgium	253,600	—	253,600
Others	250,000	—	250,000
Total	7,291,100	9,309,000	16,600,100

15 Delegate to Uchida, no. 13, Apr. 18, 1922, JFMA, 2.3.1.109.5, vol. 1.
16 Foreign Ministry Report, Apr. 1922, JFMA, 2.3.1.109.14.
17 Ibid. Delegate to Uchida, no. 53, Apr. 19, 1922, *Nihon Gaikō Bunsho,* 3:147.
18 Foreign Ministry Report on the Inter-Governmental Debts, May 1922, JFMA, 2.3.2.109.5, vol. 2.

When the Allies, without consulting Japan, sent a memorandum on April 15 to Chicherin, the Japanese issued a protest. In a memorandum to conference president Facta and also to the delegates of Great Britain, France, and Belgium, the Japanese delegation stated that it could not agree to any terms reached without its consent; it would have to consult with its government before accepting any reduction in the Russian debt.[19]

In his response on April 17 to the request for instructions on the Russian debts, Foreign Minister Uchida stated the following: Any remission of debts should be limited to intergovernmental obligations but might not include those of Japanese nationals. With regard to governmental debts, from Japan's perspective it was useless to distinguish between prewar and war debts; if Britain and France, on the basis of Article 116 of the Treaty of Versailles, were prepared to reduce the latter, Japan, with a tiny quota of German reparations, could not. And if these two countries were proposing debt reduction for the purpose of reducing their debts to the United States, this was unreasonable for Japan, which had no such obligations. Japan would adhere to its request to Soviet Russia for reparation of the Nikolaievsk incident. Even if Great Britain and France abandoned their debts, Japan should refrain from doing likewise. And if the conference adopted a resolution eliminating war debts, the Japanese delegation should reserve its attitude. Were this to occur, the delegation was authorized to separate the debt problem from the recognition of the Soviet government.[20]

On May 5, Uchida sent additional instructions, which had been adopted by the Advisory Council on Foreign Relations.[21] Japanese policy was as follows. 1) The Imperial government was not in favor of reducing or eliminating Russian debts for two reasons: because, unlike the situation in most other countries, Japan's bonds consisted almost entirely of its war debts, and because of Japan's extremely difficult internal financial conditions. 2) The Japanese delegates were to oppose any

19 Foreign Ministry Report, Apr. 1922, JFMA, 2.3.1.109.14.
20 Uchida to delegate, no. 12, Apr. 17, 1922, JFMA, 2.3.1.109.5, vol. 1.
21 The Cabinet adopted the council's decision on May 6. The Advisory Council on Foreign Relations (JACFR) was an extra-constitutional organ of the Imperial Court. It was created in July 1917 under the pretext of detaching foreign policy from the domestic political struggle. The prime minister served as the president of the body, and the other members were ministers, ex-ministers, and so forth. The Foreign Ministry was often bypassed by this organ with regard to important issues, such as the Siberian expedition, the Paris Peace Conference, and the Washington Naval Conference, until its abolition in September 1922. Cf. *Nihon Gaikōshi Jiten* [The Encyclopedia of Japanese Diplomatic History] (Tokyo, 1979), 995–6. Asada, ed., *Japan and the World,* 152–3.

recognition of the Bolshevik government or any financial assistance until Moscow accepted the repayment of its debts. 3) In regard to reducing debts, the Japanese delegation was to support France as long as the French delegation made no concession. If the tide of the conference were to turn in favor of reduction, Japan, in order to avoid responsibility for the failure of the negotiations, must accept, but with the following provision: An *aide-mémoire* was to be submitted by the delegation explaining the special Japanese situation and asking for a favorable attitude toward a future settlement of the Nikolaievsk incident. The *aide-mémoire* would explain that the state of Japanese public opinion made it impossible to abandon the idea of repayment of Russian war debts before the Nikolaievsk incident was settled. Because Japan had made considerable sacrifices during the First World War, such as responding to the Allies' request to send its naval vessels to the Mediterranean, it would now be extremely difficult to renounce its war debts.[22] Uchida's communication concluded that the Imperial government nevertheless attached importance to cooperating with the other powers and to contributing to the success of the Genoa Conference.[23] As matters turned out, however, the Russian debt problem was not resolved at Genoa.

Another problematic issue for Japan was the nonaggression pact. Introduced by Lloyd George, and based on the pact signed in Washington,[24] it gave Chicherin the opportunity to repeatedly denounce Japan's occupation of the Far Eastern Republic. On April 29, Uchida dispatched an urgent telegram dealing with the pact. Since the Imperial government had not yet prepared its position, he gave the delegation instructions for a provisional response. Japan could adhere to the pact *ad referendum,* but only if it did not violate certain conditions.[25]

Uchida considered the pact, if based on the British draft, quite similar to the Covenant of the League of Nations; therefore, without objecting to signing, the Imperial government saw no urgent necessity to accede to the nonaggression pact. But if the pact were to apply only to Europe, the delegation was ordered not to participate and to explain carefully that Japan supported the principle of nonaggression and was a member of the League of Nations and a party to the Four-Power Washington agreement, where it had voluntarily announced its support and respect for the territorial integrity of Russia. While calling for nonparticipa-

22 Uchida to delegate, no. 41, May 5, 1922, JFMA, 2.3.1.109.5, vol. 2.
23 Foreign Ministry Report, Apr. 1922, JFMA, 2.3.1.109.14.
24 Fink, *Genoa Conference,* 192.
25 Uchida to delegate, no. 32, Apr. 29, 1922, JFMA, 2.3.1.109.5, vol. 1.

tion in a pact limited to Europe, the Imperial government nonetheless feared that its absence would raise misunderstandings and incur blame.[26]

In a second scenario, if the pact included non-European states and was to extend not only to Europe but also to Asia, and if the major powers recommended that Japan sign, then the delegation should do so. But should it participate, Japan would undertake neither special responsibilities nor military or financial obligations. On the other hand, the delegation was asked to specify that the Japanese troops stationed in Siberia would not commit aggression against foreign territory.[27] On May 5, Uchida dispatched the official instructions of the Advisory Council on Foreign Relations, which were almost identical with those in his telegram of April 29.[28]

In the meeting of the Political Sub-Commission on May 16, Chicherin again criticized the Japanese occupation. Ishii, expressing his government's position, also recalled the Nikolaievsk incident:

I have no hesitation in saying that the Japanese government is anxious to withdraw its troops from the Maritime provinces as soon as they can honorably do so. But can the withdrawal of the Japanese troops take place at once without any previous arrangement being reached with a responsible government in Siberia?

His statement concluded as follows:

In regard to the concern expressed by the Russian delegate, the Japanese delegate can assure him that there will be no aggressive action on the part of the Japanese troops in Siberia and, provided that no attacks emanate from the other side, there will be no fighting in Siberia.[29]

When Chicherin persisted with his attacks and accused Japan of "aggressive intentions," Ishii answered:

. . . that he was not going to continue the discussion, but wanted to correct just one point of fact. Mr. Chicherin had just stated that Japan had demanded the annexation of Northern Siberia. The Japanese delegation would be doing their country a great injury if they passed over that statement without remark. It was absolutely untrue, and there was no foundation at all for it.[30]

The dispute erupted again on the next day, May 17. When Chicherin demanded that the nonaggression pact be extended to the Far East-

26 Uchida to delegate, no. 33, Apr. 29, 1922, ibid.   27 Ibid.
28 The Cabinet adopted the JAFCR's decision on May 6, 1922. On May 5, the JAFCR slightly changed the wording of the Foreign Ministry's draft. Uchida to delegate, no. 43, May 5, 1922, JFMA, 2.3.1.109.5, vol. 2.
29 Delegate to Uchida, no. 204, May 16, 1922, ibid.
30 Com. I/S.C.1/p.v.3, 16, ibid.

ern Republic, Ishii pointed out that the republic had neither been invited nor represented.[31] Chicherin proposed an amendment to the wording of the proposed pact to include the Far Eastern Republic, whereupon Ishii repeated that he had no mandate to conclude an agreement with a state that had not been invited to the Genoa Conference. Moreover, Ishii characterized the military agreement that had been concluded between Japan and the Far Eastern Republic, which established neutral zones, as substantially "the same thing as a non-aggression pact."[32]

To settle the conflict, President Schanzer proposed to note in the minutes that "Japan had already concluded a pact with the Far Eastern Republic."[33] Ishii accepted the wording, ". . . the Government now allied with the Russian Soviet government," *ad referendum*. However, he also realized that his government would be placed at a disadvantage if he clung to his reservations.[34]

The Japanese delegation was troubled by the *ad referendum*, but there was insufficient time to obtain instructions from the foreign ministry. Ishii, worried that his action would provide "the propagandists" with a "bait" against Japan as a spoiler of the conference,[35] decided to lift the *ad referendum* the next day. But in the meeting of the First Commission on May 18, Chicherin resumed his aggressive questioning of the non-aggression pact. Because a Japanese reply would have provoked long discussion, the delegation refrained from a public statement and sent a message to the president fully adhering to the nonaggression pact but based on Schanzer's understanding and assurances that it did not affect the Japanese expedition to Siberia. The message also added that through this nonaggression pact, Japan intended to contribute to building mutual confidence and peace.[36]

Two days after the end of the Genoa conference, the Japanese delegation recorded its general observations in a telegram to the foreign ministry. Anglo–French discord had worsened during the conference. The British had renounced their Russian debts in order to establish a new basis of economic relations; apprehensive about the future of Russia, Britain was not concerned with the German threat. France, on the other hand, attached importance to the implementation of the Versailles Treaty and the maintenance of the status quo; it worried more about the revival of Germany than about the dangers of Soviet propaganda.

31 Com. I/S.C.1/p.v.4, 23–4, ibid.   32 Com. I/S.C.1/p.v.5, 16–20, ibid.   33 Ibid., 20.
34 Delegate to Uchida, no. 209, May 18, 1922, ibid.
35 Delegate to Uchida, no. 211, May 18, 1922, ibid.   36 Ibid.

According to the Japanese observers, the British felt that the recovery of their industry depended on the stability of the continent, whereas France considered that its restoration depended on German reparation payments. Lloyd George had continuously exchanged views with the German and Russian delegates and had tried to defend them, while France had made every effort to place Germany and Russia in a "special status." The delegation reported the impression that France regarded the failure of the Genoa Conference as its victory.[37]

During the Genoa Conference, Japan, an emerging Asian power, enjoyed its status among the Great Powers but was also perplexed and wary at its unaccustomed position. This was not unlike its role at the Paris Peace Conference. Japan did not play an important role in reconstructing the postwar political and economic order in Europe, for its interests were limited to the Asian and Pacific region. The Imperial government's only common interest with the Western powers was the Russian question. For the reasons mentioned above, Japan therefore exhibited a highly conciliatory and passive attitude.

Although an Asian power, Japan would eventually watch Soviet Russia by way of European affairs; Japan's reemergence in European diplomacy took place with the anti-Comintern pact of 1936 and the Tripartite Agreement of 1940. The Genoa Conference was an early lesson for Japan in Great-Power diplomacy; this was to a large extent forgotten in the next decade. But the reconstruction of Europe at the end of this eventful twentieth century provides Japan with another chance to play a constructive role in world politics.

37 Delegate to Uchida, no. 219, May 21, 1922, ibid.

Maps

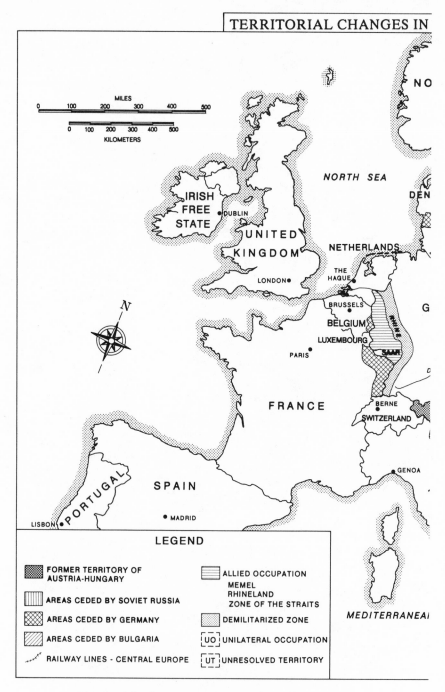

Territorial Changes in Europe After World War I

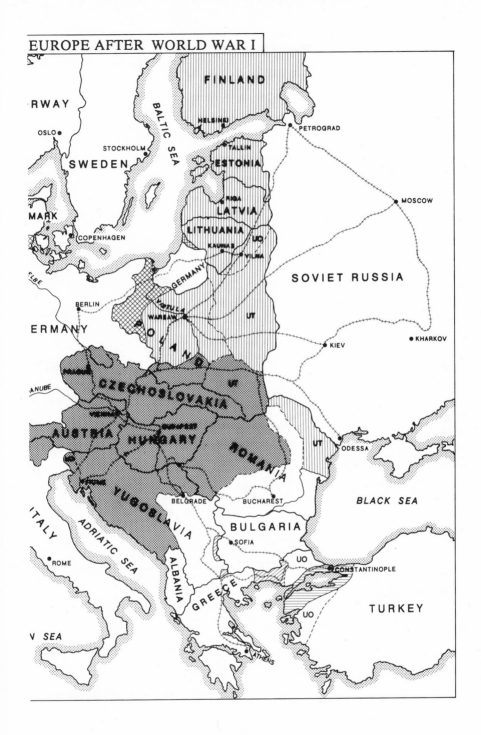

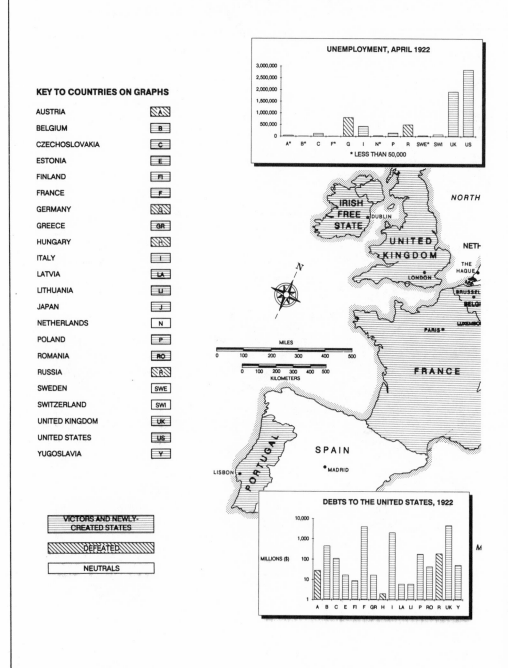

Economic Conditions in Europe on the Eve of the Genoa Conference

INFLATION, APRIL 1922

*WHOLESALE
PRICE INDEX

100,000
10,000
1,000
100
10

A F G H I J N P SWE SWI UK US

*BASED ON 1913 = 100

NORWAY
OSLO
STOCKHOLM
SWEDEN

HELSINKI
PETROGRAD

TALLIN
ESTONIA

RIGA
LATVIA

MOSCOW

SEA
DENMARK
COPENHAGEN

BALTIC SEA

LITHUANIA
KAUNAS
VILNA

DANZIG
GERMANY

SOVIET RUSSIA

IERLANDS

BERLIN
GERMANY

VISTULA WARSAW

POLAND

UM

SAAR

PRAGUE
CZECHOSLOVAKIA

VIENNA
AUSTRIA

BUDAPEST
HUNGARY

ROMANIA

BERNE
SWITZERLAND

GENOA
ITALY

YUGOSLAVIA
BELGRADE

BUCHAREST

BLACK SEA

ADRIATIC SEA

BULGARIA
SOFIA

ROME

ALBANIA

GREECE

CONSTANTINOPLE

TURKEY

MEDITERRANEAN SEA

NATIONAL DEBTS, 1922

MILLIONS $

40,000
30,000
20,000
10,000
0

A* B C* F G H* I J P* R** UK US

*FIGURES FOR 1923
**FIGURES FOR 1918

☐ INTERNAL — EXTERNAL

231

Appendix

Table 1. *Unemployment, April 1922*

Country	Number of unemployed	Percentage of population[a]
Austria	44,000	0.66
Belgium	12,900	0.17
Czechoslovakia	125,000	0.92
Denmark	50,000	1.53
France	13,000	0.03
Germany	811,000	1.35
Italy	432,000	1.11
Netherlands	42,000	0.61
Poland	149,000	0.55
Russia	503,000	0.50
Sweden	40,000	0.68
Switzerland	81,000	2.08
United Kingdom	1,926,000	4.11
United States	2,859,000[b]	2.70

[a]Censuses of 1920. Since almost no reliable figures for the size of the workforces are available, the numbers of unemployed are here expressed in percentages of the population to make them at least to a certain degree comparable.
[b]Average of 1922.
Sources: Wladimir S. Woytinsky, *Die Welt in Zahlen,* 7 vols. (Berlin, 1925–28), 1:27, 2:335–6, 344, 348–51; Brian R. Mitchell, *European Historical Statistics, 1750–1970* (New York, 1975), 19–27, 166–8; U.S. Bureau of the Census, ed., *Historical Statistics of the United States: Colonial Times to 1970,* Bicentennial ed., 2 parts (Washington, D.C., 1975), 1:9, 126.

Table 2. *Inflation, April 1922 (based on wholesale price index: 1913 = 100)*

Country	Price Index, April 1922
Austria	1,725
France	314
Germany	6,355
Hungary	200[a]
Italy	527
Japan	198
Netherlands	161
Poland	75,106
Sweden	165
Switzerland	161
United Kingdom	163
United States	143

[a]Cost of living, 1921 = 100.

Sources: Harvey E. Fisk, *The Inter-Ally Debts: An Analysis of War and Post-War Public Finance, 1914–1923* (New York and Paris, 1924), 350; Brian R. Mitchell, *European Historical Statistics, 1750–1970* (New York, 1975), 738–41; *International Labour Review* 6 (1922); U.S. Bureau of the Census, ed., *Historical Statistics of the United States: Colonial Times to 1970,* Bicentennial ed., 2 parts (Washington, D.C., 1975), 1:200.

Table 3. *National debts (close of fiscal year 1922 or 1922–3 in million dollars)*

Country	Internal debts	External debts
Austria		153[a]
Belgium	2,027	2,861
Czechoslovakia		263[a]
France	18,162	7,309
Germany	9,178	33,000[b]
Hungary		3[a]
Italy	4,268	4,282
Japan	1,292	677
Poland		421[a]
Russia		4,887[c]
United Kingdom	31,186	5,631
United States	22,963	—

[a]1923.
[b]Reparations only.
[c]1918.

Sources: U.S. Bureau of the Census, ed., *Historical Statistics of the United States: Colonial Times to 1970,* Bicentennial ed., 2 parts (Washington, D.C., 1975), 1:253; Harvey Fisk, *The Inter-Ally Debts: An Analysis of War and Post-War Public Finance, 1914–1923* (New York and Paris, 1924), 344, 346–9; Carl Parrini, "Reparations," in Alexander DeConde, ed., *Encyclopedia of American Foreign Relations,* 3 vols. (New York, 1978), 3:893–9.

Table 4. *European debts to the U.S. government (close of fiscal year 1922 or 1922–3, in million dollars)*

Country	Pre-armistice	Post-armistice	Total indebtedness
Austria		28	28
Belgium	172	282	454
Czechoslovakia		111	111
Estonia		17	17
Finland		9	9
France	1,970	2,021	3,991
Greece		17	17
Hungary		2	2
Italy	1,031	984	2,015
Latvia		6	6
Lithuania		6	6
Poland		182	182
Romania		44	44
Russia	188	5	193
United Kingdom	3,696	965	4,661
Yugoslavia	11	41	52

Sources: Harvey E. Fisk, *The Inter-Ally Debts: An Analysis of War and Post-War Public Finance, 1914–1923* (New York and Paris, 1924), 345–9; Harold G. Moulton and Leo Pasvolsky, *War Debts and World Prosperity* (Port Washington, N.Y., and London, 1932), 426; Thomas A. Bailey, *A Diplomatic History of the American People,* 10th ed. (Englewood Cliffs, N.J., 1980), 657.

Selected Bibliography

A. ARCHIVAL SOURCES

1. GOVERNMENT RECORDS

The specific records groups listed here are by no means inclusive but provide basic information on the Genoa Conference .

Austria

Haus-, Hof- und Staatsarchiv, Vienna
    Bestände 180, 687
Finanz- und Hofkammerarchiv, Vienna
    Akten des Dept. 17 aus dem Finanzarchiv

Belgium

Ministère des Affaires Etrangères, archive, Brussels
    Classement B:
    366V, 366VI, 10.071

Czechoslovakia

Státní Ústřední Archiv, Prague
    MZV-VA, projevy E. Beneše
Archiv Ministerstva Zahraničních Věcí, Prague
    Janov 1922 (12 vols.)
    II. sekce, konference, kart. 165
    Cabinet Ministry:
    věcné, kart. 15, konference, obal Janov
    kart. 56, správa veřejná
    PZ, Paris 1920–2; Berlin 1922; Bucharest 1922; London 1922; Vienna 1922
Archiv Ústavu Marxismu-Leninismu, Prague
    Benešův Archiv, Rakousko 1922

France

Archives Nationales, Paris
    AJ5/385, 413

Ministère des Affaires Etrangères, archive, Paris
  Sér. B: Relations Commerciales, Déliberations Internationales, 1920–9
    82, 86, 90, 93, 95-99, 107, 117
  Sér. Y: Internationale, 1918–40
    29, 31, 37
  Sér. Z: Europe, 1918–29: Allemagne, 236, 469, 470-472; Jugoslavie, 62; Pologne,
    137; 619, 624, 628, 633
Ministère de l'Economie et des Finances, archive, Paris
  C.A.-4, 1A/387
  B320.23; 322.54; 322.66; 322.81; 322.82
Service Historique de l'Armée, Vincennes
  6N82

Germany

Politisches Archiv des Auswärtigen Amts, Bonn
  Büro Reichsminister, 5h Genua
  Büro Reichsminister, 27
  Büro Staatssekretär, Ye
  Microfilmed Records of German Foreign Ministry
    T-120, Serial 4597H
Zentrales Staatsarchiv, Potsdam (Since 1991 Bundesarchiv, Abteilung Potsdam)
  Auswärtiges Amt, 43139

Great Britain

Public Record Office, London
Cabinet Papers:
  CAB 23: Cabinet Conclusions, 1921–2
  CAB 24: Cabinet Memoranda
  CAB 29: Allied and International Conferences (Dec. 1921–Feb. 1923)
  CAB 31: Genoa International Conference, 1922
Foreign Office Records:
  FO 371:
  General Correspondence, Political
    FO 371/5661, 5662, 6811, 7281, 7420, 7477, 7480, 7484, 7485, 7487, 7491,
    7685, 8186, 8187, 8189–8192, 8626
  FO 800:
  Foreign Secretary's Papers

Hungary

Magyar Országos Levéltár, Külügyminisztérium, Budapest
  K. 69-1922; 1922 Genoa

Italy

Archivio Centrale dello Stato, Rome
  Ministero Interno, Direzione Generale di Pubblica Sicurezza, Divisione Affari
  Generali e Riservati, 1922, Coll. A-5; Atti Speciali 1898–1940
  Segretariato Generale della Conferenza di Genova

Segreteria particolare del Duce
Ministero degli Affari Esteri, archivio, Rome
Archivio Conferenze: Posizione 52: 52/1–37 (Conferenza de Genova)
Serie Affari Politici: Italia, Russia
Archivio Storico della Banca d'Italia, Rome
Corrispondenze, pratica 3.

Japan

Foreign Ministry Archives, Tokyo
2.3.1.109 The Genoa Conference (27 Files)

Netherlands

Ministerie van Buitenlandse Zaken, Archief, The Hague
A.81/Agenda, Box 1064

Switzerland

Archives Fédérales, Berne
E 2001 (B) 3/67, 70: E 7800 4/4

United States of America

National Archives, Washington, D.C.
Records of the Department of State
RG 59, 550.E1/–
462.00R29
862.51
Records of the Treasury Department
RG 39, Treasury Bureau of Accounts
RG 56, Assistant Secretary for Foreign Loans, Albert Rathbone Files
Treasury Department, Washington, D.C.
Office of the Assistant Secretary of the Treasury for Fiscal Affairs, 63A 659, Paper-
work Management Branch
Herbert Hoover Presidential Library, West Branch, Iowa
Secretary of Commerce, Personal Files
Secretary of Commerce, Official Files
Hoover Presidential Papers, General Accession 71

2. INTERNATIONAL ARCHIVES

League of Nations Archives, Geneva
Record Group 40A

3. PRIVATE PAPERS

Belgium

Archives Générales du Royaume, Brussels
Henry Jaspar Papers

Canada
Queen's University, Kingston, Ontario
    Sir Edward Grigg (1st Baron Altrincham) Papers (available on microfilm)

Czechoslovakia
Archiv Ministerstva Zahraničních Věcí, Prague
    Vlastimil Tusar Papers

France
Archives Nationales, Paris
    Alexandre Millerand Papers
Bibliothèque Nationale, Paris
    Raymond Poincaré Papers
Ministère des Affaires Etrangères, Paris
    Camille Barrère Papers
    Léon Bourgeois Papers
    Jean Goût Papers
    Charles Laurent Papers
    Alexandre Millerand Papers
    Jacques Seydoux Papers

Germany
Politisches Archiv des Auswärtigen Amts, Bonn
    Ulrich Graf von Brockdorff-Rantzau Papers
    Karl Ritter Papers
    Carl von Schubert Papers
    Gustav Stresemann Papers (available on microfilm)
In private hands
    Carl von Schubert Papers

Great Britain
Birmingham University Library, Birmingham
    Sir Joseph Austen Chamberlain Papers
British Library, London
    Edgar Vincent (1st Viscount D'Abernon) Papers
Cambridge University Library, Cambridge
    Charles Hardinge (1st Baron Hardinge of Penshurst) Papers
Churchill College Library, Cambridge
    Maurice Hankey (1st Baron Hankey) Papers
    Philip Lloyd-Greame (1st Viscount Swinton) Papers
House of Lords Library, London
    David Lloyd George (1st Earl Lloyd George of Dwyfor) Papers
India Office Library, London
    George Nathaniel Curzon (1st Marquess Curzon of Kedleston) Papers
In private hands
    Sir Edward Grigg (1st Baron Altrincham) Papers

Italy

Archivio Centrale dello Stato, Rome
    Amedeo Giannini Papers
    Carlo Schanzer Papers
    Carlo Sforza Papers
    Andrea Torre Papers

United States

Amherst College Library, Amherst, Mass.
    Dwight W. Morrow Papers
Case Western Reserve University Library, Cleveland, Ohio
    Myron T. Herrick Papers
Corning Glass Archives, Corning, N.Y.
    Alanson B. Houghton Papers
Federal Reserve Bank of New York, N.Y.
    Benjamin Strong Papers
Harvard Business School Library, Boston, Mass.
    Thomas W. Lamont Papers
Herbert Hoover Presidential Library, West Branch, Iowa
    William R. Castle Papers
    Herbert Hoover, Secretary of Commerce, Official and Personal Papers
Hoover Institution, Stanford, Calif.
    James Logan Papers
    Louis Loucheur Papers
Houghton Library, Harvard University, Cambridge, Mass.
    William R. Castle Papers
    Ellis Loring Dresel Papers
Library of Congress, Washington, D.C.
    David E. Finley Papers
    Leland Harrison Papers
    Charles E. Hughes Papers
Ohio Historical Society, Columbus, Ohio
    Warren G. Harding Papers (available on microfilm)
Olin Library, Cornell University, Ithaca, N.Y.
    Jacob G. Schurman Papers
Pierpont Morgan Library, New York, N.Y.
    J. P. Morgan Papers
Sterling Library, Yale University, New Haven, Conn.
    Russell C. Leffingwell Papers
Van Horne House, Van Hornesville, N.Y.
    Owen D. Young Papers
In private hands
    Burton J. Hendrick Papers

B. PUBLISHED DOCUMENTARY SOURCES

Belgium

Ministère des Affaires Etrangères. *Documents diplomatiques belges, 1920-1940.* Vol. 1: 1920-1924. Brussels, 1964.

France

Ministère des Affaires Etrangères. *Documents diplomatiques. Conférence économique internationale de Gênes,* 9 avril-19 mai 1922. Paris, 1922

Germany

Akten zur Deutschen Auswärtigen Politik 1918-1945. Series A-E. 1950-.
Akten der Reichskanzlei: Weimarer Republik. Das Kabinett Cuno. Ed. K.-H. Harbeck. Boppard, 1968.
Akten der Reichskanzlei: Weimarer Republik. Die Kabinette Wirth I und II. Ed. J. Schulze-Bidlingmaier. Boppard, 1977.
Auswärtiges Amt. *Material über die Konferenz von Genua.* Berlin, 1922.
Deutsch-sowjetische Beziehungen von den Verhandlungen in Brest-Litowsk bis zum Abschluss des Rapallo-Vertrages. Ed. Ministerium für Auswärtige Angelegenheiten der DDR and Ministerium für Auswärtige Angelegenheiten der UdSSR. 2 vols. Berlin, 1967 and 1971.
Verhandlungen des Reichstags. Stenographische Berichte. Berlin, 1919-.

Great Britain

Foreign Office. *Documents on British Foreign Policy, 1919-1939.* First Series, vols. 14-20. London, 1966-76.
Hansard. *House of Commons Debates.* London, 1920-2.
Parliament. Papers by Command:
    Cmd. 1217. *Trade Agreement between His Britannic Majesty's Government and the Government of the Russian Socialist Federal Soviet Republic.* London, 1921.
    Cmd. 1667. *Papers Relating to the International Economic Conference of Genoa, April-May 1922.* London, 1922.
    Cmd. 1812. *Inter-allied Conferences on Reparations and Inter-allied Debts held in London and Paris, December 1922 and January 1923.* London, 1923.
    Cmd. 2258. *Minutes of the London Conference on Reparations, August 1922.* London, 1924.

Italy

Commissione per la Pubblicazione dei Documenti Diplomatici. *I Documenti Diplomatici Italiani.* Ser. 7, vol. 1. Rome, 1953.
Ministero deglo Affari Esteri. *Les documents de la Conférence de Gênes.* Ed. A. Giannini. Rome, 1922.

Japan

Nihon Gaikô Bunsho (Documents on Japanese Foreign Policy). Taishô 11-nen (1922), vol. 3. Tokyo, 1977.

Netherlands

Departement van Buitenlandsche Zaken. *Documenten betreffende de Buitenlandse Politiek van Nederland, 1919–1945.* Ser. A, vols. 2 and 3. The Hague, 1980.

Soviet Russia

Soviet Documents on Foreign Policy. Ed. by Jane Degras. London and New York, 1951.
Ministerstvo Inostrannykh Del (Ministry of Foreign Affairs). *Dokumenty vneshnei politiki SSSR.* Vols. 4 and 5. Moscow, 1962.
Soviet Russia and the West, 1920–1927: A Documentary Study. Ed. by Xenia Eudin and Harold H. Fisher. Palo Alto, Calif., 1957.

Switzerland

Documents diplomatiques suisses. Vol. 8. Berne, 1988.

United States

Department of State. *Papers Relating to the Foreign Relations of the United States.* 1922, vols. 1 and 2, Washington, D.C., 1938.
United States Congress. *Congressional Record,* 1921 and 1922.

Multilateral

Reparation Commission. *Official Documents Relative to the Amount of Payments to be Effected by Germany under Reparations Account.* 33 vols. London, 1922–30.
Die Sachverständigengutachten. Der Dawes- und McKenna-Bericht. Mit Anlagen. Frankfurt/ M., 1924.

C. NEWSPAPERS

L'Avanti
Chicago Tribune
Corriere della Sera
Deutsche Allgemeine Zeitung
Financial Times, London
Frankfurter Zeitung
Isvestia
Manchester Guardian
Le Matin
Morning Post
Neue Zürcher Zeitung
New York Commercial
New York Herald
New York Times

New York World
News of the World
The Observer
L'Oeuvre
Il Paese
Prager Presse
Il Secolo
Le Soir, Brussels
Le Temps
The Times, London
Toronto Daily Star
Vorwärts
Vossische Zeitung
Washington Post

D. DIARIES, MEMOIRS, SPEECHES, COLLECTED WORKS, AND WRITINGS BY CONTEMPORARIES

Bergmann, Carl. *Der Weg der Reparation.* Frankfurt/M., 1926.

Beneš, Edouard. *Problémy nové Evropy a zahraniční politika Československa, 1919–1924.* Prague, 1924.

Blücher, Wipert von. *Deutschlands Weg nach Rapallo.* Wiesbaden, 1951.

Charles-Roux, François. *Souvenirs diplomatiques: Une grande ambassade à Rome.* Paris, 1961.

Child, Richard W. *A Diplomat Looks at Europe.* New York, 1925.

Conti, Ettore. *Dal taccuino di un borghese.* 2nd ed. Milan, 1971.

D'Abernon, Viscount Edgar. *An Ambassador of Peace.* 3 vols., London, 1929.

Furst, Gaston. *De Versailles aux experts.* Nancy, 1927.

Gregory, John D. *On the Edge of Diplomacy.* London, 1928.

Hardinge, Charles, Baron Hardinge of Penshurst. *Old Diplomacy.* London, 1947.

Hoover, Herbert. *The Memoirs of Herbert Hoover.* 3 vols., New York, 1952.

Ishii, Viscount Kikujiro. *Diplomatic Commentaries.* Translated and edited by W. L. Langdon. Baltimore and London, 1936.

Joffe, Adolf A. *Ot Genuy do Gaagi.* Moscow, 1923.

Jones, Thomas. *Whitehall Diary.* Vol. 1, 1916–23. Oxford, 1969.

Kennedy, A . L. *Old Diplomacy and New.* London, 1922.

Kessler, Harry Graf. *Tagebücher, 1918–1937.* Frankfurt/M., 1961.

Keynes, John M. *The Economic Consequences of the Peace.* London, 1919.

—*The Collected Writings of John Maynard Keynes.* Vol. 17: *Activities, 1920–1922. Treaty Revision and Reconstruction.* Edited by Elizabeth Johnson. London and New York, 1977.

Laroche, Jules. *Au Quai d'Orsay avec Briand et Poincaré, 1913–1926.* Paris, 1957.

Lenin, V. I. *Collected Works.* vols. 32, 33, 42, 45. Moscow, 1965–71.

Lloyd George, Francis. *Lloyd George: A Diary.* Edited by A. J. P. Taylor. New York, 1971.

Loucheur, Louis. *Carnets secrets, 1908–1932.* Brussels, 1962.

Lyubimov, N. N., and A. N. Erlikh. *Genuezkaia Konferenciia.* Moscow, 1963.

Magnago, V. *La crisi della pace da Genova.* Rome, 1922.

Marceilin, L. *Politique et politiciens d'après-guerre.* 3 vols. Paris, 1924.

Mills, John Saxon. *The Genoa Conference.* New York, 1922.

Monnet, Jean. *Mémoires.* Paris, 1976.

Pierrefeu, Jean de. *La Saison diplomatique: Gênes (avril–mai 1922).* Paris, 1928.

Prittwitz and Gaffron, Friedrich von. *Zwischen Petersburg und Washington.* Munich, 1952.

Rathenau, Walther. *Gesammelte Reden.* Berlin, 1924.

—*Tagebuch, 1907–1922.* Edited by Hartmut Pogge von Strandmann. Düsseldorf, 1967.

Rheinbaben, Werner Freiherr von. *Viermal Deutschland.* Berlin, 1954.

The Riddell Diaries, 1908–1923. Edited by John M. McEwen. London, 1986.

Schanzer, Carlo. *Il mondo tra la pace e la guerra.* Rome, 1932.

Scheffer, Paul. *Augenzeuge im Staate Lenins. Ein Korrespondent berichtet aus Moskau, 1921–1930.* Munich, 1972.

Schlesinger, Moritz. *Erinnerungen eines Aussenseiters im auswärtigen Dienst.* Cologne, 1977.

Scott, Charles Prestwick. *The Political Diaries of C. P. Scott, 1911–1928.* Edited by Trevor Wilson. London, 1970.

Seydoux, Jacques. *De Versailles aux Plan Young.* Paris, 1932.

Steed, Wickham H. *Through Thirty Years.* 2 vols. London, 1924.

Stein, B. E. *Genuezkaia Konferenciia.* Moscow, 1922.

Stein, Ludwig. *Aus dem Leben eines Optimisten.* Berlin, 1930.

Stresemann, Gustav. *Vermächtnis.* 3 vols. Edited by H. Bernhard. Berlin, 1932–3.

Swinton, Viscount (Philip Lloyd-Greame). *I Remember.* London and New York, 1949.

Troeltsch, Ernst. *Spektator-Briefe: Aufsätze über die deutsche Revolution und die Weltpolitik 1918–22.* Tübingen, 1924.

Weiss, Louise. *Mémoires d'une européenne.* Vol. 2. Paris, 1969.

Wenger, Antoine. *Rome et Moscou, 1900–1950.* Paris, 1987.

E. MONOGRAPHS AND ARTICLES

Ádám, Magda. *Richtung Selbstvernichtung. Die Kleine Entente 1920–1938.* Budapest, 1988.

—*The Little Entente and Europe.* Budapest, 1989.

Ando, Yoshio, ed. *Ryotaisenkan no Nihon Shihonshugi* (Capitalism in Japan between the Two World Wars). Tokyo, 1979.

Artaud, Denise. *La Question des dettes interalliées et la reconstruction de l'Europe, 1917–1929.* 2 vols. Lille and Paris, 1978.

Asada, Sadao, ed. *Japan and the World 1853–1952: A Bibliographic Guide to Japanese Scholarship in Foreign Relations.* New York, 1989.

Bariéty, Jacques. *Les Relations franco-allemandes après la première guerre-mondiale.* Paris, 1977.

Beaverbrook, Lord. *The Decline and Fall of Lloyd George.* London, 1963.

Bentley, M. *The Liberal Mind, 1914–1929.* Cambridge, 1977.

Berg, Manfred. "Gustav Stresemann und die Vereinigten Staaten von Amerika. Weltwirtschaftliche Verflechtung und Revisionspolitik 1907–1929." Diss. Heidelberg, 1988.

Bournazel, Renata. *Rapallo: naissance d'un mythe. La politique de la peur dans la France du Bloc National.* Paris, 1974.

Brandes, Joseph. *Herbert Hoover and Economic Diplomacy: Department of Commerce Policy, 1921–1928.* Pittsburgh, 1962.

Buckingham, Peter H. *International Normalcy: The Open Door Peace with the Former Central Powers, 1921–1929.* Wilmington, Del., 1983.

Büsch, Otto, and Gerald D. Feldman, eds. *Historische Prozesse der deutschen Inflation, 1914 bis 1924.* Berlin, 1978.

Campbell, F. Gregory. *Confrontation in Central Europe: Weimar Germany and Czechoslovakia.* Chicago, 1975.

Campbell, John. *F. E. Smith, First Earl of Birkenhead.* London, 1986.

Carr, Edward H. *The Bolshevik Revolution.* Vol. 3. London, 1966.

—*International Relations Between the Two World Wars, 1919–1939.* New York, 1966.

Chandler, Lester. *Benjamin Strong: Central Banker.* Washington, D. C., 1958.

Chossudovsky, Evgeni M. *Chicherin and the Evolution of Soviet Foreign Policy and Diplomacy.* Geneva, 1973.

—"Genoa Revisited. Russia and Coexistence." *Foreign Affairs* 50 (1972):554–77.

Chubaryan, A. O. *V. I. Lenin i formirovaniye sovietskoy vneshnei politiki.* Moscow, 1972.

Cienciala, Anna M., and Titus Komarnicki. *From Versailles to Locarno: Keys to Polish Foreign Policy, 1919–1925.* Lawrence, Kan., 1984.

Clarke, Peter. *The Keynesian Revolution in the Making, 1924–1936.* London, 1988.

La Conferenza de Genova e il Trattato de Rapallo (1922): Atti del covegno italo-sovietico, Genova-Rapallo, 8–11 guigno 1972. Rome, 1974.

Costigliola, Frank. *Awkward Dominion: American Political, Economic, and Cultural Relations with Europe, 1919–1933.* Ithaca, N. Y., 1984.

Cowling, Maurice. *The Impact of Labour 1920–1924: The Beginning of Modern British Politics.* Cambridge, 1971.

Cross, J. A. *Lord Swinton.* Oxford, 1982.

Day, Richard. *Leon Trotsky and the Politics of Economic Isolation.* Cambridge, 1973.

Dohrmann, Bernd. *Die englische Europapolitik in der Wirtschaftskrise, 1921–1923.* Munich and Vienna, 1980.

Ellis, L. Ethan. *Republican Foreign Policy, 1921–1933.* New Brunswick, N. J., 1968.

Enssle, Manfred J. *Stresemann's Territorial Revisionism: Germany, Belgium, and the Eupen-Malmédy Question, 1919–1929.* Wiesbaden, 1980.

Erdmann, Karl Dietrich. "Deutschland, Rapallo und der Westen." *VfZG* 11 (1963):105–65.

Feldman, Gerald D. *Iron and Steel in the German Inflation, 1916–1923.* Princeton, 1977.

—*Vom Weltkrieg zur Weltwirtschaftskrise. Studien zur deutschen Wirtschafts- und Sozialgeschichte, 1914–1932.* Göttingen, 1984.

Feldman, Gerald D., et al., eds. *The German Inflation Reconsidered: A Preliminary Balance.* Berlin and New York, 1982.

—*The Experience of Inflation: International and Comparative Studies.* Berlin and New York 1984.

—*The Adaption to Inflation.* Berlin and New York, 1986.

—*Konsequenzen der Inflation.* Berlin, 1989.

Felix, David. *Walther Rathenau and the Weimar Republic: The Politics of Reparations.* Baltimore and London, 1971.

Fink, Carole. *The Genoa Conference: European Diplomacy, 1921–1922.* Chapel Hill and London, 1984.

—"European Politics and Security at the Genoa Conference of 1922," in C. Fink, I. V. Hull, and M. Knox, eds. *German Nationalism and the European Response, 1890–1945.* Norman and London, 1985, 135–56.

Fischer, Louis. *Oil Imperialism: The International Struggle for Petroleum.* New York, 1926.

—*The Soviets in World Affairs: A History of the Relations Between the Soviet Union and the Rest of the World, 1917–1929.* 2 vols. Princeton, 1951.

Fisk, Harvey E. *The Inter-Ally Debts: An Analysis of War and Post-War Public Finance, 1914–1923.* New York and Paris, 1924.

Fleury, Antoine. "La Suisse et la réorganisation de l'économie mondiale: l'expérience du premier après-guerre." *Relations Internationales* 30 (1982):141–57.

—"La Politique étrangère de la Suisse et la 'Nouvelle Diplomatie.'" *Itinera* 7 (1987):54–75.

Frohn, Axel. "Der 'Rapallo-Mythos' und die deutsch-amerikanischen Beziehungen," in J. Dülffer et al., eds. *Deutschland in Europa: Kontinuität und Bruch. Gedenkschrift für Andreas Hillgruber.* Frankfurt/M., 1990, 135–53.

Fursenko, Alexander A. "S.Sh.A. i Genuezkaia Konferenciia 1922 g," in Victor I. Rutenburg, ed. *Problemy istorii mezhdunarodnyky otnoshenii.* Leningrad, 1972.

—*Neftianye voiny v konze 19–nachale 20 veka.* Leningrad, 1985.

—"Neftjanoe Dossier Gosudarstvennogo Departamenta S.Sh.A. 1920-ch gg," in A. A. Fursenko, ed. *Problemy istochnikovedenia vneshnei politiki S.Sh.A.* Leningrad, 1987, 150–63.

—*Problemy istochnikovedenia vneshnei politiki.* Leningrad, 1987.

Gaimushô Gaikô Shiryô Kan Nihon Gaikôshi Jiten Hensan Iinkai, ed. *Nihon Gaikôshi Jiten* (The Encyclopedia of Japanese Diplomatic History). Tokyo, 1979.

Gajanová, Alena. *ČSR a středoevropska politika velmocí, 1918–1938.* Prague, 1967.

—"La Politique extérieure tchécoslovaque et la 'question russe' á la Conférence de Gênes." *Historica* 8 (1964):135–76.

Galandauer, Jan. *Od Hainfeldu ke vzniku KSČ. České dělnické hnutí v letech, 1889–1921.* Prague, 1986.

Gauss, Julia. "Motta an der Konferenz von Genua." *Revue Suisse d'Histoire* 4 (1978):453–81.

Gescher, Dieter B. *Die Vereinigten Staaten von Nordamerika und die Reparationen 1920–1924.* Bonn, 1956.

Gibb, George, and Evelyn Knowlton. *The Resurgent Years, 1911–1927.* New York, 1956.

Glad, Betty. *Charles Evans Hughes and the Illusions of Innocence: A Study in American Diplomacy.* Urbana, Ill., 1966.

Goldbach, Marie-Luise. *Karl Radek und die deutsch-sowjetischen Beziehungen 1918–1923.* Bonn, 1973.

Graml, Hermann. "Die Rapallo-Politik im Urteil der westdeutschen Forschung." *VfZG* 18 (1970):366–91.

Griffiths, Franklyn. *Genoa Plus 51: Changing Soviet Perspectives in Europe.* Toronto, 1973.

Heideking, Jürgen. *Areopag der Diplomaten. Die Pariser Botschafterkonferenz der alliierten Hauptmächte und die Probleme der europäischen Politik, 1920–1931.* Husum, 1979.

—"Oberster Rat – Botschafterkonferenz – Völkerbund: Drei Formen multilateraler Diplomatie nach dem Ersten Weltkrieg." *HZ* 231 (1980):589–630.

Helbig, Herbert. *Die Träger der Rapallo-Politik.* Göttingen, 1958.

Hiden, John. *The Baltic States and Weimar Ostpolitik.* Cambridge, 1987.

Hogan, Michael J. *Informal Entente: The Private Structure of Cooperation in Anglo-American Economic Diplomacy, 1918–1928.* Columbia, Mo., 1977.

Hogenhuis-Seliverstoff, Anne. *Les Relations franco-soviétiques, 1917–1924.* Paris, 1981.

Holtfrerich, Carl-Ludwig. *Die deutsche Inflation, 1914–1923.* Berlin, 1980.

Hosoya, Chihiro, *Siberia Shuppei no Shiteki Kenkyû* (A Study of the Siberian Intervention). Tokyo, 1955.

—*Ryotaisenkan no Nihon Gaikô* (The Foreign Policy of Japan between the Two World Wars). Tokyo, 1988.

Hosaya, Chichiro, and Makoto Saito, eds. *Washington taisei to Nichi-Bei Kankei* (The Washington System and Japanese-American Relations). Tokyo, 1970.

Iriye, Akira. *After Imperialism: The Search for a New Order in the Far East, 1921–1931.* Cambridge, 1965.

Iriye, Akira, and Tadashi Aruga, eds. *Senkanki no Nihon Gaikô* (The Diplomacy of Japan during the Inter-War Period). Tokyo, 1984.

Jazkova, Alla A. *Malaja Antanta v evropejszkoj politike* (The Little Entente and European Politics). Moscow, 1974.

Kaplan, Jay L. "France's Road to Genoa: Strategic, Economic, and Ideological Factors in French Foreign Diplomacy, 1921–1922." Ph.D. diss., Columbia University, 1974.

Kennan, George F. *Russia and the West under Lenin and Stalin.* New York, 1961.

Kent, Bruce, *The Spoils of War: The Politics, Economics, and Diplomacy of Reparations, 1918–1932.* New York, 1989.

Kerekes, Lájos. *Von St. Germain bis Genf. Oesterreich und seine Nachbarn, 1918–1922.* Vienna, Cologne, and Graz, 1979.

Kinnear, Michael. *The Fall of Lloyd George: The Political Crisis of 1922.* London, 1973.

Klein, Fritz. *Die diplomatischen Beziehungen Deutschlands zur Sowjetunion, 1917–1932.* Berlin, 1953.

Koskoff, David E. *The Mellons: The Chronicle of America's Richest Family.* New York, 1978.

Krüger, Peter. "Das Reparationsproblem der Weimarer Republik in fragwürdiger Sicht. Kritische Überlegungen zur neuesten Forschung." *VfZG* 29 (1981):21–47.

—*Die Aussenpolitik der Republik von Weimar.* Darmstadt, 1985.

Laubach, Ernst. *Die Politik der Kabinette Wirth, 1921/22.* Lübeck and Hamburg, 1968.

—"Maltzans Aufzeichnungen über die letzten Vorgänge vor dem Abschluss des Rapallo-Vertrages." *Jahrbücher für Geschichte Osteuropas* 22 (1974):556–79.

Lauren, Paul Gordon. *Diplomats and Bureaucrats: The First Institutional Response to Twentieth Century Diplomacy in France and Germany.* Stanford, Calif., 1976.

Leffler, Melvyn P. *The Elusive Quest: America's Pursuit of European Stability and French Security, 1919–1933.* Chapel Hill and London, 1979.

Link, Werner. *Die amerikanische Stabilisierungspolitik in Deutschland, 1921–1933. Die Vereinigten Staaten und der Wiederaufstieg Deutschlands nach dem Ersten Weltkrieg.* Düsseldorf, 1970.

Linke, Hans Günther. *Deutsch-sowjetische Beziehungen bis Rapallo.* Cologne, 1970.

Longu, Dov. "Soviet-Rumanian Relations and the Bessarabian Question in the Early 1920s." *South Eastern Europe* 6 (1979):29–45.

Macartney, Carlile A., and Alan W. Palmer. *Independent Eastern Europe.* New York, 1966.

Maier, Charles S. *Recasting Bourgeois Europe: Stabilization in France, Germany, and Italy in the Decade After World War I.* New ed. Princeton, 1989.

Marks, Sally. *The Illusion of Peace: International Relations in Europe, 1918–1933.* New York, 1976.

—"The Myths of Reparations." *Central European History* 11 (1978):231–55.

—*Innocent Abroad: Belgium at the Paris Peace Conference of 1919.* Chapel Hill and London, 1981.

McDougall, Walter A. *France's Rhineland Diplomacy, 1914–1924: The Last Bid for a Balance of Power in Europe.* Princeton, 1978.

McNeil, William. *American Money and the Weimar Republic: Economics and Politics in the Era of the Great Depression.* New York, 1986.

Meyer, Richard. *Bankers' Diplomacy: Monetary Stabilization in the 1920s.* New York, 1970.

Mikulicz, Sergiusz. *Od Genui do Rapallo.* Warsaw, 1966.

Morgan, Kenneth O. *Lloyd George.* London, 1974.

—*Consensus and Disunity: The Lloyd George Coalition Government, 1918–1922.* Oxford, 1979.

Moulton, Harold G., and Leo Pasvolsky. *War Debts and World Prosperity.* London, 1932.

Mouton, Marie-Renée. "Société des Nations et reconstruction financière de l'Europe: La conférence de Bruxelles (24 septembre–8 octobre 1920)." *Relations Internationales* 39 (1984):309–31.

Murray, Robert K. *The Harding Era: Warren G. Harding and His Administration.* Minneapolis, 1969.

Nish, Ian H. *Alliance in Decline: A Study in Anglo-Japanese Relations, 1908–1923.* London, 1972.

Northedge, F. S. *The Troubled Giant: Britain among the Great Powers, 1916–1939.* London, 1966.

Olivová, Věra. "Postoy československé buržoasie k Sovětskemu svazu v době jednání o prazatimní smlouvu z roku 1922." *Československý Časopis Historický* 3 (1953):294–323.

—"Die russische Linie in der tschechoslowakischen Aussenpolitik, 1918–1938," in *Die Entstehung der Tschechoslowakischen Republik und ihre international-politische Stellung. Zum 50. Gründungsjubiläum der ČSR.* Prague, 1968.

Orde, Anne. *British Policy and European Reconstruction After the First World War.* Cambridge, 1990.

Palyi, Melchior. *The Twilight of Gold, 1914–1936.* Chicago, 1972.

Parrini, Carl P. *Heir to Empire: United States Economic Diplomacy, 1916–1923.* Pittsburgh, 1969.

Pasvolsky, Leo, and Harold G. Moulton. *Russian Debts and Russian Reconstruction: A Study of the Relation of Russia's Foreign Debts to Her Economic Recovery.* New York, 1924.

Petracchi, Giorgio. *La Russia rivoluzionaria nella politica italiana. Le relazioni italo-sovietiche, 1917–1925.* Bari, 1982.

Pietri, Nicole. *La Reconstruction financière de l'Autriche, 1921–1926.* Geneva, 1970.

Pogge von Strandmann, Hartmut. "Grossindustrie und Rapallopolitik: Deutsch-sowjetische Handelsbeziehungen in der Weimarer Republik." *HZ* 222 (1976):265–341.

—"Rapallo – Strategy in Preventive Diplomacy: New Sources and New Interpretations," in V. R. Berghahn and M. Kitchen, eds., *Germany in the Age of Total War.* London, 1981, 123–46.

Pusey, Merlo J. *Charles Evans Hughes.* 2 vols., New York, 1951.

Recker, Marie-Luise. *England und der Donauraum 1919–1929. Probleme einer europäischen Nachkriegsordnung.* Stuttgart, 1976.

Rhodes, Anthony. *The Vatican in the Age of Dictators.* London, 1973.

Rhodes, Benjamin. "The United States and the War Debt Question, 1917–1934." Ph.D. diss., University of Colorado, 1965.

Rigby, Thomas H. *Lenin's Government: Sovnarkom, 1917–1922.* Cambridge and New York, 1979.

Rowland, Benjamin M., ed. *Balance of Power or Hegemony: The Interwar Monetary System.* New York, 1976.

Rumi, Giorgio. *Alle origini della politica estera fascista, 1918–1923.* Bari, 1968.

Rupieper, Hermann-Josef. *The Cuno Government and Reparations, 1922–1923.* The Hague, 1979.

Saint-Aubin, Laurent de. *Les Aspects monétaires de la conférence de Gênes.* Paris, 1986.

Saltiel, Jean-Pierre. *Commerce extérieur et croissance économique en Russie et en URSS, 1861–1940.* Paris, 1977.

Sayers, Richard S. *The Bank of England, 1891–1944.* 3 vols., Cambridge, 1976.

Schieder, Theodor. *Die Probleme des Rapallo-Vertrags. Eine Studie über die deutsch-russischen Beziehungen 1922–1926.* Cologne, 1956.

—"Die Entstehungsgeschichte des Rapallo-Vertrags." *HZ* 204 (1967):545–609.

Schlesinger, Arthur M., Jr. *The Crisis of the Old Order, 1919–1933.* Boston, 1957.

Schmidt, Gustav, ed. *Konstellationen internationaler Politik, 1924–1932: Politische und wirtschaftliche Faktoren in den Beziehungen zwischen Westeuropa und den Vereinigten Staaten.* Bochum, 1983.

Schuker, Stephen. *The End of French Predominance in Europe: The Financial Crisis of 1924 and the Adoption of the Dawes-Plan.* Chapel Hill and London, 1976.

—*American 'Reparations' to Germany, 1919–1933: Implications for the Third-World Debt Crisis.* Princeton, 1988.

Schulin, Ernst. "Noch etwas zur Entstehung des Rapallo-Vertrages," in H. von Hentig and A. Nitschke, eds. *Was die Wirklichkeit lehrt: Golo Mann zum 70. Geburtstag.* Frankfurt/M., 1979, 177–202.

Schwabe, Klaus. *Woodrow Wilson, Revolutionary Germany, and Peacemaking: Missionary Diplomacy and the Realities of Power.* Chapel Hill and London, 1985.

Senn, Alfred Erich. *The Great Powers, Lithuania, and the Vilna Question, 1920–1928.* Leiden, 1966.

Silverman, Dan P. *Reconstructing Europe After the Great War.* Cambridge, Mass., 1982.

Shishkin, V. A. *Sovetskoe gosudarstvo i strany zapada, 1917–1923. Ocherki stanovlenija ekonomicheskih otnoshenij.* Leningrad, 1969.

—*Polosa priznani i vneshne ekonomicheskaia politika SSSR 1924–1925.* Leningrad, 1983.

Skidelski, Robert. *Politicians and the Slump.* London, 1967.

—*J. Maynard Keynes: Hopes Betrayed, 1883–1920.* New York, 1986.

Soják, Vladimir, ed. *O československé zahraniční politice, 1918–1939.* Prague, 1956.

Sokin, M. *Kljuchi ot bronirovannych Komnat.* Moscow, 1970.

Stamm, Christoph. *Lloyd George zwischen Innen- und Aussenpolitik. Die britische Deutschlandpolitik 1921/22.* Cologne, 1977.

Stehlin, Stuart A. *Weimar and the Vatican, 1919–1933.* Princeton, 1983.

Stettler, Peter. *Das aussenpolitische Bewusstsein in der Schweiz, 1920–1930.* Zurich, 1969.

Stirk, Peter M. R., ed. *European Unity in Context: The Interwar Period.* London and New York, 1989.

Taylor, A. J. P., ed. *Lloyd George: Twelve Essays.* London, 1971.

Trachtenberg, Marc. *Reparation in World Politics: France and European Economic Diplomacy, 1916–1923.* New York, 1980.

Trush, M. I. *Vneshnepoliticskaja dejatel'nost V. I. Lenina, 1921–1923.* Moscow, 1967.

Ueta, Takako. *Chiikiteki Anzenhosho no Shiteki Kenkyû* (The Regional Security System Under the League of Nations: A Historical Development). Tokyo, 1989.

Uldricks, Teddy J. *Diplomacy and Ideology*. Beverly Hills, 1979.

Ullman, Richard H. *Britain and the Russian Civil War*. Princeton, 1968.

—*The Anglo-Soviet Accord*. Princeton, 1973.

van Meter, Robert H., Jr. "The United States and European Recovery, 1918–1923." Ph.D. diss., University of Wisconsin, 1971.

Veneruso, Danilo. *La vigilia del fascismo: Il primo ministero Facta nella crisi dello stato liberale in Italia*. Bologna, 1968.

Vinaver, V. *O jugoslavsko-sovietskoj trgovini izmedu dva rats*. Sarajevo, 1957.

Walters, Francis P. *A History of the League of Nations*. 2nd ed. London and New York 1965.

Wandycz, Piotr S. *France and Her Eastern Allies, 1919–1925*. Minneapolis, 1962.

Weill-Raynal, Etienne. *Les Réparations allemandes et la France*. 3 vols., Paris, 1938–47.

White, Stephen. *Britain and the Bolshevik Revolution*. London, 1979.

—*The Origins of Detente: The Genoa Conference and Soviet-Western Relations, 1921–1922*. Cambridge, 1985.

Williams, Andrew. *Labour and Russia: The Attitude of the Labour Party to the Soviet Union, 1924–1934*. Manchester, 1989.

Wilson, Joan Hoff. *American Business and Foreign Policy, 1921–1933*. Lexington, Ky., 1971.

Wilson, Trevor. *The Downfall of the Liberal Party, 1914–1935*. London, 1966.

Winter, J. M. "Arthur Henderson, the Russian Revolution and the Reconstruction of the Labour Party." *Historical Journal* 15 (1972):733–73.

Ziebura, Gilbert. *Weltwirtschaft und Weltpolitik 1922/24–1931*. Frankfurt/M., 1984.

Zimmermann, Ludwig. *Deutsche Aussenpolitik in der Aera der Weimarer Republik*. Göttingen, 1958.

Contributors

Professor Magda Ádám
Institute of History
Hungarian Academy of Sciences
Budapest

Dr. Manfred Berg
John F. Kennedy Institute for North
    American Studies
Free University of Berlin

Professor Carole Fink
The Ohio State University
Columbus, Ohio

Professor Antoine Fleury
Institut Universitaire de Hautes
    Etudes Internationales
Geneva

Dr. Axel Frohn
German Historical Institute
Washington, D.C.

Professor Alexander Fursenko
Institute of the History of the USSR
Leningrad

Dr. Frank Hadler
Institute of General History
Academy of Sciences, Berlin

Professor Dr. Jürgen Heideking
University of Tübingen

Professor Anne Hogenhuis
European Institute of Public
    Administration
Maastricht, the Netherlands

Professor Dr. Peter Krüger
University of Marburg

Professor Sally Marks
Providence, Rhode Island

Professor Giorgio Petracchi
Università degli Studi di Firenze
Florence

Professor Stephen A. Schuker
University of Virginia
Charlottesville, Virginia

Professor Takako Ueta
International Christian University
Tokyo

Professor Andrew Williams
Darwin College
The University of Kent
Canterbury, England

Index